Towards an Economic Sociology of Law

Edited by

Diamond Ashiagbor, Prabha Kotiswaran, and Amanda Perry-Kessaris

Blackwell Publishing was acquired by John Wiley & Sons in February 2007. Blackwell's publishing programme has been merged with Wiley's global Scientific, Technical, and Medical business to form Wiley-Blackwell.

Editorial Offices
350 Main Street, Malden, MA 02148-5020, USA
9600 Garsington Road, Oxford OX4 2DQ, UK

For details of our global editorial offices, for customer services, and for information about how to apply for permission to reuse the copyright material in this book please see our website at www.wiley.com/wiley-blackwell

Registered Office
John Wiley & Sons Ltd, The Atrium, Southern Gate, Chichester, West Sussex PO19 8SQ.

The right of Diamond Ashiagbor, Prabha Kotiswaran, and Amanda Perry-Kessaris to be identified as the authors of the Editorial Material in this work has been asserted in accordance with the Copyright, Designs and Patents Act 1988.

Library of Congress Cataloging-in-Publication Data
Towards an economic sociology of law / edited by Diamond Ashiagbor, Prabha Kotiswaran, and Amanda Perry-Kessaris.
   pages cm
  Includes bibliographical references.
  ISBN 978-1-4443-6152-0 (alk. paper)
  1. Law and economics–Social aspects. 2. Sociological jurisprudence–Economic aspects. 3. Economics–Sociological aspects. I. Ashiagbor, Diamond, editor of compilation. II. Kotiswaran, Prabha, editor of compilation. III. Perry-Kessaris, Amanda, editor of compilation.
  K487.E3T69 2013
  340'.115–dc23
                                          2013003250

A catalogue record for this title is available from the British Library.

ISBN: 978-1-4443-6152-0

Set in the United Kingdom by Godiva Publishing Services Ltd
Printed in Singapore by Fabulous Printers Pte Ltd

Contents

Contents

JOURNAL OF LAW AND SOCIETY
VOLUME 40, NUMBER 1, MARCH 2013
ISSN: 0263-323X, pp. 1–6

Introduction: Moving Towards an Economic Sociology of Law

DIAMOND ASHIAGBOR,* PRABHA KOTISWARAN,** AND AMANDA PERRY-KESSARIS*

This special issue represents a milestone in our on-going journeys towards an 'economic sociology of law' – that is, shared understandings of how and why one might use sociologically-inspired approaches (analytical, empirical, and normative) to investigate relationships between legal and economic phenomena; and of what might be gained and lost in the process.

We three editors set off on our journeys separately and some time ago. For the first, the trigger was an engagement with the social dimension of regional integration, and the 'embedded liberal bargain' between European states. For the second, it was an interest in the role of national legal systems as a determinant of foreign direct investment in South Asia. For the third editor, it was a frustration with feminist legal theorizing which, in presenting the commodification of sex as nothing but violence, obliterated the economic agency of women.

By early 2011 we had assembled a caravan – an economic sociology of law reading group – along with faculty and students from across London and the south east of England.[1] Together we have gone back to the classics and neo-classics,[2] outwards to heterodox economics and legal anthropology,[3]

* School of African and Oriental Studies, University of London, Thornhaugh Street, Russell Square, London WC1H 0XG, England
da40@soas.ac.uk   a.perry-kessaris@soas.ac.uk
** Dickson Poon School of Law, King's College London, Strand, London WC2R 2LS, England
prabha.kotiswaran@kcl.ac.uk

1 See <http://www.soas.ac.uk/law/events/readinggroups/esol>.
2 Such as M. Weber, 'The Economic System and the Normative Orders' in *Max Weber on Law in Economy and Society*, ed. M. Rheinstein, transl. by E. Shils and M. Rheinstein (1967) 11–40; K. Polanyi, 'The Self-Regulating Market and the Fictitious Commodities: Labor, Land, and Money' in *The Great Transformation* (1944) ch. 6; H. de Soto, 'The Costs and Importance of the Law' in *The Other Path: The Invisible Revolution in the Third World* (1990) ch. 5.
3 B. Fine, 'Social capital in wonderland: the World Bank behind the looking glass' (2008) 8 *Progress in Development Studies* 261–9; E.F. Schumacher, 'Buddhist

1

across to feminist and postcolonial perspectives,[4] and from the empirical to the abstract.[5] Our search has been for lessons, examples, warnings, connections, and opportunities, whether lost or not yet found.

In September 2012, we invited a small group of participants and discussants to a two-day workshop entitled 'Towards an Economic Sociology of Law', supported by the *Journal of Law and Society* and the School of Law at the School of Oriental and African Studies, University of London. This volume reproduces the intellectual energy of half the participants, with the remaining papers to follow in a special issue of the *International Journal of Law in Context* in June 2013.

We set the scene for the workshop by locating economic sociology of law within the broader tradition of the sociology of law. We noted the pervasive and consistent influence of Weber on social theory throughout the twentieth and twenty-first centuries: Weber's sociological analysis of law and the economy can clearly be seen as a prototype for an economic sociology of law.[6] His work has also had a significant influence on policy makers, as evidenced within discourse on development, governance, and the rule of law: Weber's observations on the central role of 'rational' legal systems in the emergence of modern capitalism and in economic development more generally have been implicitly and explicitly co-opted by the World Bank.[7]

We noted that Karl Polanyi's dramatic and troubling probing of economic history, as set out in particular in *The Great Transformation* (1944), has tended to receive less attention than this, by now familiar, Weberian perspective. Interest in the Polanyian perspective is undergoing a revival,

---

economics' in S*mall is Beautiful: a study of economics as if people mattered* (1973) ch. 4; D. McCloskey, *The Secret Sins of Economics* (2002); A. Riles, *Collateral Knowledge: Legal Reasoning in the Global Financial Markets* (2011) chs. 4 and 5.

4 R. Birla, 'Introduction' and 'Hedging bets: Speculation, gambling and market ethics 1890–1930' in *Stages of Capital: Law, Culture, and Market Governance in Late Colonial India* (2009) 1–32, 143–98; P. Kotiswaran, 'Born unto Brothels: Toward a Legal Ethnography of Sex Work in an Indian Red-Light Area' (2008) 33 *Law & Social Inquiry* 579–629.

5 For example, R. Hale, 'Bargaining, Duress, and Economic Liberty' (1943) 43 *Columbia Law Rev.* 603–28; M. Callon, 'What does it mean to say that economics is performative?', CSI Working Papers Series no. 5 (2006).

6 R. Swedberg, 'The case for an economic sociology of law' (2003) 32 *Theory and Society* 1–37. See, also, D. Trubek, 'Max Weber on Law and the Rise of Capitalism' (1972) *Wisconsin Law Rev.* 720–53 and D. Kennedy, 'The Disenchantment of Logically Formal Legal Rationality, or Max Weber's Sociology in the Genealogy of the Contemporary Mode of Western Legal Thought' (2004) 55 *Hastings Law J.* 1031–76.

7 A. Santos 'The World Bank's uses of the "Rule of Law" promise in economic development' in *The New Law and Economic Development: A Critical Appraisal*, eds. D. Trubek and A. Santos (2006) 272–3; I.F.I. Shihata et al., *The World Bank in a Changing World: Selected Essays* (1991); and C. Thomas, 'Re-Reading Weber in Law and Development: A Critical Intellectual History of "Good Governance" Reform', Cornell Law Faculty publications, paper 118 (2008).

2

which attests to a wider resurgence of intellectual attentiveness to the 'social embeddedness' of market societies. In particular, those working in the discipline of economic sociology draw on Polanyi to challenge 'economics imperialism',[8] most especially the assumption of the self-regulating market economy, by asserting the importance of both state action and social relations as constitutive of markets.[9]

We also observed that it is only relatively recently that legal scholars have also begun to draw upon economic sociology, whether in terms of insights from Polanyian- or Weberian-inspired scholarship, or from what may be termed the 'new economic sociology', owing more to Granovetter.[10] Our workshop was aimed at remedying some of the resulting gaps. It sought to bring to the fore work which has been in the tradition – if not using the language – of economic sociology of law, and to uncover connections between Polanyian and Weberian approaches to the intersection between law, economy, and society. Sabine Frerichs has responded in this volume by placing the (non-contemporaneous) 'historical' scholarship of Weber and Polyani as the first of three 'generations' in the evolution of economic sociology of law, followed by 'legal realists' and 'constructivist socio-legal' scholars.[11] Frerichs goes on to explore money as a double-sided 'social phenomenon' – an 'economic commodity' that 'hinges on the market' and a 'legal relation' that 'depends on the state' – and reveals that the 'resulting tension features prominently in the works of Max Weber and Karl Polanyi' (p. 7).

Furthermore, the workshop was intended to generate new analytical frames which go beyond both the often 'over-socialized' views of social action presented in 'law and society', and the characteristically 'under-socialized' analyses of social action offered by 'law and economics'.[12] So it is that in this volume we find Andrew Lang reaching for 'the sociology of knowledge, including the sociology of science' as new and 'powerful intellectual resources for rethinking the role of law within economic life' (p. 155). Similarly, Ritu Birla sets out a postcolonial approach to economic sociology of law in which the 'legal regimes' and 'political economies of modern colonialisms and colonized societies' are examined 'not only as an empirical project to "fill in" the big historical picture of law's role in

8 See B. Fine and D. Milonakis, *From Political Economy to Freakonomics: Method, the Social and the Historical in the Evolution of Economic Theory* (2008).
9 See, for example, T. Halliday and B.G. Carruthers, *Bankrupt: Global Lawmaking and Systemic Financial Crisis* (2009); B. Lange and D. Thomas (eds.), *Northern Ireland Legal Q.* 4 (2011), special issue on socializing economic relationships; C. Joerges and J. Falke (eds.), *Karl Polanyi, Globalisation and the Potential of Law in Transnational Markets* (2011).
10 M. Granovetter, 'Economic Action and Social Structure: the Problem of Embeddedness' (1985) 91 *Am. J. of Sociology* 481–93.
11 S. Frerichs, this volume, pp. 7–26. See, also, F. Block in this volume, pp. 27–48.
12 Granovetter, op. cit., n. 10; G Krippner et al., 'Polanyi symposium: a conversation on embeddedness' (2004) 2 *Socio-Economic Rev.* 109–35.

3

economic life with new global case studies and translations of culture', but also to 'chart colonial genealogies of contemporary forms of governing more broadly' (p. 92).[13] While Birla herself explores market governance as a colonial mode of constituting the market in India, Amanda Perry-Kessaris identifies postcolonial undertones in the constitution of the Cypriot wind energy market, which was largely 'downloaded' in the course of Europeanization (p. 76).

An important theme emerging from this project, which echoes earlier conversations among economic sociologists,[14] is the receding utility of that touchstone of economic sociology: 'embeddedness'. A number of contributors focused on the concept's oxymoronic and ill-defined qualities. It is ill-defined in that, as Fred Block notes, '[e]mbeddedness is a relatively blunt instrument for analysing different types of market structures and arrangements' (p. 39). 'What is embedded', demands Roger Cotterrell, and 'in what is it embedded?' (p. 53). So economic sociology of law would do well to look to other approaches to flesh out the concept. For example, as Prabha Kotiswaran notes, we ought to refer to feminists who offer the family as the very glue that facilitates the embedding of the market in the social while managing to project a disembedded view (p. 117). Embeddedness is oxymoronic because, in speaking of the economic as (embedded in) the social, we suggest that they are at once distinct and the same. Perhaps more troubling is the potential of the concept of embeddedness to obscure the co-constitutive nature of the social and economic by presenting 'the social' as ameliorating the excesses of 'the market'. As Kenneth Veitch shows, capitalism has always benefited in some general way from the reproduction of labour by the welfare state.[15] These ties have become explicit under contemporary neo-liberalism: the welfare state subsidizes the market. Thus, 'in Polanyi's terms ... the institutions that once contributed to ensuring the embeddedness of the market economy in society now play an important role in processes of disembedding' (p. 137). Furthermore, the concept of 'embeddedness' does not seem adequately to challenge the tendency of some economic sociologists to adopt a narrow understanding of market activity, and either ignoring or relegating to the 'economic periphery' – what Viviana Zelizer calls the 'quasi-economies'[16] of households, informal economies, and trust networks.

Here, Roger Cotterrell offers a measured setting aside of embeddedness in favour of an attention to the existence (or absence) of 'communal networks' (p. 55), some of which may focus on primarily economic values and interests; others will not. Some of the empirical and analytical implications of this approach are demonstrated by Amanda Perry-Kessaris in her

13 R. Birla, this volume, pp. 92–114.
14 Krippner et al., op. cit., n. 11.
15 K. Veitch, this volume, pp. 137–54.
16 V. Zelizer, *Economic lives: how culture shapes the economy* (2011) 8.

4

examination of interactions between wind-farm, government, and civil society actors in Cyprus.[17] Fred Block also proposes an alternative to the embeddedness frame, this time drawn from Zelizer's concept of 'relational work'. Here attention is paid to transactions (rather than networks), and to how social actors themselves define their connections 'usually by implicitly or explicitly contrasting it with other known types of relationship, defining the types of transactions in which they will engage, and identifying appropriate media of exchange' (p. 41).

Some of the contributors also interrogate the much problematized, yet persistent, public–private divide. Ritu Birla uses the example of corporate legal personality to show the divide is intensely contested, while Kenneth Veitch uses the contemporary British welfare state to show how the divide reappears, but also dissolves, in the form of Clinical Commissioning Groups, workfare schemes, and the return of private law mechanisms such as contract. Likewise Prabha Kotiswaran points to the fact that the division of labour among feminist legal scholars in the care-work and sex-work debates, and resulting legal reform efforts, rely heavily on the family/market dichotomy (pp. 119 ff.). Despite their fluidity, the categories of public and private exert a profound influence on the legal consciousness of economic actors. Ritu Birla observes this phenomenon in 'the relationships between the legal subject and *homo economicus*, ... telescoped through the figure of the corporate person' (p. 93); Andrew Lang sees it in the 'cognitive infrastructure' that 'helps to constitute particular kinds of economic rationality' by giving 'meaning to what counts as "rational" action in different market contexts' (p. 166).

In selecting our contributors we consciously sought methodological diversity – hence the presence of legal historians, sociologists, and lawyers trained in more than one discipline. Yet they were all attuned to the observation made elsewhere by Roger Cotterrell that in a sociologically-inspired approach:

> the social phenomena of law must be understood empirically (through detailed examination of variation and continuity in actual historical patterns of social co-existence, rather than in relation to idealized or abstractly imagined social conditions).[18]

We also paid attention to the fact that economic sociology of law is an effective tool for exploring diverse substantive legal fields such as labour,[19] the corporate form,[20] social policy, gender, high-frequency trading, money,

---

17 A. Perry-Kessaris, this volume, pp. 68–91.
18 R. Cotterrell, 'Why Must Legal Ideas Be Interpreted Sociologically?' (1998) 25 *J. of Law and Society* 183.
19 See contributions by D. Ashiagbor, A. Blackett, R. Dukes, K. Rittich, and D. Tsikata in the *International J. of Law in Context* special issue (2013, forthcoming).
20 See Birla, op. cit., n. 13, and P. Ireland in *International J. of Law in Context*, id.

5

climate change, the construction of economic rationalities,[21] and micro-finance.[22] Clearly our best hope for robust progress is in pooling resources across these and other fields of inquiry.

This volume, the accompanying forthcoming special issue of the *International Journal of Law in Context*, and our on-going reading group present an especially timely intervention into debates around the regulation of market economies, not least in light of the many reassessments and self-estrangements that have been prompted by the continuing economic crisis.[23] '[T]here is nothing', writes Fred Block in this volume, 'like a global economic crisis to accelerate critical thinking about our ways of organizing economic activity' (p. 28). So, in the spirit of London 2012 – *citius, altius, fortius* (faster, higher and, most of all, stronger) – we hope to proceed towards, through, and most probably beyond an economic sociology of law.

---

21 See, respectively, contributions in this volume by Veitch, Kotiswaran, Cotterrell, Frerichs, Perry-Kessaris, and Lang.
22 See contribution by A. Haldar, *International J. of Law in Context*, op. cit., n. 19.
23 See, for example, the infamous testimony to the United States Congress of Alan Greenspan, former chairman of the US Federal Reserve, quoted in R. Patel, *The Value of Nothing* (2011) 6; R. Posner, *A Failure of Capitalism: The Crisis of '08 and the Descent into Depression* (2008); Zelizer, op. cit., n. 16.

6

JOURNAL OF LAW AND SOCIETY
VOLUME 40, NUMBER 1, MARCH 2013
ISSN: 0263-323X, pp. 7–26

From Credit to Crisis: Max Weber, Karl Polanyi, and the Other Side of the Coin

SABINE FRERICHS*

The predicament of modern capitalism, and of contemporary finance capitalism in particular, is the fine line between credit and crisis. Recent developments from the American sub-prime mortgage crisis to the European sovereign debt crisis revived debates about the nature of money and all sorts of derivatives. Money is a social phenomenon which has always two sides: an economic and a legal one. As an economic commodity, it hinges on the market; as a legal relation, it depends on the state. The resulting tension features prominently in the works of Max Weber and Karl Polanyi. Both studied the market society of the late-nineteenth and early-twentieth century, including its monetary institutions. Moreover, both were also aware of the political function of their related writings. The following review allows us to establish links between law, economy, and society and thus exemplify the economic sociology of law as it is foreshadowed by the sociological classics.

INTRODUCTION: WEBER AND POLANYI ON MONETARY CAPITALISM

This volume is concerned with sociological perspectives on law and economy, or with the interrelations of law and economy in (modern) society. Somewhat paradoxically, the road towards an 'economic sociology of law' – as this field is dubbed – leads, in the first instance, back to the sociological classics.[1] As representatives of an integrated view on law, economy, and society, we can thus name Karl Marx, Emile Durkheim, and Max Weber,

* *Centre of Excellence in Foundations of European Law and Polity, P.O. Box 4, 00014 University of Helsinki, Helsinki, Finland*
sabine.frerichs@helsinki.fi

1 S. Frerichs, 'The Legal Constitution of Market Society: Probing the Economic Sociology of Law' (2009) 10(3) *Economic Sociology – European Electronic Newsletter* 20–5.

7

who are also known as founding fathers of the sociological discipline, as well as Karl Polanyi, whose legacy is strongest in economic sociology. Following the invitation of the editors, I will focus on intersections of law and economy in the work of Max Weber (1864–1920) on the one hand, and Karl Polanyi (1886–1964) on the other, concerning their respective views on money, which is an economic commodity and a legal relation at the same time.

In order to compare and contrast the viewpoints of Weber and Polanyi, I will focus on aspects of their work which are indeed comparable: namely, essays and chapters which have been written from a sociological (or social-scientific) point of view, but with a wider political or politically-interested audience in mind. In Burawoy's terms, they are not targeted at an 'academic audience' only – the natural forum for a strictly 'professional sociology' as well as a more self-reflective 'critical sociology' – but are also aimed at an 'extra-academic audience', be it policy-makers or the wider public.[2] My point of comparison thus belongs to what is referred to as 'policy sociology' or 'public sociology', to which both Weber and Polanyi contributed. This does not mean that they merged 'is' and 'ought' questions in the scientific core of their work, but that at least some of their arguments also fulfilled a political function. The writings which I will draw upon contain an analysis of their time against the backdrop of historical developments of the (late) nineteenth century, which concern the regulation, or self-regulation, of markets. Weber and Polanyi are thus contemporaries although, according to their birth years (which are more than twenty years apart), they are not of the same generation, and differ in their lifetimes and respective experiences (Weber died soon after the First World War, while Polanyi also witnessed the Second World War). Inasmuch as we will be concerned with their differing accounts of monetary capitalism, and the political conclusions they draw, it is also worth noting that both scholars stem from entrepreneurial families which had once benefited from the 'rise' of the market economy and which were equally affected by its 'fall', which spiralled into two world wars.

Roth speaks of Weber's and Polanyi's 'contrary interpretation of liberal capitalism'.[3] By this, he refers to a regime of 'multilateral world trade' which is based on 'private enterprise' and market-based 'currency and credit arrangements'.[4] Accordingly, the 'liberal world economy' is built on 'the relatively free movement of persons, capital, goods, and information in an arena of stable or moderately flexible exchange rates'.[5] This regime is the reference, or even subject matter, of key texts of both Weber and Polanyi,

---

2 M. Burawoy, '2004 Presidential Address [to the American Sociological Association]' (2005) 70 *Am. Sociological Rev.* 4–28, at 9–11.
3 G. Roth, 'The Near-Death of Liberal Capitalism: Perceptions from the Weber to the Polanyi Brothers' (2003) 31 *Politics and Society* 263–82, at 264.
4 id., p. 263.
5 id., pp. 263–4.

8

some of which will be analysed and illustrated in more detail below. For Weber, I will draw on two articles on 'Stock and Commodity Exchanges', which were originally published in 1894[6] and 1896[7] as well as his inaugural lecture as a professor of economics in Freiburg in 1895, entitled 'The National State and Economic Policy'.[8] As Weber had completed doctoral and postdoctoral dissertations in jurisprudence, these pieces mark, at the same time, his reorientation from law to economics, before he turned, in his later years, to the new discipline of sociology.[9] However, Weber's post-humously published *magnum opus, Economy and Society*, subtitled 'An Outline of Interpretive Sociology',[10] also contains elaborate parts which can, besides their analytical value, best be understood as a critique of market regulation as it stood and developed in the late-nineteenth and early-twentieth century. As for Polanyi, my main source will naturally be *The Great Transformation*[11] which is concerned with the 'rise and fall of market economy' in the 'long' nineteenth century. However, besides this famous treatise, which was completed, in a rush, at the height of the Second World War and thus clearly had a political function, I will also draw on two shorter pieces which date back to the late 1950s and early 1960s, respectively: 'The Economy as Instituted Process'[12] and 'Money Objects and Money Uses'.[13] While these essays are characterized by a much more scholarly tone, they nevertheless round off Polanyi's criticism of 'formal' economics and its ideological function in science and society. Hence, all these texts have been selected with a focus on the political side of Weber's and Polanyi's work, and on how they conceive of core ideas and institutions of economic liberalism, such as self-regulating markets and related currency and credit arrangements. Most strikingly, Weber and Polanyi diverge in their reconstruction and interpretation of the catastrophe of their time: the chain of events which culminated in the two world wars. Whereas Polanyi holds that the 'crisis of liberal capitalism' has to be understood as a 'cause' of the

6 M. Weber, 'Stock and Commodity Exchanges' (2000/1894) 29 *Theory and Society* 305–38.
7 M. Weber, 'Commerce on the Stock and Commodity Exchanges' (2000/1896) 29 *Theory and Society* 339–71.
8 M. Weber, 'The National State and Economic Policy (Freiburg Address)' (1980/1895) 9 *Economy and Society* 428–44.
9 R. Swedberg, 'Max Weber's Contribution to the Economic Sociology of Law' (2006) 2 *Annual Rev. of Law and Social Science* 61–81, at 74–7.
10 M. Weber, *Economy and Society: An Outline of Interpretive Sociology*, ed. G. Roth (1978/1922).
11 K. Polanyi, *The Great Transformation* (1957/1944).
12 K. Polanyi, 'The Economy as Instituted Process' in *Trade and Market in the Early Empires: Economies in History and Theory*, eds. K. Polanyi, C.M. Arensberg, and H.W. Pearson (1957) 243–70.
13 K. Polanyi, 'Money Objects and Money Uses' in *The Livelihood of Man*, ed. H.W. Pearson (1977/1964) 97–121.

First World War (the ramifications of which had already laid the ground for the Second World War), Weber considers the downturn of the market economy its 'consequence'.[14]

WEBER ON NATIONAL STATE AND ECONOMIC POLICY (1895)

Weber's Freiburg address, given at the age of just over thirty, is considered representative of his political writings, which are notably concerned with German national development. As to the relevance of this inaugural lecture, it is noted:

> While Weber later might then have in a similar context expressed himself in a more temperate fashion, it must be recognised that the question of power and the national state is one that retains a central importance until his death.[15]

What Weber emphasizes in his new position as a professor of economics, who combined 'a practical legal training with a grounding in a historical approach to political economy',[16] is the role that the latter plays with regard to the development of the nation-state – in this case the German one. One of his main points is that, despite being a science which strives as such for objective knowledge, political economy is, as a 'political science', always also value-related.[17] And the 'standards of value' which it naturally adopts are the interests of the nation-state.[18] In other words, '[a]s a science of explanation and analysis political economy is *international*'.[19] However, in its policy function it is, first of all, oriented towards the nation-state: 'The economic policy of a German state, and the standard of value adopted by a German economic theorist, can therefore be nothing other than a German policy and a German standard.'[20] Thus understood, economics is 'a servant of [national] politics' and has to advance 'the interests of national *power*' in its international (political and economic) context.[21] At the time of Weber's writing, this context is a liberal regime of multilateral world trade which is increasingly challenged by national protectionism. Considering the 'lasting power-political interests of the nation',[22] Weber himself favours 'nationalist' economic policies, which pursue the 'reason of state'. However, for him, this does not imply an agenda of 'blind' protectionism. In fact, the national

---

14 Roth, op. cit., n. 3, 266–7.
15 K. Tribe, 'Introduction to Weber' (1980) 9 *Economy and Society* 420–7, at 422–3.
16 S. Lestition, 'Historical Preface to Max Weber, "Stock and Commodity Exchanges"' (2000) 29 *Theory and Society* 289–304, at 293.
17 Weber, op. cit., n. 8, p. 438.
18 id., p. 437.
19 id. (original emphasis).
20 id.
21 id., p. 438 (original emphasis).
22 id.

10

interest would be compromised if one simply advocated ' "state assistance" instead of "self-help", state regulation of economic life instead of the free play of economic forces'.[23] Hence, to Weber, 'the question of whether, and how far, the state should intervene in economic life, and when it should rather untie the economic forces of the nation and tear down the barriers in the way of their free development' requires thorough economic reasoning, which is oriented towards the 'economic and political interests of our nation's power, and the vehicle of that power, the German national state'.[24]

Two further aspects are worth mentioning. The first aspect concerns Weber's merits as a forerunner of the economic sociology of law.[25] In this regard, we can note that his Freiburg address already contains a link between economics and jurisprudence, if only at the margins of his overall argument and with little sociological framing. Weber lays stress on the 'advance in the popularity of the economic method of approach'[26] across scientific disciplines and fields of interest. Accordingly, economic issues have become central for history, law, and politics alike. As to the law, he quotes '[o]ne of our most ingenious theorists [who] was self-confident enough to believe he could characterize jurisprudence as "the handmaiden of political economy".'[27] Interestingly, Weber – a lawyer turned economist himself – confirms this view:

> And one thing is certainly true: the economic form of analysis has penetrated into jurisprudence itself. Even its most intimate regions, the treatises on the Pandects, are beginning to be quietly haunted by economic ideas. And in the verdicts of the courts of law it is not rare to find so-called 'economic grounds' put in where legal concepts are unable to fill the bill.[28]

Thus understood, legal rationality is increasingly complemented by economic rationality. The second aspect I want to note is Weber's intention to raise the profile of political-economic thinking in the (prospective) leadership of the German nation-state, which he hopes to be the bourgeoisie. Tribe summarizes the political situation in Germany at the end of the nineteenth century as follows: 'the ruling class have become incapable of the proper rule of the nation, the proletariat are immature and the bourgeoisie unschooled and unready.'[29] In his Freiburg address, Weber identifies himself as a member of

23 id., pp. 438–9.
24 id., p. 439.
25 R. Swedberg, 'The case for an economic sociology of law' (2003) 32 *Theory and Society* 1–37; Swedberg, op. cit., n. 9.
26 Weber, op. cit., n. 8, p. 439.
27 id. Weber gives no name, but probably refers to a statement by Bernhard Windscheid, see M. Weber, 'Der Nationalstaat und die Volkswirtschaftspolitik: Akademische Antritsrede' in *Gesamtausgabe Max Weber, Vol. 4(2): Landarbeiterfrage, Nationalstaat und Volkswirtschaftspolitik: Schriften und Reden 1892–1899*, ed. W.J. Mommsen (1993/1894) 543–74, at 562, fn. 42.
28 id.
29 Tribe, op. cit., n. 15, p. 424.

11

the bourgeoisie: 'I feel myself to be a bourgeois, and I have been brought up to share their views and ideals.'[30] The 'interventionist nature' of his speech is more specifically to be seen in a call to his fellows to take political responsibility for the development of the German nation[31] – and to consider in this regard, the laws of the market. Claiming that the question 'whether the German bourgeoisie is at present ripe to be the leading political class of the nation' cannot be answered 'in the affirmative *today*', his point is thus not least that the potential leaders are still lacking the necessary economic expertise.[32]

WEBER ON STOCK AND COMMODITY EXCHANGES (1894/1896)

Roth qualifies Weber as a 'cosmopolitan nationalist',[33] for whom the power interests of the German nation-state are intricately linked with its insertion in a liberal world trade regime. Accordingly, Weber favoured 'Germany's rapid industrialization' and a 'relatively free access to the world market', which was '[a]gainst the powerful agrarian interests'.[34] In the dispute over 'liberalism' versus 'protectionism' in (national) economic policy, Weber thus favoured free markets over state intervention – at least as long as this was in the interest of the German nation-state and national economy. Against this background, Weber's writings on stock and commodity exchange, which will be discussed next, also have a political function. His motivation appears to be the 'need for a strong capital market and efficient commodity exchanges for the sake of strengthening the German economy on the world market'.[35] At the same time, the two pamphlets – which were originally published in a series called Göttingen Workers' Library – are an effort in the economic education of a non-academic audience, in this case the 'socialist-oriented working class and its fledgling leaders'.[36] Far from being a 'socialist of the lectern' (*Kathedersozialist*), Weber was interested in establishing links between the interests of 'bourgeoisie' and 'proletariat'.[37] The immediate political context for his intervention was marked by calls for a ' "committee of inquiry" ' which would 'examine the commercial practices and social interests operative at the exchanges', in what was a climate of heightened 'interest-group based politics' and a looming 'great depression'.[38] Reportedly, the goal of that conservative initiative was to counteract

30 Weber, op. cit., n. 8, p. 444.
31 Tribe, op. cit., n. 15, p. 424.
32 Weber, op. cit., n. 8, p. 444 (original emphasis).
33 Roth, op. cit., n. 3, p. 267.
34 id., pp. 267–8.
35 id., p. 267.
36 Lestition, op. cit., n. 16, p. 301.
37 id., p. 296.
38 id., p. 289.

12

speculation at the stock and commodity exchanges, which would harm the national interest, or any form of 'abuse' at the expense of 'important interest groups in German society (especially the "agrarians")'.[39] In fact, the German *fin de siècle* offered all the ingredients of a financial crisis, including:

> the collapse of some otherwise reputable banks in 1891–1893, the publicity surrounding some spectacular personal bankruptcies, and public outrage over the suspension of payments on state debt bonds issued by the governments of Argentina, Portugal, and Greece.[40]

Demands to curb speculation notably aimed at 'futures trading in grain', the workings of which seemed to jeopardize agrarian interests, namely, in price stability.[41]

As a young professor of economics, Weber gave 'specialized courses in finance, such as "On Money, Banking and Stock Exchange Transactions" [...] and "Stock and Commodity Exchanges and their Law".'[42] At the same time, he was – at least preliminarily – appointed as 'expert adviser' to the Exchange Commission, which *Reichstag* and *Bundesrat* established to supervise the stock and commodity exchanges, as well as to the 'subcommittee set up to examine the grain trade on the exchanges in particular'.[43] Weber's message to his non-academic (or non-economic) audience is, in part, very basic, but it still pursues a political purpose. Accordingly, '[t]he stock and commodity exchange is an institution created by modern *large-scale commerce*' that is 'indispensible' for modern economies which are based on interdependence and the increasing '*community of exchange*', which ultimately spans 'the totality of all civilized peoples'.[44] The largest share of foreign trade was, in Weber's times, made up by '*mass articles*', such as grain, coal and iron, and cotton, and it seemed only natural to him that a modern bourse system was required to 'serve this gigantic process of exchange'.[45] With pedagogical intent, Weber emphasizes that 'stock [and commodity] exchanges and ["normal"] markets are the same in essence, especially through the analogous purposes they serve', and only differ in scope.[46] By way of examples, he demonstrates that modern bourses are not all about 'gambling' but that they fulfil rational functions for the national economy. In the second pamphlet,[47] Weber elaborates on the 'rationality and functionality of futures trading' and, in doing so, mitigates criticisms by the agrarian lobby.[48] The main argument is that future contracts (for example,

39 id.
40 id.
41 id., p. 292.
42 id., p. 293.
43 id., p. 292.
44 Weber, op. cit., n. 6, pp. 306–7 (original emphasis).
45 id., p. 309 (original emphasis).
46 id., p. 310.
47 Weber, op. cit., n. 7.
48 Lestition, op. cit., n. 16, p. 301.

13

about buying or selling a certain amount of grain for a fixed price at a specific date in the future) help traders and producers to control market-related risks – such as uneven supply, changing prices – and might actually bring about greater stability and predictability for all. In the first pamphlet, Weber further dwells on securities, including government bonds, and 'commercial notes of exchange'. Accordingly, the economic function of certified promises for payment would not be understood 'from looking at their legal meaning' only.[49] Moreover, Weber points out that stock and commodity exchanges increase not only the number of 'securitized claims', but also the extent of 'mutual owing-of payments [*Tributpflichtigkeit*]' within a society[50]– provided that the property relations are fairly even. The circulation of credit and debt would then become the normal state of affairs: everybody owns (shares or bonds) and everybody owes (dividends, interests, or simply taxes) at the same time.

WEBER ON MONETARY SYSTEM AND MONETARY POLICY (1922)

Weber's *Economy and Society*,[51] which he could not finalize during his lifetime, likewise contains sections with a clear political function. In the end, Weber 'poured most of his energies into the longest chapter', entitled the 'Sociological Categories of Economic Action'.[52] This is 'a chapter that despite its abstractness reflects the economic policy issues of the day' and is 'in a sense Weber's economic testament'.[53] Particularly relevant in this context is Weber's discussion of the function of money in the market economy. However, he notes that 'the present discussion is not an essay in monetary theory' but is 'concerned primarily with certain elementary socio-logical consequences of the use of money'.[54] Whereas the terminological clarifications at the beginning of his argument might be little contested, Weber later also takes up 'some of the most recent economic controversies' and notably discusses Georg Friedrich Knapp's *State Theory of Money* (1905), which 'had become extremely controversial between the schools of theoretical and historical economics'.[55] For Knapp, a 'theory of money' has to take into account that '[m]oney is a creature of law' and that '[t]he soul of currency is not in the material of the pieces, but in the legal ordinances which regulate their use'.[56] Weber considers Knapp's theory formally

---

49 Weber, op. cit., n. 6, p. 313.
50 id., p. 320 (original emphasis).
51 Weber, op. cit., n. 10.
52 Roth, op. cit., n. 3, p. 270.
53 id.
54 Weber, op. cit., n. 10, p. 76.
55 Roth, op. cit., n. 3, p. 271.
56 G.F. Knapp, *Staatliche Theorie des Geldes* (1905), cited in Roth, id.

correct, but deficient in substantive terms: whereas money was, as a (legal) means of payment, 'legitimated by the state', he emphasizes that, as an (economic) means of exchange, its 'value was determined by the market'.[57] Among the 'sociological consequences' of the use of money, 'which is merely a formal matter when seen from an economic point of view',[58] Weber lists new options for indirect exchange over space and time, a precise accountancy of assets, credits, and debts, a unitary assessment of costs and benefits of market chances, and the incentives this yields for a profit-making orientation. However, all this depends on the given 'market situation'[59] which is itself contingent on the given degree of market freedom, or the extent of market regulation, including formal restrictions (through state law) as well as substantive restrictions (through market power). According to Weber, the precondition of rational monetary accounting and profit-making behaviour is 'the battle of man with man', that is, effective competition and the balancing of supply and demand via the price mechanism.[60] All market prices therefore reflect certain constellations of power. In this regard, '[m]oney is not a mere "voucher for unspecified utilities", which could be altered at will', but reflects given economic interests and market forces.[61] One can thus distinguish between the 'formal, legal validity [of money] as a means of payment', which often includes a 'legal compulsion for its formal use as a means of exchange', and its '"substantive" validity', which is derived from 'its valuation in relation to marketable goods', that is, its actual purchasing power.[62]

To fulfil its function as a *formally* rational means of payment and exchange, money requires free and efficient markets. However, Weber points out that the price mechanism does not automatically yield results which are also regarded as *substantively* rational (such as a fair and equal distribution of wealth). For him, '[f]ormal and substantive rationality, no matter by what standard the latter is measured, are always in principle separate', even though they may coincide in practice.[63] Whereas by the 'experience of the last few decades' Weber considers market economies superior to planned economies, he also notes that such a claim can only be made on empirical grounds, and with regard to certain value standards.[64] The fact that formally highly rational market economies can lead to substantively irrational results is depicted as 'one of the important sources of all "social" problems, and above all, of the problems of socialism'.[65] His underlying

57 Roth, id., p. 272.
58 Weber, op. cit., n. 10, p. 77.
59 id., p. 80.
60 id., p. 91.
61 id., p. 106.
62 id., p. 167.
63 id., p. 106.
64 id.
65 id., p. 109.

worry seems to be that a market economy that does not sufficiently further social progress (lack of substantial rationality) might be replaced with a planned economy that no longer follows the price mechanism (lack of formal rationality). One type of rationality would thus be traded off against the other. The conflict between formal and substantive rationality also extends to 'monetary matters', with the 'formal rationality of the market economy [being] oriented primarily to profitability, currency stability, and exchange parity', whereas 'substantive (*material*) social ideals' often motivate more generous, or permissive, monetary policies.[66] What Weber criticizes about the latter is an overreliance on 'paper money', which can be generated at will by the state and thus further inflation, against so-called 'market money', which is still backed by (marketable) material values, such as gold or silver. While in the latter case, the creation of money is naturally limited, this does not hold true for administrative money: 'In this case, there is no doubt that it is the free decision of the political authorities which is the regulator of the quantity of money, unimpeded by any such mechanical restraints.'[67] The risk – or 'irrational factor' – which Weber notes here is that, in times of war or financial crisis, monetary policy could easily be dominated by 'interests' in excessive money creation.[68] While paper money always implies debts, one of the strongest motives for monetary inflation *within* a national economy is its (reductive) effect on outstanding *foreign* debts, either public or private. But 'someone would have to bear the costs' of this trick: namely, those with a relatively fixed income, little weight in the political process, and little power in the market place.[69]

BETWEEN STATES AND MARKETS: THE TWO SIDES OF THE COIN

In his essay 'Heads or Tails? Two Sides of the Coin',[70] Keith Hart invites us to take a closer look at the coins in our pockets: 'On one side is "heads" – the symbol of the political authority which minted the coin; on the other side is "tails" – the precise specification of the amount the coin is worth as payment in exchange.'[71] The two sides of the coin are explained with the 'double bind' of money between states and markets, that is, between top-down and bottom-up forms of social organization.[72] Accordingly, the symbolism of 'heads' reminds us of the fact 'that states underwrite currencies and that money is originally a relation between persons in society', whereas

---

66 Roth, op. cit., n. 3, p. 272.
67 Weber, op. cit., n. 10, p. 190.
68 id.
69 id., p. 185.
70 K. Hart, 'Heads or Tails? Two Sides of the Coin' (1986) 21 *Man* 637–56.
71 id., p. 638.
72 id.

16

'tails' stands for the nominal value money has on the market, 'independent of the persons engaged in any particular transaction'.[73]

According to Hart, most theories of money are preoccupied with only one side of the coin. In historical terms, 'English utilitarianism' furthered commodity theories of money, which define money as an economic good to be exchanged on the market, whereas 'German idealism' produced theories of money as a symbol of legal relations, which are backed by the state.[74] However, the two leading ideologies of the nineteenth century were also 'cross-cutting', which Hart tries to capture by distinguishing between 'formal' and 'substantive' versions of the respective paradigms.[75] As to the market paradigm, formalist perspectives are represented by classical economic liberalism 'which regards money solely as a commodity, subject to the laws of competitive markets'.[76] A more substantive argument is inherent in the idea of a civil society – or a civilized market society – as being based on trust. In both accounts, the 'law of the market' is of an economic nature, perhaps with an emphasis on competition in the former and on cooperation in the latter case. As to the state paradigm, Hart specifies a formalist view of '[m]oney as the expression of state policy [which] emphasises the role of law and government intervention'.[77] This is contrasted with a more substantive understanding of money as an expression of national culture and tradition. In both cases, the market is subject to regulation, either in the form of state law or customary law.

Against this background, we can situate Weber between the two poles of state law and market law, or rather, as moving from one side to the other. On the one hand, his work is inspired by German idealism, and he is himself listed as a member of the 'youngest' generation of the German historical school of economics, which is rooted in the same tradition. In this regard, Weber naturally starts from a concept of money as a legal artefact. On the other hand, he not only draws upon but also takes issue with Knapp's 'State Theory of Money',[78] which exemplifies the formalist version of the state paradigm.[79] Whereas Knapp held 'that money was a standard of credit issued by the state and that the state's freedom of manoeuvre in monetary policy should not be restricted by an international system anchored in the timeless exchangeability of gold',[80] Weber emphasizes the risks of such a policy, namely, in times of crisis. His aim is, therefore, to strengthen the commodity character of money against its possible inflation on paper. Such arguments

---

73 id.
74 id., pp. 643–4.
75 id., p. 645.
76 id.
77 id., p. 646.
78 Knapp, op. cit., n. 56.
79 Hart, op. cit., n. 70, p. 646.
80 id., p. 644.

17

mark Weber 'as a sympathetic critic of the liberal tradition in economics', who even adopts some of its elements.[81] We can compare this with Marx's position, for whom it is claimed that '[i]n matters of monetary theory Marx adhered broadly to classical orthodoxy'.[82] However, this statement has to be taken with a grain of salt, inasmuch as Marx also exposes how money is 'fetishized' in modern capitalism and, first of all, by liberal economics.[83] For Nelson, Marx's theory of money is, therefore, not a 'conventional commodity theory of money' but a 'theory of the money commodity'.[84] In contrast to classical economists who focus on the material or market value of goods, Marx ultimately defines commodity 'in philosophical or social terms as alienated human being'.[85] In this framing, the money commodity represents human labour, or the 'value' yielded by its exploitation in the production process. Moreover, Marx's theory also differs from economic liberalism in its harsh criticism of the 'cult' of legal concepts which would only legitimate the existing relations of production.[86] Accordingly, it is notably 'politicians and lawyers' who justify and reify given inequalities in terms of 'natural' property rights.[87]

POLANYI ON THE EFFECTS OF THE GOLD STANDARD (1944)

Polanyi works in the Marxian legacy, but develops his own view of the market economy and its relation with money. In terms of an economic sociology of law, his work is less explicit but no less inspiring than Weber's.[88] In the following, we will first focus on two chapters in *The Great Transformation*[89] – 'The Hundred Years' Peace' and 'Self-Regulation Impaired' – which together account for both the relative stability of nineteenth-century civilization and its accelerating crisis at the end. For Polanyi, this social formation 'rested on four institutions': the 'balance-of-power system', the 'gold standard', the 'self-regulating market', and the 'liberal state'.[90] While he notes that 'two of these institutions were economic,

81 id., p. 651.
82 id., p. 643.
83 id.
84 A. Nelson, 'Marx's Theory of the Money Commodity' (2001) 33 *History of Economics Rev.* 44–63, at 45.
85 id.
86 K. Marx (and F. Engels), *The German Ideology*, ch. 3: Saint Max (part B, s. I) (1845), at <http://www.marxists.org/archive/marx/works/1845/german-ideology/ch03k.htm>.
87 id.
88 S. Frerichs, 'Re-embedding Neo-liberal Constitutionalism: A Polanyian Case for the Economic Sociology of Law' in *Karl Polanyi, Globalisation and the Potential of Law in Transnational Markets*, eds. C. Joerges and J. Falke (2011) 65–84.
89 Polanyi, op. cit., n. 11.
90 id., p. 3.

18

two political',[91] he actually criticizes the 'institutional separation of society into an economic and political sphere'.[92] His analysis thus reflects what he considers normatively and objectively dangerous: the 'disembedding' of the market from social regulation. Nevertheless, the two economic institutions – gold standard and self-regulating market – help to explain the 'hundred year's peace' between the Congress of Vienna and the First World War. As to the gold standard (a monetary system based on the convertibility of currencies into gold which guaranteed a fixed exchange rate between the participating countries), Polanyi introduces this as 'an attempt to extend the domestic market system to the international field'[93] and as an instrument to discipline national monetary policies.[94] Its ultimate collapse is seen as the 'proximate cause of the catastrophe' which unfolded in the two world wars.[95] Moreover, Polanyi emphasizes the 'powerful social instrumentality' of international networks of banking and finance, whose business was premised on the gold standard and, indirectly, on the maintenance of peace.[96] Their activities were 'not restricted to the financing of governments' but also 'comprised foreign investment in industry, public utilities, and banks, as well as long-term loans to public and private corporations abroad'.[97] Hence, by way of monetary integration, '[t]rade had become linked with peace'.[98] The attained state of 'globalization' is illustrated as follows:

> By the fourth quarter of the nineteenth century, world commodity prices were the central reality in the lives of millions of Continental peasants; the repercussions of the London money market were daily noted by businessmen all over the world; and governments discussed plans for the future in light of the situation on the world capital markets.[99]

Polanyi also notes a 'growing peace interest inside every nation where the investment habit had taken root'.[100] In fact, '[b]esides the international center, *haute finance* proper, there were some half dozen national centers hiving around their banks of issue and stock exchanges', reflecting the same economic logic.[101]

However, the experience that 'national independence and sovereignty were now the functions of currency and credit'[102] evoked strong reactions by

91 id.
92 id., p. 71.
93 id., p. 3.
94 id., p. 14.
95 id.
96 id., p. 9.
97 id., p. 11.
98 id., p. 15.
99 id., p. 18.
100 id., p. 14.
101 id., p. 11.
102 id., p. 18.

19

those who had to bear the costs of the indifferent rule of the market. As to the gold standard, Block notes:

> In theory, if a country is in a deficit position in a given year because its citizens spent more abroad than they earned, gold flows out of that country's reserves to clear payments due to foreigners. The domestic supply of money and credit automatically shrinks, interest rates rise, prices and wages fall, demand for imports declines, and exports become more competitive.[103]

In practice, such a process of deflation meant 'dramatic declines in wages and farm income, increases in unemployment, and a sharp rise in business and bank failures'.[104] To mitigate the costs of 'adjustment' for workers and farmers, and business in general, national governments increasingly resorted to countermeasures, thus heralding a new era of protectionism – and imperialism. In this sense, the gold standard 'forced nations to consolidate themselves around heightened national, and then, imperial boundaries'.[105] Polanyi speaks specifically of 'the half century 1879–1929', in which 'Western societies developed into closely knit units, in which powerful disruptive strains were latent'.[106] Notably, the agrarian sector suffered from a protracted crisis at that time:

> Among continental farmers, the decreasing price of grain, associated with the long and difficult economic depression in the 1870s, that continued until the early 1890s, fuelled protectionist sentiments and encouraged their alignment with the rising industrialist class.[107]

This was not without precedence. Already, at the beginning of the nineteenth century, the gold standard was imposed 'against the backdrop of a severe rural crisis that had begun right at the end of the Napoleonic Wars' and caused much distress in the agrarian sector.[108] 'Moreover, the deflationary pressures did not end with the success of restoration; the gold standard simply made the pressures on the rural economy permanent.'[109] As important in the present context is, however, the fact that the new protectionism also implied a shift in monetary policies: 'The new crustacean type of nation expressed its identity through national token currencies safeguarded by a type of sovereignty more jealous and absolute than anything known before.'[110] Whereas from the

---

103 F. Block, 'Introduction' to new edition of Polyanyi's *The Great Transformation* (2001, 2nd edn.) xviii, at xxx–xxxi (reference omitted).
104 id., p. xxxi.
105 id., p. xxxii.
106 Polanyi, op. cit., n. 11, p. 201.
107 R. Väyrynen, 'Peace, Market, and Society: Karl Polanyi's Contribution to Theory of War and Peace', paper prepared for the 43th Annual Convention of the International Studies Association, New Orleans, 23–27 March 2002, URL <http://isanet.ccit.arizona.edu/noarchive/vayrynen.html> (reference omitted).
108 F. Block and M. Somers, 'In the Shadow of Speenhamland: Social Policy and the Old Poor Law' (2003) 31 *Politics and Society* 283–323, at 309.
109 id., p. 310.
110 Polanyi, op. cit., n. 11, p. 202.

viewpoint of economic liberalism, national currencies, if backed by gold, did not matter as such since the market would watch over their exchange relations, they now developed a life of their own. In the end, 'the monetary system was the strongest among the economic forces integrating the nation'.[111] Rather than furthering liberalism, it fostered nationalism.

POLANYI ON THE (DE-)COMMODIFICATION OF MONEY (1944)

This historical account of the economic premises and social consequences of the gold standard is complemented by a more theoretical account of money as a 'fictitious commodity', which Polanyi likewise develops in *The Great Transformation*. A good starting point to introduce this perspective is Polanyi's criticism of Marx in this respect. As Polanyi notes, '[b]elief in the gold standard was the faith of the age'.[112] More precisely, the idea 'that bank notes have value because they represent gold' was shared by 'capitalists and socialists' alike:[113]

> Whether the gold itself has value for the reason that it embodies labor, as the socialists held, or for the reason that it is useful and scarce, as the orthodox doctrine ran, made for once no difference. [...] Karl Marx had gone to great pains to show up Proudhon's utopian labor notes (which were to replace currency) as based on self-delusion; and *Das Kapital* implied the commodity theory of money, in its Ricardian form.[114]

Also in the chapter in which the concept of the fictitious commodities is introduced, Polanyi distances himself, in a footnote, from 'Marx's assertion of the fetish character of the value of commodities [which] refers to the exchange value of genuine commodities and [therefore] has nothing in common with the fictitious commodities mentioned in the text.'[115] For Polanyi, fictitious commodities – namely, land, labour, and money – are key to the functioning of the self-regulating market, which he considers a dangerous utopia. All these production factors are fictitious commodities in that they are traded on the market but have not been produced for the market in the first place. As to land and labour, Polanyi argues that 'labor is only another name for a human activity which goes with life itself' and 'land is only another name for nature, which is not produced by man'.[116] By an act of 'commodification', the natural productivity of man and nature is thus turned into land and labour. With regard to money, Polanyi distinguishes between

111 id., p. 204.
112 id., p. 25.
113 id.
114 id.
115 id., p. 72, fn. 3.
116 id., p. 72.

21

money as mere purchasing power and money as a marketable commodity. Accordingly, 'actual money' is 'merely a token of purchasing power which [...] comes into being through the mechanism of banking or state finance'.[117] In this picture, a national token currency follows a political logic, whereas commodity money follows an economic logic. As a 'self-regulating mechanism of supplying credit', the gold standard furthers the commodity form of money. In contrast, national central banking allows for a 'manipulation' or, rather, the management of currency exchange and money supply.[118]

In the realm of money, Polanyi's 'double movement' is thus embodied by the 'commodifying' gold standard on the one hand, and 'decommodifying' central banking on the other. Polanyi notes that, in practice:

> the institutional separation of the political and economic spheres had never been complete, and it was precisely in the matter of currency that it was necessarily incomplete; the state, whose Mint seemed merely to certify the weight of coins, was in fact the guarantor of the value of token money, which it accepted in payment for taxes and otherwise.[119]

Replicating the distinction between (market-based) commodity money and (state-based) fiat money, Polanyi continues:

> This money was *not* a means of exchange, it was a means of payment; it was not a commodity, it was purchasing power; far from having utility itself, it was merely a counter embodying a quantified claim to things that might be purchased.[120]

Considering that a lack of monetary steering would not only exacerbate crises but also jeopardize the 'expansion of production and trade' due to the rigidities inherent to commodity money,[121] Polanyi clearly sympathizes with a 'non-essentialist' theory of money, such as that of John Maynard Keynes: 'In the Keynesian system the role of money is purely pragmatic', that is, 'the presence of money is here taken for granted, not conceptually deduced'.[122] Rather than locating central banks on the side of fiat money only, one can also argue that they mediate between 'international gold standard' and 'national credit money' and, hence, between an economic logic, which 'rests on the means of exchange', and a political logic, which 'embodies the collective identity on which the means of payment is based'.[123] At any rate,

---

117 id.
118 id., p. 195.
119 id., p. 196.
120 id. (original emphasis).
121 id., p. 193.
122 K. Polanyi, 'The Semantics of Money-Uses' in *Primitive, Archaic, and Modern Economies: Essays of Karl Polanyi*, ed. G. Dalton (1971/1957) 175–203, at 196.
123 J. Maucourant, 'Polanyi on Institutions and Money: An Interpretation Suggested by a Reading of Commons, Mitchell and Veblen' in *Economy and Society: Money, Capitalism and Transition*, eds. A. Fikret and P. Devine (2001) 150–71, at <http://hal.archives-ouvertes.fr/docs/00/55/87/10/PDF/Black_Rose_Books_R.pdf > 12.

governments – or central banks, for that matter – can and do create money, namely, in the form of public debts, which establish a monetary link between present wealth holders and future taxpayers, and between public and private interests.[124] A related point to be mentioned is the juridical form that monetary policies take, both in their international-economic and national-political orientation. As to the former, the legal stipulation of the 'taboos of money'[125] is best expressed in the following passage:

> In all matters relevant to the world monetary system, similar institutions were established everywhere, such as representative bodies, written constitutions defining their jurisdiction and regulating the publication of budgets, the promulgation of laws, the ratification of treaties, the methods of incurring financial obligations, the rules of public accountancy, the rights of foreigners, the jurisdiction of courts, the domicile of bills of exchange, and thus, by implication, the status of the bank of issue, of foreign bondholders, of creditors of all description.[126]

Hence, no money without law.

POLANYI ON EMPIRICAL ECONOMIES AND MONEY USES (1977)

Finally, we will turn to writings which are less political but nevertheless criticize the dominant role that economics has assumed in modern society – and in the social sciences. Already in *The Great Transformation*, Polanyi asserts that 'there is hardly an anthropological or sociological assumption – whether explicit or implicit – contained in the philosophy of economic liberalism that has not been refuted'.[127] In 'Economy as Instituted Process',[128] he now explicitly distinguishes between two meanings of the term 'economic', which would compete (and often be confounded) in the social sciences: its formal meaning and its substantive meaning. Accordingly, the formal meaning forms the basis of 'formal economics', which starts from the problem of 'scarcity' and is preoccupied with rational means-ends relations. For Polanyi, this understanding of economics is confined to the modern market economy, and thus not suited to describe other kinds of empirical economies across times and space. He therefore suggests a more substantive understanding of the human economy, which starts from the problem of 'subsistence' and studies 'the manner in which the economic process is instituted' in particular societies.[129] Attention would notably be given to the

---

124 A. Davis, 'Endogenous Institutions and the Politics of Property: Comparing and Contrasting Douglass North and Karl Polanyi in the Case of Finance' (2008) 42 *J. of Economic Issues* 1101–22.
125 Polanyi, op. cit., n. 11, p. 205.
126 id.
127 id., p. 269.
128 Polanyi, op. cit., n. 12, pp. 243–5.
129 id., p. 245.

23

'great variety of institutions other than markets, in which man's livelihood was [or is] embedded'.[130] Such an empirical approach would not be hampered by the (narrow) presumptions of the economic discipline, which mark the work of many social scientists – Polanyi's list of names includes here, besides Marshall, Pareto, and Durkheim, also Weber and Parsons.[131] To the same effect, he speaks of an 'economistic fallacy'[132] and, with regard to the presumable interdependence of market, trade, and money, of a 'catallactic fallacy'.[133] Whereas in *The Great Transformation* the dominance of a market perspective on society was mostly addressed as a political problem, it is now pointed out as a methodological problem. However, even in his later writings Polanyi does not do without a reference to 'the lapse of the gold standard', which entailed 'a recession of the world role of markets from their nineteenth century peak'.[134] Moreover, he notes that the implications of his criticism of 'catallactic definitions of trade, money and market' have to be seen 'in the light of the gradual institutional transformation that has been in progress since the first World War'.[135] Polanyi thus substantiates the need for a substantive economic approach also in political terms.

According to the substantive view, 'the human economy is [...] embedded and enmeshed in institutions, economic and noneconomic', which includes the effects and influences of religion, government, technology – and of 'monetary institutions'.[136] As to the latter, we can draw on Polanyi's more specific writings on 'money uses', in which he is, however, more interested in reassessing the role of money in traditional societies than in modern ones.[137] His major distinction is, in this respect, between (our) modern '"all-purpose" money' and the '"limited purpose"' or 'special purpose money' of earlier times.[138] The basic idea is that only today's money includes all possible 'money uses', whereas in earlier moneys they are institutionally distinguished and spread over different 'money objects' (for example, lifestock as a measure of wealth; cowrie shells as a means of exchange; a substantial dowry as a condition for marriage). It is interesting to note that the qualification of modern money as 'all-purpose' money, which is as such singled out from all other moneys, is contested – and even attributed to Polanyi's own modernist bias. In fact, the 'money uses' which Polanyi discusses in more detail – 'means of payment, standard of value or money of

130 id.
131 id., p. 244.
132 id., p. 245, fn. 1, mentioning Hume, Spencer, Knight, and Northrop.
133 Polanyi, op. cit., n. 13, p. 104, mentioning Smith, Ricardo, Spencer, Durkheim, Mauss, and Simmel.
134 Polanyi, op. cit., n. 12, p. 256.
135 id., pp. 269–70.
136 id., p. 250.
137 Polanyi, op. cit., n. 122; Polanyi, op. cit., n. 13.
138 Polanyi, op. cit., n. 12, pp. 264–6; Polanyi, op. cit., n. 13, p. 120.

24

account; store of wealth; and medium of exchange' – are 'derived from the
monetary theory of the market economy'.[139] On the positive side, explora-
tions into earlier moneys may also give insight into the substance of modern
money, which is neglected in 'formal economics', or else reduced to the
dichotomy between commodity money and fiat money. In fact, Polanyi's
definition of money as 'semantic system' whose symbols are often 'attached
to physical objects' but sometimes only 'represented by a word or cypher'[140]
is inclusive enough to also cover the 'financialization' of contemporary
economies. Moreover, all money uses discussed in Polanyi's anthropological
review have references to the law. Payment means 'settling an obligation by
handing over quantifiable objects'[141] and has a 'propinquity' to punishment:
'Thus payment was due alike from the guilty, the impure, the weak and
lowly; it was owed to the gods and their priests, the honoured, and the
strong.'[142] A standard of value is required for 'individual exchange' as well
as 'central administration'.[143] The latter is notably interested in the
accounting of tributes and taxes from subjects or citizens, which is a matter
of public law. Storage of wealth, or staples, is the origin of 'staple finance,
i.e., the rudimentary form of money and credit finance',[144] with lending and
borrowing again creating extended legal obligations. And before markets and
the price mechanism developed, exchange rates had been fixed 'by virtue of
custom, statute, or proclamation'.[145]

CONCLUSION: BACK TO THE CLASSICS – OR BETTER BEYOND?

In *The Great Transformation*, Polanyi criticizes the 'market-view of society
which equated economics with contractual relationships, and contractual
relations with freedom', and which imagines the individual as an independent actor who is 'in nobody's debt'.[146] In such a perspective, '[s]ociety as a
whole remained invisible',[147] but also the law and the legal nature of money
are neglected. In contrast, Weber interprets the interdependencies which
arise from increasing exchange on markets and at bourses as bringing about a
society, in which everybody is virtually in everybody's debt. This illustrates
that money is not only a thing but also a relation, an insight that Polanyi and
Weber seem to share.[148] At the same time, Weber lays more emphasis on

139 Polanyi, op. cit., n. 13, p. 97.
140 id., pp. 97–8.
141 id., p. 102.
142 id., p. 105.
143 id., p. 108.
144 id., p. 115.
145 id., p. 119.
146 Polanyi, op. cit., n. 11, p. 258.
147 id.
148 Hart, op. cit., n. 70, pp. 638–9.

money as a commodity, which derives its value from the market, whereas Polanyi highlights the responsibility of the state in shaping the underlying legal relations. In their assessment of monetary policies Weber and Polanyi come, each at their time of writing, apparently to opposite conclusions: the former seems to be more rigid, the latter more permissive in this respect.

As recent developments show – from the American sub-prime mortgage crisis to the European sovereign debt crisis – the ambiguity of money, which is expressed in the 'two sides of the coin', has not lost its topicality. While it thus seems worthwhile to go back to Weber's and Polanyi's classical accounts of money in the market economy, this does not suffice to put the 'economic sociology of law' on the track of the twenty-first century. Both sociologists are representative of historical scholarship, which can be considered the 'first generation' of socio-legal thinking, and, in a way, also pioneers of a realist understanding of law, as forwarded by the 'second generation'. But their writings bear little traces of a constructivist point of view, which has come into fashion in the 'third generation' of socio-legal thinking.[149]

The question is thus not only what we can learn from the classics, but also what we could teach them in return. To give but an idea of constructivist theorizing about money, we conclude with Maurer,[150] who argues that there are actually more than two sides of the coin. In this regard, he not only objects to the 'classical accounts of Marx, Weber, and Simmel' but also criticizes contemporary scholars for still retelling 'the story of the "great transformation" from socially embedded to disembedded and abstracted economic forms [and money uses]', even when they amend the narrative here and there.[151] Moreover, he claims that '[t]he telling of the tale and the criticisms of the tale [...] may in fact constitute money today, its indeterminacy, its openness'.[152] The same performative effect might be implicated by continued use of the dichotomy of commodity money and fiat money, economic thing and legal relation. This means that it cannot capture the 'reality' of modern finance besides our talk about it and our mysterious and precarious belief in its functioning. If money is neither made from gold nor guilt, what remains?

149 S. Frerichs, 'Studying Law, Economy, and Society: A Short History of Socio-legal Thinking' (2012) Helsinki Legal Studies Research Paper no. 19, at <http://ssrn.com/abstract_id=2022891>.
150 B. Maurer, 'The Anthropology of Money' (2006) 35 Annual Rev. of Anthropology 15–36.
151 id., p. 15.
152 id., p. 17.

JOURNAL OF LAW AND SOCIETY
VOLUME 40, NUMBER 1, MARCH 2013
ISSN: 0263-323X, pp. 27–48

Relational Work and the Law: Recapturing the Legal Realist Critique of Market Fundamentalism

FRED BLOCK*

A global financial crisis seems a propitious time to renew a dialogue between legal scholarship and the field of economic sociology. In the 1920s and 1930s, legal realist scholars developed insightful analyses of market processes. But since post-war mainstream legal scholarship has largely ignored this aspect of legal realism, economic sociology might be helpful in refocusing legal scholarship on what happens in actual market settings. One tool is Zelizer's concept of relational work; that in market transactions, actors must define the nature of their relationship, what is to be exchanged, and by what media. Relational work has an enormous impact on the outcomes of transactions, but it is largely ignored in economic accounts. An empirical study of variations in relational work across economic settings could provide a strong foundation for rethinking the relationship between law and economic activity.

INTRODUCTION

Bringing insights from economic sociology into legal scholarship requires considerable humility, as legal thinkers have been struggling with the empirical realities of economic activity for many years, and the ideas of important sociologists have been part of the background intellectual culture

* Department of Sociology, University of California at Davis, Davis, California 95616, United States of America
flblock@ucdavis.edu

I am deeply grateful to Karl Klare for educating me on key issues in legal scholarship and for providing extensive feedback on multiple drafts of this article. I could not have written this without him, but I alone am responsible for the remaining weaknesses. I have also drawn here on work done with Margaret Somers. Thanks also to Viviana Zelizer for our on-going conversation and for specific suggestions on an earlier draft. I am also grateful to the editors for their initial invitation and for their suggestions for strengthening this article.

27

of legal thinkers for three or four generations. It is hardly as though law and sociology have developed in splendid isolation from each other. On the contrary, some key transformations in legal thinking in the past century and a half have followed closely shifts in related academic disciplines.[1] Moreover, for almost half a century, an organized law and society movement has been working to deepen the connections between legal scholarship and the social sciences.[2]

There is, however, something special about the current moment that provides a possible opportunity to initiate a new phase in the engagement between these fields.[3] First, in the same way that the prospect of a hanging concentrates the mind, there is nothing like a global economic crisis to accelerate critical thinking about our ways of organizing economic activity. We have long recognized that the Great Depression of the 1930s produced enormous intellectual breakthroughs in economic knowledge, and it might well be possible that the global financial crisis that began in 2008 is similarly generative.

Second, mainstream legal thinking, particularly in the United States, has for some time faced a crisis in its understanding of economic activity. This crisis results from the marginalization of the key insights of legal realist scholars of the 1920s and 1930s who had developed a theoretically sophisticated analysis of the actual workings of markets. The failure of more legal scholars to build on the insights of the realists created an opening in legal academia for a revival of market fundamentalism – an exaggerated reverence for market self-regulation that has had huge influence in the courts, in public policy, and in political debate. This article will argue that ideas developed by economic sociologists could help legal thinkers to bring the critical insights of legal realism back into the mainstream of legal debate while simultaneously pushing market fundamentalist ideas back into marginality.

Economic sociology is a relatively young field of scholarly inquiry. It grew up in the United States in the 1980s very much in response to the market fundamentalism of the Reagan administration and the imperialist impulses of neo-classical economics. A number of scholars from different theoretical traditions came together and recognized that what they were doing could be termed economic sociology, and from there, the usual activities of building a new academic field were set in motion.[4] Conferences

---

1 See, for example, M. Horwitz, *The Transformation of American Law 1870–1960* (1992).

2 L. Friedman, 'The Law and Society Movement' (1986) 38 *Stanford Law Rev.* 763; A. Sarat, 'Vitality Amidst Fragmentation: On the Emergence of Postrealist Law and Society Scholarship' in *The Blackwell Companion to Law and Society,* ed. A. Sarat (2004) 1.

3 To be sure, an interdisciplinary group of law and society scholars have been pursuing this project of renewal for some time. See, for example, the New Legal Realism Conversations, at <http://newlegalrealism.wordpress.com/>.

4 R. Swedberg, 'Economic Sociology: Past and Present' (1987) 35 *Current Sociology* 1.

28

were organized, specific organizational entities and journals created, and new courses established at both the undergraduate and graduate level. Now, almost three decades later, the field has become well-established in the United States and internationally and it has attracted several new cohorts of extremely productive scholars.

To be sure, this initiative had a distinct advantage from the start. Sociology in the United States recognizes three canonical figures who shaped the basic questions of the discipline – Karl Marx, Emile Durkheim, and Max Weber. All three of these figures can, in fact, be claimed retrospectively as economic sociologists. Moreover, the term 'economic sociology' had a certain currency during the lifetimes of Durkheim and Weber and in central Europe, extending through the inter-war period.[5] Hence, the universe of classical antecedents for contemporary economic sociology can easily be expanded to include Werner Sombart, George Simmel, Joseph Schumpeter, and Karl Polanyi. This 'classical' lineage has been extremely valuable in legitimating the project of contemporary economic sociologists.

Surprisingly, however, there has been relatively little work done in tracing out this historical lineage of economic sociology within the United States itself. There are occasional references to Thorstein Veblen and John Commons as figures who straddled the boundary between institutional economics and economic sociology, but to date, there are few serious treatments of their work by contemporary economic sociologists.

The more serious scandal is that contemporary economic sociologists have largely ignored the theoretical contributions of the legal realists, a group of legal scholars active particularly in the 1920s and 1930s who developed a powerful critique of what were then the dominant forms of legal reasoning.[6] Since a significant element of that mainstream jurisprudence was a defence of 'freedom of contract', some of the legal realists directly challenged free market economic ideas.[7] These thinkers independently elaborated many of the key insights that have become central to contemporary economic sociology.

The centrepiece of contemporary economic sociology has been the argument that markets do not exist in the abstract; they are embedded in law, politics, culture, and social arrangements. To understand how particular markets are functioning, one has to look at the way that they are embedded

---

5 C. Trigilia, *Economic Sociology* (2002).
6 There is intense scholarly debate on who is included under the rubric of legal realism and its precise period. See Horwitz, op. cit., n. 1; J.W. Singer, 'Legal Realism Now' (1988) 76 *California Law Rev.* 465.
7 Of these, the most important figure was Robert Lee Hale. See B. Fried, *The Progressive Assault on Laissez-Faire: Robert Hale and the First Law and Economics Movement* (1998); D. Kennedy, 'The Stakes of Law, or Hale and Foucault' in *Sexy Dressing Etc.* (1993).

in society. But these are precisely the arguments that the legal realists elaborated in their critique of the jurisprudence of the early twentieth century – often referenced as Lochnerism.[8] Critics of *Lochner* argued in systematic fashion that markets are not natural; they are socially constructed and that the relative power of different market actors is directly shaped by the particular legal rules and institutional practices that have structured that particular market.[9]

This article, however, is not intended to address this contemporary sociological neglect of the legal realist tradition; rather, the goal is to use insights from current economic sociology to revisit the theoretical project in which the realists were engaged. At the risk of distortion, I am going to offer an extremely condensed version of the contribution and trajectory of the legal realists. This begins with Singer's argument that the legal realists mounted a two-sided challenge to Lochnerism.[10] One part of the challenge focused on the formalism of the dominant legal tradition which imagined that judicial rulings are simply a question of applying broad legal principles to particular cases, and that any judge who engages in the proper form of legal reasoning will be bound to reach the same conclusion. Against these claims, the realists insisted that most cases worth hearing involved conflicts between opposing legal principles and that there are always gaps and ambiguities in any field of law that make it impossible to apply principles mechanically. Furthermore, as Davis and Klare state it: 'Legal concepts are not self-defining and cannot determine outcomes.'[11] The point is that judges do not simply find the applicable law; they make law by adjudicating among conflicting principles and differentiating the particular case in front of them from other seemingly similar cases.

The second part of the legal realist challenge was a direct assault on the public/private distinction that has acted as a powerful constraint on direct and indirect forms of regulation of economic activity. As was articulated by Karl Polanyi, Anglo-American thought has long been shaped by 'social naturalism' – the idea that society is governed by the same laws that govern nature.[12] The classical economists, Malthus and Ricardo, building on the foundation established by John Locke, argued that the economy – the sphere in which private contracting takes place – exists both analytically and

---

8 *Lochner* v. *New York*, 198 U.S. 45 (1905) was a Supreme Court decision that overruled state regulations on the hours worked by bakers because the legislation infringed on the 'liberty of contract' of employers.

9 D. Davis and K. Klare, 'Transformative Constitutionalism and the Common and Customary Law' (2010) 26 *South African J. on Human Rights* 403.

10 Singer, op. cit., n. 6.

11 Davis and Klare, op. cit., n. 9, p. 439.

12 K. Polanyi, *The Great Transformation* (2001/1944); M. Somers and F. Block, 'From Poverty to Perversity: Ideas Markets, and Institutions over 200 Years of Welfare Debate' (2005) 70 *Am. Sociological Rev.* 260; M. Somers, *Genealogies of Citizenship* (2008).

30

historically prior to the emergence of government institutions. Moreover, government has a solemn obligation not to interfere with or disrupt the workings of that economic realm which must necessarily be governed by economic principles such as the law of supply and demand. The failure of government to respect the boundary between the public sphere and the private sphere of economic activity will produce both economic disaster and tyranny.

Some of the legal realists, particularly Hale, recognized the social naturalism that was at the heart of Lochnerism and they proceeded to attack it directly. They showed that markets simply do not exist independently of the legal rules that govern them. The nature of contract and property, for example, were not handed down with the Commandments on Mount Sinai; they are defined by legislatures and courts in different ways at different times. Moreover, 'the so-called "freedom of contract" consists of negotiation conducted and agreements made within a governmentally structured framework of mutual pressure and coercion.'[13] And there is no way for the law to remain neutral in this negotiation process; whether judges decide to act or not act in a particular instance, and precisely how they act if they choose to do so, influence the relative power of the contracting parties.

The legal realists had some successes in their attacks on legal formalism. The dominant tendencies within post-war jurisprudence have adopted legal realist arguments that what judges must do is to elaborate intermediate concepts and balancing tests that allow them to deal with conflicting principles and the inevitable gaps in existing frameworks.[14] Nevertheless, formalist errors have returned through the back door precisely because mainstream legal thinking has largely rejected the legal realist assault on the public/private divide.

Beginning during the Second World War, some liberal legal theorists who had been supportive of the New Deal's key reforms began to worry about the threat of governmental overreach, and they started a gradual and uneven retreat from the legal realists' critique of the public/private distinction. As Horwitz argues, F.A. Hayek's 1944 polemic, *The Road to Serfdom,* influenced the thinking of some mainstream lawyers.[15] Hayek's argument was that when government failed to respect the public/private boundary as happened in Soviet Russia and Nazi Germany, totalitarianism was the inevitable outcome. But he insisted that even gradualist reforms such as those of the New Deal and European social democracies that occurred under democratic auspices, would push those societies down the 'road to serfdom'. To be sure, Hayek presented no real evidence to support this claim, but he very successfully invoked the arguments of social naturalism to cast doubt

13 Davis and Klare, op. cit., n. 9, p. 447.
14 Singer, op. cit. n. 6 , p. 503.
15 Horwitz, op. cit., n. 1, p. 228.

31

on the historic achievements of the New Deal. As mainstream legal thinkers sought to avoid this danger by reconstructing some kind of wall of separation between the public and the private, they slid back into formalist errors.[16]

CONSEQUENCES OF MARKET FUNDAMENTALISM

It is now well understood that decades of well-funded counterattacks against New Deal jurisprudence have significantly transformed both legal and popular understandings of the appropriate conditions for government regulation of market activity. To be sure, defenders of markets acknowledge that there are certain conditions under which markets fail, and in such instances, the normal restraints that favour respecting the public/private divide may be suspended. But conservative law and economics scholars have insisted that such failures are always the exception; the normal state is – as social naturalism insists – market success. These thinkers, often with significant support from right-wing funders, have waged extensive intellectual and political campaigns to assert that a particular market failure occurs far less frequently than has been alleged by their opponents.[17] Whether we are talking about antitrust violations, involuntary unemployment, various types of externalities, or even the existence of financial bubbles, vast literatures have been produced to 'prove' that such market failures occur either infrequently or never.

While these arguments sometimes include the mobilization of empirical data, it is almost always the case that the key part of the argument is derived deductively from economic first principles. We know how a self-regulating economy works and from these basic mechanisms, as illustrated through mathematical proofs, it should be self-evident that the particular alleged market failure cannot occur. For example, in Milton Friedman's classic argument, there can be no such thing as a financial bubble – the systematic and sustained overpricing of financial assets. Rational actors know that they should buy low and sell high. If they see an overpriced asset, they will not purchase it, so it follows that soon the asset price will come down to a level that is closer to its correct market price.

The consequence is that arguments that are reminiscent of Lochnerism have gained increasing influence in the legal arena.[18] The legal realist focus on the empirical reality of actual market situations has given way to a more

16 Singer, op. cit., n. 6.
17 S.M. Teles, *The Rise of the Conservative Legal Movement* (2008).
18 Everson and Joerges find suggestions of Lochnerism in recent European Court of Justice decisions on the freedom of firms to trade across national lines. M. Everson and C. Joerges, 'Reconfiguring the Politics-Law Relationship in the Integration Project through Conflicts-Law Constitutionalism' (2012) 18 *European Law J.* 644–66.

abstract and deductive approach in which the analysis of markets relies heavily on economic theory. What conservative law and economics scholars have successfully done is tilt the lenses used by both jurists and legislators in a way that focuses on abstract ideas about how markets work and leaves the reality of the market situation largely out of focus. The consequence is that abstract principles such as freedom of contract are again able to trump a close examination of the actual balance of power in market situations.

But this shift has produced a consequence that is even more serious than a threatened revival of Lochnerism. The restoration of uncritical acceptance of the public/private divide by many legal scholars and widespread embrace of social naturalism actually threaten the effective functioning of economic institutions. This happens when those who have significant power within the current system pursue their economic self-interest in destabilizing ways. It was, after all, bad behaviour by mortgage brokers, investment banks, and rating agencies that lay behind the global financial crisis.[19] And just in the year 2012, there have been two new major financial scandals. First, we found that bankers had been deliberately manipulating the London Interbank Offer Rate (Libor) – the presumably objective index that determines lending rates around the world. Second, bankers at the London office of JPMorgan Chase racked up huge losses because they were again engaging in dangerous speculation involving complex derivatives.

These on-going financial scandals are indicative of a deep confusion in our culture about the relationship between markets, behaviour, and the salvation of the soul. This confusion is exemplified by a 2002 case that occurred far from Wall Street. Robert Courtney was a pharmacist practicing in Kansas City, Missouri and a deacon in a local congregation of the Assembly of God, a Christian fundamentalist denomination.[20] In 2002, he pleaded guilty in federal court to twenty counts of tampering with and adulterating chemotherapy drugs that he was providing to local oncologists for their patients. The dilution of the drugs that sold at a very high price for each individual dose allowed him to increase his earnings very significantly. After sentencing, he explained to the court that he needed extra money because he had pledged $1 million to the building fund of his church.

Obviously, this case can be seen as simply an instance of individual pathology; someone who made a strange split between his religious beliefs and his business behaviour. But against the backdrop of a series of major financial scandals from ENRON down to the present, many of them engineered by individuals who presented themselves as deeply committed to one or another religious faith, another interpretation seems appropriate.[21]

---

19 While the literature is now vast, for a valuable overview see B. McLean and J. Nocera, *All the Devils are Here* (2010).

20 R. Draper, 'The Toxic Pharmacist' *New York Times,* 8 June 2003.

21 In the ENRON case, both Kenneth Lay, the CEO and later chair, and Andrew Fastow, the treasurer, were visibly religious men.

33

Some people seem to believe that religious injunctions simply do not apply to business transactions – even when those transactions have grave consequences for other people.

This belief, however, is not that peculiar given that the rhetoric of the self-regulating free market suggests that when individuals pursue their economic self-interest without restraint, the invisible hand of the market will miraculously produce social order out of the chaos of self-aggrandizing individuals. None other than Milton Friedman mocked the idea of corporate social responsibility by saying that the only responsibility of business was to pursue profits in the marketplace. He saw no need to include even the standard caveats against the use of force or fraud. And in their widely read popularization of free market ideas, *Free to Choose,* Milton and Rose Friedman are explicit that all forms of government regulation are an undesirable restriction on individual freedom:

> Today you are not free to offer your services as a lawyer, a physician, a dentist, a plumber, a barber, a mortician, or engage in a host of other occupations, without first getting a permit or a license from a government official. [22]

Is it any wonder that under the influence of this kind of libertarian ideology, even very religious people have come to believe that everything is permitted when one is seeking profit in a competitive marketplace?

Moreover, these misunderstandings about individual ethics in market settings were at the centre of the global financial crisis. Starting in the 1990s, various financial intermediaries came to realize that packaging mortgages into mortgage bonds could be a highly lucrative business. Investors were drawn to these mortgage-backed securities because they paid a substantially higher interest rate than government debt, and they were comparatively safe as indicated by their AAA ratings. For the banks that bundled mortgages into securities, this was an extremely lucrative business because they earned significant fees on these transactions, and they could also earn a significant spread by borrowing at very low rates to hold these higher-yielding assets on their own books.

The problems in this lucrative market came in late 2003 when the volume of conventional mortgages suddenly reached a peak and began to decline.[23] It was at this point that the investment bankers turned aggressively towards securitizing sub-prime mortgage loans – a type of loan that had emerged to serve lower-income households with problematic credit histories. Sub-prime lending had been rising before 2003, and it often took a predatory form.[24] The backdrop was that the overall rise in housing prices in many metro-

---

22 M. and R. Friedman, *Free to Choose* (1981) 57.
23 N. Fligstein and A. Goldstein, 'The Anatomy of the Mortgage Securitization Crisis' in *Markets on Trial*, eds. M. Lounsbury and P. Hirsch (2010).
24 J. Hernandez, 'Redlining Revisited: Mortgage Lending Patterns in Sacramento 1930–2004' (2009) 33 *International J. of Urban and Regional Research* 291.

© 2013 The Author. Journal of Law and Society © 2013 Cardiff University Law School

politan areas was also driving up the prices of single family houses in poor neighbourhoods dominated by racial minorities. This created a situation in which the inability of a borrower to service a loan ceased to be a significant problem for the mortgage lender. Assuming they had made an adequate profit on the initial transaction, they could foreclose on the house quickly and resell it at a higher price to another borrower whose sub-prime loan was equally or even more profitable. In fact, many of these sub-prime loans went not to new purchasers but to established homeowners. A mortgage broker would knock on the door and offer to refinance the person's loan at a relatively low rate with the promise that the person would receive $20,000 of cash in the transaction. The fine print of the loan agreement, however, showed that the initial teaser rate would rise dramatically in 24 months or if any of the penalty conditions occurred. The homeowner would typically lose their home and the lender would then 'flip' the house once more.

The interest by the big banks in securitizing sub-prime loans suddenly transformed the calculus for the mortgage brokers; they no longer had to worry about reselling foreclosed houses at a higher price. They could simply sell the loan along with hundreds of others to the bundler and make all of their profits at the front end. Suddenly, there was a dramatic increase in the quantity of sub-prime loans, and we know now that a very high percentage of those that were written in 2004 to 2007 ultimately went into default. As the markets began to perceive these high default rates, the value of the hundreds of billions of mortgage-backed securities based on sub-prime loans fell precipitously, creating the toxic debt that weighed down the balance sheet of financial institutions around the world.

But much less attention has been focused on the devastation that this lending produced in many minority neighbourhoods across the country.[25] Hundreds of thousands of minority households lost their homes and much of their saving as a consequence of this boom in predatory lending. The impact was particularly dramatic in cities such as Cleveland and Detroit where entire neighbourhoods were devastated as foreclosed homes were abandoned, looted, and ultimately demolished.

It is striking, however, that these actions by mortgage brokers in writing hundreds of thousands of bad loans that devastated minority communities and contributed significantly to a global financial crisis, has created a relatively modest legal response. The Dodd-Frank Act passed in 2010 did add significant new regulation of mortgage lending, but with a few exceptions, a whole range of other responses including criminal prosecutions, large-scale restitution to impacted communities, and even the invalidation of

25 But see R. Dyal-Chand, 'Exporting the Ownership Society: A Case Study on the Economic Impact of Property Rights' (2007), at <http://ssrn.com/abstract=968689> or <http://dx.doi.org/10.2139/ssrn.968689>.

35

thousands of questionable mortgage contracts have not materialized.[26] For example, after an intensive investigation, the Justice Department decided not to pursue criminal charges against Angelo Mozillo, the CEO of Countrywide Financial that had been the nation's largest writer of sub-prime mortgage loans.

But the most serious issue here is the failure by courts to recognize that the honesty or good faith of the parties is a precondition for any valid contract, including a mortgage loan. Despite a significant body of legal scholarship that elaborates the necessity that both sides act in good faith in contractual settings,[27] the courts appear to rely on the abstract approach of conservative law and economics scholars who argue that 'voluntary' contracts are inherently optimizing. Little remains of the legal realist's focus on the actual bargaining power of the parties in the transaction which would highlight, in sub-prime lending, the huge power differential between minority homeowners with limited education and unscrupulous but very well-connected mortgage brokers.

Again, the biggest danger here is that without any legal restraint, dishonest and predatory behaviours become the norm in market settings. Perhaps we have already reached this tipping point. But a vast amount of thinking has made clear that when individuals pursue their self-interest without restraint, it tends to destabilize markets and make it harder to achieve the optimal results promised by neo-classical economics.

CAN ECONOMIC SOCIOLOGY HELP WITH THESE PROBLEMS?

Is it possible to recapture the insights of the legal realists, effectively challenge social naturalism, and elaborate a sounder empirical analysis of how actual markets work?[28] Fortunately, research in economic sociology provides some promising leads for this project. Two contributions, in particular, are relevant and complementary. The first is a body of work inspired

---

26 To be sure, the Dodd-Frank legislation created the Consumer Financial Protection Bureau (CFPB) which has the potential to significantly impact the relational work done in consumer financial markets both by new regulations and by providing key resources to consumers. However, it is still very uncertain whether the CFPB will be able to realize this potential, given the resistance and political clout of the financial services industry.

27 S. Macaulay, 'Relational Contracts Floating on a Sea of Custom? Thoughts about the Ideas of Ian Macneil and Lisa Bernstein' (2000) 94 *Northwestern University Law Rev.* 775; I. Macneil, 'Contracting Worlds and Essential Contracts Theory' (2000) 9 *Social & Legal Studies* 431; R.E. Speidel, 'The "Duty" of Good Faith in Contract Performance and Enforcement' (1996) 46 *J. of Legal Education* 537.

28 For a somewhat different strategy for accomplishing the same ultimate goal, see R. Cotterrell, 'Rethinking "Embeddedness": Law, Economy, and Community' in this volume, pp. 49–67.

by Karl Polanyi's mid twentieth-century insight that the human economy is always and everywhere embedded in politics, law, culture, and particular ideas.[29] The second is a more recent body of work developed by Viviana Zelizer that explores the relational work that is done in actual market situations.[30]

1. *Karl Polanyi*

Karl Polanyi (1886–1964) was one of many refugee intellectuals displaced from Central Europe in the turbulent period between the world wars.[31] But unlike other refugee intellectuals who later became influential scholars, Polanyi had not pursued an academic career in central Europe; he had worked mostly as an economic journalist in Vienna in the 1920s. While he was ultimately able to gain tenuous employment in the Economics Department at Columbia University after the Second World War, he never attained the secure disciplinary identity of such contemporaries as Karl Mannheim, Hannah Arendt, or Leo Strauss. The consequence was that it took additional decades before his work received the recognition it deserves.

But the ironies of history are also a factor in the delayed recognition. Polanyi's book, *The Great Transformation*, is the most eloquent and carefully argued critique of free market economic ideas produced in the twentieth century. But the book was published at a time when those ideas had already been widely discredited and Keynesian economics and support for an emerging welfare state were in the ascendant. Just as with the legal realist critiques of Lochnerism, Polanyi's critique of Malthus and Ricardo did not seem particularly relevant for the three decades of Keynesian hegemony. It was only when the tables were turned in the 1970s by the discrediting of Keynesian ideas and the coronation of Friedman and Hayek as key wise men for Ronald Reagan and Margaret Thatcher that Polanyi's critique became suddenly relevant. In the decades of market fundamentalism that began in the 1980s, Karl Polanyi's work has been rediscovered by an expanding number of scholars and activists.

Polanyi's work is relevant because he independently traversed the same intellectual ground as the legal realists; this led him to argue for a much more empirical and substantive analysis of how markets work.[32] In fact, Polanyi

---

29 Polanyi, op. cit., n. 12.

30 V. Zelizer, *The Purchase of Intimacy* (2006); V. Zelizer, 'How I Became a Relational Economic Sociologist and What Does that Mean?' (2012) 40 *Politics & Society* 145.

31 F. Block, 'Karl Polanyi and the Writing of *The Great Transformation*' (2003) 32 *Theory and Society* 275; F. Block and M. Somers, 'Beyond the Economistic Fallacy: The Holistic Social Science of Karl Polanyi' in *Vision and Method in Historical Sociology,* ed. T. Skocpol (1984); G. Dale, *Karl Polanyi: The Limits of the Market* (2010).

32 Polanyi probably had little familiarity with legal realism when he wrote *The Great Transformation*, but he was aware of the institutionalist tradition in United States

developed his ideas in direct response to the effort of Ludwig von Mises and Friedrich Hayek to revive free market economic ideas in Vienna in the 1920s.[33] These theorists of the Austrian economic tradition argued that a 'collectivist conspiracy' in the last decades of the nineteenth century had effectively undermined the free market arrangements that had produced spectacular European economic growth in the decades following Napoleon's final defeat in 1815. They insisted that protectionist trade policies and misguided efforts by governments to artificially improve living standards had undermined global free trade and the international gold standard mechanism. The outbreak of the First World War was the initial product of this misguided collectivism and the economic turbulence of the inter-war years was the second. For von Mises and Hayek – just as for Milton Friedman half a century later – the only way to return to prosperity was to embrace the time-honoured principles of laissez-faire and small government.

As already noted, Polanyi directly attacked the social naturalism embedded in Anglo-American thought. Polanyi also understood that social naturalism depended upon a particular theory of knowledge (that Somers and I term 'theoretical realism') – the belief that behind the level of appearances, there are invisible theoretical structures that account for those appearances.[34] In the same way that the internal mechanisms of a clock shape the configuration of the hands at any given time, the hidden laws of nature shape what we are able to perceive directly with our senses. For this reason, it was not scientific to rely on empirical observations; they could be deeply misleading. Malthus and Ricardo thought that just as Newton discovered the laws of motion governing planetary movements, they were discovering the underlying natural laws that determined what actually happened in the economy.

Polanyi saw that the classical economists had successfully constructed a closed system that was effectively protected from empirical disconfirmation. He recognized that the only way to challenge this theoretical construction was to both prove that the self-regulating market was a fiction and adopt a different way of thinking about human economies that started from the empirical realities of what people did to secure their livelihoods in different times and places. It was for this reason that he argued that the project in the nineteenth century of constructing a self-regulating market was doomed to failure.

One of his most powerful arguments is that land, labour, and money are treated as commodities by market theorists, but the definition of a true

economics. See W.C. Neale, 'Karl Polanyi and American Institutionalism: A Strange Case of Convergence' in *The Life and Work of Karl Polanyi,* ed. K. Polanyi-Levitt (1990).

33 Another key antagonist for Polanyi was A.V. Dicey, an English constitutional theorist who was also a key exemplar of free market orthodoxy for some of the legal realists.
34 Somers and Block, op. cit., n. 12.

commodity is something produced for sale on a market. Land, however, is subdivided nature, labour is the activity of human beings, and money is the supply of currency and credit that are created by the monetary system; none of these were produced for sale on a market. In his terms, these are all fictitious commodities, but everyone has to pretend that their supply and demand will respond to price signals in the same way as true commodities. But since they cannot, government has to be involved from the very beginning in managing the supply and demand for these fictitious commodities.

Polanyi makes a second powerful argument that shows a deep conflict between freedom of contract and the self-regulating market:

> Theoretically, laissez-faire or freedom of contract implied the freedom of workers to withhold their labor either individually or jointly, if they so decided; it implied also the freedom of business to concert on selling prices irrespective of the wishes of the consumers. But in practice such freedom conflicted with the institutions of a self-regulating market, and *in such a conflict the self-regulating market was invariably accorded preference* ... No more conclusive proof could be offered of the inevitability of antiliberal or 'collectivist' methods under the conditions of modern industrial society than the fact that even economic liberals themselves regularly used such methods in decisively important fields of industrial organization.[35]

In other words, the self-regulating market is not and cannot be simply freedom of contract writ large. Moreover, the self-regulating market cannot be self-regulating; even its strongest supporters recognize that its daily survival depends upon instruments of government regulation.

As with the legal realists, Polanyi is insisting that when we look at the realities of actual market economies, what we find significantly diverges from what free market theory tells us. This leads him to the argument that markets are always embedded; they are shaped by political, legal, and cultural practices. Even the project of creating a self-regulating market system has to be understood as a political project designed to structure markets in a particular way, which includes ideationally embedding them within the ideology of free markets or the fiction of a meaningful public/private divide.[36]

But while Polanyi provides us with powerful theoretical tools to challenge free market ideas, researchers have found that embeddedness is a relatively blunt instrument for analysing different types of market structures and arrangements.[37] While we need to focus on differences in how markets are embedded, so far there has been little success in setting up a persuasive

---

35 Polanyi, op. cit., n. 12, p. 155.
36 It is also important to understand that Polanyi is clearly rejecting a dualism in which markets are destructive and social constraints are good. On the contrary, he is arguing that both are necessary and it is the specifics of a given market situation that need to be analysed and perhaps remedied.
37 F. Block, 'Relational Work in Market Economies: An Introduction' (2012) 40 *Politics & Society* 1.

39

typology of different forms of embeddedness. Moreover, analysis that sees embeddedness as a quantitative variable, with some markets being more embedded than others, lead to greater confusion.[38]

2. *Viviana Zelizer*

It is precisely on this last issue where the work of Viviana Zelizer becomes relevant. Zelizer is an Argentinian-born economic sociologist who received her PhD in the United States and has been teaching at Princeton for several decades. Her intellectual project has been to challenge the well-worn claim that the expanding role of markets in social life will inevitably undermine the emotional and affective ties that link people together in communities, in families, and in other intimate relations. While such predictions can be found in Shakespeare, Marx, Simmel, and many others, Zelizer has consistently challenged the claim that commercialization and commodification inevitably impoverish our emotional lives.[39]

Particularly in her more recent work, Zelizer explicitly links this project to a feminist standpoint.[40] Some conservatives have long argued that the ideal of gender equality in which women pursue work and careers in the same way as men will ultimately destroy family life and turn intimate relations into something resembling market transactions. Zelizer sees in this argument the same slippery slope causality that is found in Marxist critiques of commodification. Her counter-argument is that these slippery-slope claims ignore the capacity of people to build and maintain powerful affective and reciprocal relations with each other even when commercial relationships and the rhetoric of self-interest are dominant.

In *The Purchase of Intimacy*, Zelizer argues that it is completely mistaken to see intimate relations and economic exchanges as two 'hostile worlds' that need to be kept separated from each other for fear of contamination. On the contrary, she shows empirically that these are 'connected worlds' because people in intimate relations are routinely making economic exchanges. Even in the ambiguous realm of courtship where couples are exploring whether or not their temporary emotional connection should be deepened through the legal recognition of marriage, there are routinely exchanges that involve money or other items of value. And yet, the parties are still able to differ-entiate their relationship from a commercial transaction in which intimacy is exchanged for money. It should be obvious that Zelizer's framework applies to the public/private divide as well; while liberal jurisprudence treats these as

---

38 G. Krippner, 'The Elusive Market: Embeddedness and the Paradigm of Economic Sociology' (2002) 30 *Theory and Society* 775; K. Gemici, 'Karl Polanyi and the Antinomies of Embeddedness' (2008) 6 *Socio-Economic Rev.* 5.

39 V. Zelizer, *Pricing the Priceless Child* (1994); V. Zelizer, *Economic Lives: How Culture Shapes the Economy* (2011).

40 Zelizer, op. cit., n. 30.

separate worlds, they are, as both Polanyi and the legal realists recognized, deeply interconnected worlds. People manage the connected worlds of intimacy and the market, Zelizer argues, by engaging in 'relational work' – a process of defining the nature of their connections – usually by implicitly or explicitly contrasting it with other known types of relationship, defining the types of transactions in which they will engage, and identifying appropriate media of exchange. Often, this process ends up with what Zelizer terms a 'relational package' which usually corresponds with familiar social categories such as that of 'friends', 'lovers', or 'spouses'.

Zelizer insists that people do not do this relational work as isolated individuals; they draw on available cultural resources and beliefs and, ultimately, they depend on the relational work done by the legal system to ratify their choices. For example, she describes a lawsuit concerning an intimate relationship between a white man and a former slave woman in the ante-bellum period that involved a significant transfer of assets. Others challenged the transfer in court and the Supreme Court of Louisiana had to do its own relational work to fit their relationship into the established legal categories. While there was no doubt that these two people had lived together for some time in a loving relationship, the court ruled that the woman was a concubine and that meant that the transfer was not legally valid.

In more recent work, Zelizer goes on to argue that relational work takes place across all economic interactions – even those far from the realm of intimacy.[41] Actors engage in a similar process of defining the nature of the relationship which includes establishing what is to be exchanged and what are the appropriate media of exchange. To be sure, certain economic transactions are highly routinized. When we stand in the express line at the supermarket to buy a quart of milk or when we rent a car at the airport, the transaction is highly scripted and can be completed with a minimum of spoken words. But when we attempt to carry out similar routinized transactions in an unfamiliar foreign country, we are quickly reminded that there are significant variations in the way such transactions are executed. The existence of this scripted relational work is the reason tourists buy guidebooks to find out about, for example, local tipping practices and why international businesses need consultants to find out the informal and formal rules governing transactions in each particular foreign country.

At the other end of the continuum, there are many types of transactions that cannot rely on scripted behavior alone, because participants – as individuals or as representatives of organizations – must perform in a way that seems authentic and responsive to the other party. So, for example, to negotiate a substantial loan or to secure certain types of employment or to work out a complex partnership between two organizations, the parties might

41 id.

41

rely on standard legal agreements but they all must present themselves to each other in ways that generate trust and credibility. And in these on-going exchanges, these performance demands continue, especially when the parties face issues that were not anticipated at the outset.[42]

However, the nature of these performances can be highly variable. At one extreme lies the predatory mortgage brokers discussed earlier who often behaved like the proverbial con man, pretending to be very concerned about the welfare of the borrowers while manipulating them into signing a predatory loan with very high interest rates and other negative conditions such as strong penalties for prepayment or renegotiation. At the other, a loan officer at the local credit union might resemble the kindly banker who is genuinely concerned that the borrowers be able to afford the loan and sustain their payments over the life of the loan. At the same time, of course, the performance of the borrowers could also vary between the extremes of misrepresenting key facts on the one hand to fully and honestly disclosing factors that might interfere with people's ability to keep up their loan payments on the other. The point is that how these market participants do their relational work has significant consequences for the price and terms of the resulting loans, as well as for the performance of the loan into the future. As we have seen, systematically dishonest relational work in the mortgage market was a key contributor to the global financial crisis.

In short, Zelizer's concept of relational work has the potential to help us escape from the extremely simplified view of economic transactions that is taken by conventional economic analysis. With the conventional assumptions of perfect information and self-executing contracts, there is no reason to look inside the economic transaction to see how it is being constructed by the participants. But Zelizer's concepts help us to recapture what the legal realists saw – the economic transaction as a social relationship that is characterized by the same kind of differences in power, information, and sincerity that pervade other social relationships. Moreover, these differences impact not only the prices and terms established by the contract, but also whether the contract is likely to be sustained over time and the probability that its outcome will meet or exceed the expectations of the parties.

She also helps us see that courts inevitably do their own legal relational work in which they ratify or deny the validity of the understandings that plaintiffs and defendants have reached. Moreover, in deciding whether a particular contract is valid or invalid, courts never have the option of being neutral arbiters who simply apply the law. Their legal reasoning inevitably involves categorizing the relationships and behaviours in ways that determine how the case will be decided. Moreover, sometimes courts create new understandings and perspectives that then influence how ordinary people construct their relationships.

---

42 In the legal literature, these longer-term arrangements are referred to as 'relational contracts': Speidel, op. cit., n. 27.

42

To be sure, lawyers already know the importance of what goes on inside of contractual arrangements. A lot of the legal advice they dispense to clients is actually about how the clients should perform the relational work involved in dealing with counter-parties or regulators. For example, they are often explaining the specific disclosure obligations in different market settings.

Nevertheless, what is powerful in Zelizer's contribution is that by giving a name to a set of practices, she makes them more visible and makes it easier to bring them out of the background and into the foreground. In short, the relational work idea is offering us a different set of lenses for studying transactions that brings behaviour and context into sharper focus and pushes the more abstract arguments of economic theory into the background.[43]

Her work, in short, has the possibility of opening up a broad empirical agenda for analysing the specifics of how relational work takes place in different market settings.[44] This kind of empirical work might be able to deliver on the promise of the embeddedness concept – allowing us to recognize systematic variations in the ways in which different markets are structured and show how these different structures produce different outcomes that might or might not improve the efficiency with which resources are used. In short, there is a promise of a body of scholarship produced by both sociologists and legal scholars that recaptures the legal realist focus on what actually happens in market exchanges.

For example, Zelizer's approach alerts us to the importance of disclosure and discovery in contractual settings.[45] In the real world, economic transactions occur under conditions of imperfect and asymmetrical information and pervasive uncertainty. To deal with the information problems, parties to a transaction have to engage in significant disclosure that often includes information that might be inconsistent with effective impression management. Such inconvenient disclosures are important to avoid both an unproductive contract that has to be quickly terminated and to create the trust necessary for joint discovery. Joint discovery is often the goal of contractual relationships; the two parties have to pool their knowledge in order to produce new information or new understandings. In fact, a significant portion of contemporary contracts are explicitly designed to produce something novel and unique – a remodelled kitchen, a new software programme or a newly designed part for a car. Yet we have had remarkably little

---

43 F. Block, 'Contesting Markets All the Way Down' (2012) 68 *J. of Australian Political Economy* 27.

44 The 2012 special issue of *Politics & Society* on relational work includes more empirical articles that represent a start on this effort: see J. Whitford, 'Waltzing, Relational Work, and the Construction (or Not) of Collaboration in Manufacturing Industries'; J. Haylett, 'One Woman Helping: Another Egg Donation as a Case of Relational Work'; D. Biscotti et al., 'Constructing "Disinterested" Academic Science: Relational Work in University-Industry Research Collaborations' (2012) 40 *Politics & Society* 249–72, 223–47, and 273–308 respectively.

45 Block, op. cit., n. 37.

research focusing on the question of what arrangements are optimal for effective joint discovery.

INNOVATION AND RELATIONAL WORK

This final section is intended to suggest briefly how a focus on relational work in the context of innovation can challenge certain legal rules that have historically been defended as improving economic efficiency. The mainstream view has been that strict enforcement of intellectual property rights, such as patents, has been an indispensable element in the international economic successes of the United States by creating strong incentives for firms to invest in research and development. But when one looks more closely at the actual organization of the innovation system and the centrality of certain types of relational work for its effective functioning, it becomes obvious that the current legal regime is not optimizing the efficient use of resources.

A generation ago, the United States innovation system was centered in industrial laboratories organized by the largest corporations that won the bulk of new patents and were responsible for most of the new commercial innovations.[46] But three key developments have transformed this picture. First, many of the large corporations have eliminated their research laboratories or have significantly downsized their research efforts. This has been a fairly systematic response to a more intensely competitive environment in which financial markets emphasize the goal of maximizing shareholder value. So, for example, with a few exceptions such as Google, Microsoft, and IBM, most corporate laboratories now have to focus on projects with fairly immediate commercial payoffs. Most other firms have embraced the slogan of 'open innovation' which indicates that their focus is on collaborations with other organizations or simply purchasing innovations that they see as promising.[47]

Second, the public sector role in the innovation system has expanded dramatically because across many different industries, innovation is increasingly linked to advances in science that generally occur in university and federal laboratories. The pharmaceutical industry is typical here; over the last generation, most of the major new prescription drugs emerged out of cutting-edge biological research done at universities or at National Institutes

---

46 F. Block and M. Keller, 'Where do innovations come from? Transformations in the US Economy, 1970–2006' (2009) 7 *Socio-Economic Rev.* 459; D. Mowery, *'Plus ca change*: Industrial R&D in the "third industrial revolution"' (2009) 18 *Industrial and Corporate Change* 1.

47 M. Keller and F. Block, 'Explaining the transformation in the US innovation system; the impact of a small government program' (2013) 11 *Socio-Economic Rev.* (forthcoming).

44

of Health laboratories.[48] In our study of the sources of prize-winning innovations between the 1970s and 2000s, there was clear evidence that inter-organizational collaborations involving public entities had become central to the innovation system.[49]

Third, there has been a dramatic expansion in the role that small firms (fewer than 500 employees) play in the innovation system. Firms that started as spin-offs from universities, federal laboratories, or larger private firms, often receiving initial assistance from one or another federal agency, now play a critical role in moving new technologies from the laboratory to the commercial space. This growing importance is reflected by the fact that small firms are winning an increasing share of patents, and PhD scientists and engineers are now more likely to work at small firms than at large firms.[50]

These three trends all suggest that innovation is now a networked process. Scholars have recognized for some time that the United States corporate system has been shifting from vertical integration to a network form of organization. Instead of attempting to organize all stages of the production process under one roof, most firms are now dependent on long-term collaborations with a range of other firms that provide both products and services. But nowhere is this network system more developed than with the innovation process. As Lester and Piore argue, most innovations now emerge out of inter-organizational collaborations that often include multiple entities, some public and some private. In their argument, when technologists with different skills come together to work on a shared problem, they gradually develop trust and a common language which sometimes serves as a basis for joint discovery of new products or processes.[51]

But building this trust requires overcoming fears that one's collaborators might act against one's own interests. Biscotti et al. report on interviews with scientists in universities and in private firms engaged in university–industry collaborations in agricultural science.[52] They report that industry scientists were concerned that university researchers might compromise their firm's intellectual property by publishing results before patent applications had been submitted. University scientists whose primary professional rewards came through publishing in peer-review journals had the reciprocal anxiety that the business partners might block the timely publication of important research findings. When the collaboration is between two or more private firms, anxieties are intense that one of the other partners will simply steal key pieces of intellectual property.

48 S. Vallas, D.L. Kleinman, and D. Biscotti, 'Political Structures and the Making of U.S. Biotechnology' in *State of Innovation*, eds. F. Block and M.R. Keller (2011).
49 Block and Keller, op. cit., n. 46.
50 id.; Keller and Block, op. cit. n. 47.
51 R.K. Lester and M. Piore, *Innovation — the Missing Dimension* (2004).
52 Biscotti et al., op. cit., n. 44.

45

All of this suggests the centrality of relational work to effective innovation. Both at the managerial level and at the level of individual scientists and engineers, there is an interactional process that is indispensable for creating the kind of trust that is needed for people to share ideas and information. We also know that public agencies have been able to play a critical role in this process. Lester and Piore emphasize the importance of collaborative public spaces in which technologists feel free to share ideas because public officials serve as honest brokers to discourage freeriding.[53] Schrank and Whitford develop this argument by noting that government officials can avert network failures by validating the competence of partners and by discouraging opportunistic behaviour by one party or the other.[54] For example, in the federally administered Small Business Innovation Research programme, defence department officials use the application materials by small firms as a legal record to protect them from losing control of their intellectual property in negotiations with larger firms.[55]

While this example affirms the need for mechanisms to protect the ideas of small firms that have become an essential part of this innovation system, there are severe problems with the functioning of the existing patent system that were not addressed in the 2011 America Invents legislation that was supposed to update the United States patent system. First, the grounds for distrust among network partners are enormously intensified by the patent system since the danger is real that one party will quietly defect and file for ownership of ideas that have emerged out of a collective process, giving them exclusive rights for a twenty-year period. Second, the inventions that have become eligible for patents have moved ever closer to the scientific frontier as, for example, in patents on specific genes or on bioengineered organisms. Such decisions undermine the distinction between fundamental research and research that has immediate commercial applications so that scientists themselves no longer know what information should be shared and what should be kept hidden. Third, small firms are systematically disadvantaged in dealing with the system of intellectual property because they simply cannot afford the expensive litigation that has now become routine for giant corporations.[56] Finally, in an era of ubiquitous innovation, the existing patent system depends on patent officers making hundreds of thousands of decisions each year evaluating the merit and originality of particular applications. Surprisingly, free market theorists have been largely silent on the question of whether mid-level government officials have the

53 Lester and Piore, op. cit., n. 51.
54 A. Schrank and J. Whitford, 'The Anatomy of Network Failure' (2011) 29 Sociological Theory 151.
55 Keller and Block, op. cit. n. 47.
56 S.M. Benjamin and A.K. Rai, 'Fixing Innovation Policy: A Structural Perspective' (2008) 77 George Washington Law Rev. 1.

training and knowledge necessary to make these profoundly consequential decisions.[57]

Obviously, this is not the place to propose alternatives to the existing intellectual property regime. The point is simply that an empirical focus on the actual location and dynamics of innovation in the current economy suggests that there is a fundamental tension between gaining ownership rights over critical pieces of knowledge and the development of the inter-organizational collaborations on which key technological breakthroughs depend. Given our economy's growing dependence on these scientific collaborations, we need to find ways to make it far easier to negotiate the relational work necessary for joint discoveries.

CONCLUSION

We learn from Polanyi and the legal realists that there is no such thing as a self-regulating market economy. The only kind of market economy that can work is one that is regulated and this requires active and ongoing action by legislators and courts to decide what are appropriate and what are inappropriate actions by market participants. Zelizer reminds us that how actors behave in market situations is highly variable and has extremely important consequences for the ability of a society to use economic resources efficiently. How people do the actual relational work that is part of every economic transaction matters.

As a society, we need not stand idly by when that confused Kansas City pharmacist has become a familiar cultural type. When people mistakenly imagine that economic transactions require no ethical underpinning and that all is fair in love, war, and markets, there are things that can be done. Part of the response is in scholarly contributions such as this one in which we remind our audiences that the same Adam Smith who is endlessly invoked by free market theorists had also published *The Theory of Moral Sentiments* in 1759 with its emphasis on moral norms as the foundation for any market activity.

Another response is to pursue democratic debate where we actively engage our fellow citizens in arguing that the Golden Rule is necessarily at the foundation of any vision of a society where market transactions are widespread. Without deeply held norms of reciprocity, honesty, and mutual respect, the market will inevitably slide into a Hobbesian nightmare.[58] And

---

57 For further elaborations of this critique, see L. Burlamaqui, A.C. Castro, and R. Kattel, eds., *Knowledge Governance: Reasserting the Public Interest* (2012).

58 I have done this in several pieces stressing the need to reconstruct a moral economy: see F. Block, 'The Right's Moral Trouble' *The Nation,* 30 September 2002; F. Block, 'Breaking with Market Fundamentalism: Toward Domestic and Global Reform' in *Globalization and Beyond*, eds. J. Shefner and P. Fernandez-Kelly (2011).

finally, the legal system has to support these moral norms. It is through law – as created by legislatures and judiciaries – that we communicate our moral norms and provide individuals in daily life with the support they need to incorporate those norms into their relational work.

Moreover, in constructing the legal framework in which market transactions occur, legislators and judges do not have the option to stay out of the realm of voluntary contract. Those who see economic transactions solely in terms of arms-length, buyer-beware bargaining, while ignoring the obligations on both parties, are embarking on what is a very dangerous road. When they ignore the relational work that goes on in actual contractual settings, they are reinforcing the socially and economically destructive ideas that contracts are self-executing and that market participants have no obligation but to pursue their own self-interest. We have already seen in the global financial crisis the horrendous consequences of that theoretical illusion.

48

JOURNAL OF LAW AND SOCIETY
VOLUME 40, NUMBER 1, MARCH 2013
ISSN: 0263-323X, pp. 49–67

Rethinking 'Embeddedness': Law, Economy, Community

ROGER COTTERRELL*

Ideas (of Karl Polanyi and others) that economies and markets are 'socially embedded' are central to recent research in economic sociology, closely paralleling socio-legal claims for studying law in 'social context'. But the concept of embeddedness is imprecise and inadequate: a sociology of law and economy cannot rely on it but must address intellectual and moral-political concerns that its use reflects. Max Weber's writings on law and economy have inspired advocates of a new economic sociology of law, but some of Weber's key claims may be outdated, and he treats law and economy as distinct spheres rather than as facets of the social. Sociological research on law and economy should focus on 'networks of community' and their regulation, thus illuminating the social character of both law and economic relations. Viewing the social (including economic life) through a 'community lens' makes it possible to analyse cultural factors in regulating markets, while emphasizing links between economic relations and other aspects of social life.

INTRODUCTION

Recent calls for 'a sociological analysis of the role of law in economic life'[1] have not gone unheeded. A large literature aimed at developing such an analysis now exists. In fact, many important contributions have been made throughout the modern history of sociology of law. It has not needed the current revival of efforts to shape a distinct field of 'economic sociology' to

* *Department of Law, Queen Mary, University of London, Mile End Road, London E1 4NS, England*
r.b.m.cotterrell@qmul.ac.uk

I am grateful to Prabha Kotiswaran and Amanda Perry-Kessaris for their comments, and to participants in the SOAS Workshop on Economic Sociology of Law (September 2012) who discussed a version of this article presented there.

1 R. Swedberg, 'The case for an economic sociology of law' (2003) 32 *Theory and Society* 1–37, at 1.

provoke this development. Nevertheless, interest in the prospects for an 'economic sociology of law', as a kind of offspring from the new economic sociology (which has not itself been much concerned with law), surely reflect some shared inspirations – especially a sense that much new thinking beyond mainstream economics is needed to address the social and political aspects of major economic crises. In this context the question of law's place in regulating economic relations and structures is becoming more urgent: a response to the need, which the new economic sociologists see, to relocate the economic firmly in the social and the political, so as to understand in new ways the nature of economic life, its conditions of existence, and its broad consequences in society.

The concept of embeddedness has been called 'the core concept – or lowest common denominator – of economic sociology'.[2] 'More than most sub-fields of sociology, economic sociology is built on one key idea ... "embeddedness" ...'; the idea is 'so ubiquitous, it would be hard to get rid of it even if we wanted to'.[3] Its broad significance is to affirm that in some way the economy (or the market) is embedded in wider arenas of social and political life; that it is not 'autonomous' and cannot (or cannot safely) be treated as operating independent of legal and political controls and free of direct social accountability for its operation.

The idea 'exercises a general appeal for those who are dissatisfied with the narrow focus of orthodox economics'.[4] Yet, because embeddedness is interpreted in contradictory ways it has become 'a source of enormous confusion'.[5] Mark Granovetter, the scholar most strongly associated with its revival from the mid-1980s, admitted two decades later that 'I rarely use "embeddedness" anymore, because it has become ... stretched to mean almost anything, so that it therefore means nothing.'[6] There might then be reasons to avoid it, were it not that it has been invoked as a basis for economic sociology of law[7] and that, as noted earlier, it remains 'ubiquitous'.

My main purpose here is to rethink embeddedness: to suggest for socio-legal inquiry a more precise way of conceptualizing the kinds of linkages between economic and other social relations that the idea of embeddedness is intended to highlight. The article argues that 'the social' – the social environment in which law operates – should be seen as composed of *net-*

---

2 S. Frerichs, 'The Legal Constitution of Market Society: Probing the Economic Sociology of Law' (2009) 10(3) *Economic Sociology* 20–25, at 20.

3 G. Krippner et al., 'Polanyi Symposium: A Conversation on Embeddedness' (2004) 2 *Socio-Economic Rev.* 109–35, at 110, 125.

4 G. Dale, *Karl Polanyi: The Limits of the Market* (2010) 195.

5 F. Block, 'Introduction' to K. Polanyi, *The Great Transformation: The Political and Economic Origins of Our Time* (2001) xxiii.

6 In Krippner et al., op. cit., n. 3, p. 113.

7 See, for example, Frerichs, op. cit, n. 2, and many of the essays in C. Joerges and J. Falke (eds.), *Karl Polanyi, Globalisation and the Potential of Law in Transnational Markets* (2011).

50

works of community. Some of these networks (including some of the most powerful) are dominated by (but rarely exclusively made up of) economic relations – that is, instrumental relations centred on common or convergent projects focused on profit making or mutual material welfare.

Fundamentally, in this approach, the economic appears as an *aspect* of the social. As such, it has regulatory conditions and requirements that reflect not only the particular characteristics of economic relations but also their situation as part of networks of community that may be held together by a variety of bonds (for example, shared values, allegiances or customary practices, as well as by a convergence of economic interests). Sociology of law should concern itself with the interplay of different types of social relations in communal networks, focusing on the regulatory issues these present.[8] Within this project, research on regulating economic relations should be integral. Adopting such an approach, a sociology of law and economy can build beyond the idea of embeddedness.

THE ALWAYS (OR SOMETIMES) 'EMBEDDED' ECONOMY (AND LAW)

Use of the embeddedness concept in economic sociology has posed theoretical and methodological problems that show striking parallels with some no less fundamental problems that have haunted sociology of law since its modern founding a century ago. This is a main reason why it is necessary here to look at the ambiguities which 'embeddedness' has presented.

In Granovetter's influential usage, the term expresses a need to situate the study of economic relations in social networks that surround and support them.[9] This may seem not unlike treating 'the economic' as located in networks of community. But whereas the latter approach focuses on communal structures of the social in general, with the economic seen as *an aspect* of these, Granovetter keeps a focus on the economic, treating social networks as *contexts* for this. In doing so, he has been sharply criticized by Greta Krippner for encouraging a view of the economic sphere (or 'the market') as a given not needing sociological inquiry, so that economic sociology would be restricted to analysing the social contexts of the market, not the market as such. Krippner declares that Granovetter 'has run the ship aground on a conception ... that insists on the separate nature of economy and society'.[10] In other words, ironically, the effort to embed economy in

8 See, also, A. Perry-Kessaris, 'Reading the story of law and embeddedness through a community lens: a Polanyi-meets-Cotterrell economic sociology of law?' (2011) 62 *Northern Ireland Legal Q.* 401–13.
9 M. Granovetter, 'Economic Action and Social Structure: The Problem of Embeddedness' (1985) 91 *Am. J. of Sociology* 481–510.
10 Krippner et al., op. cit., n. 3, pp. 112–13.

51

society has ended with an entrenchment of *their separation*.[11] While the social contexts of market relations and institutions are put at the centre of study, the market itself is left as a kind of 'black box', beyond sociological analysis.[12] Whether or not this critique is accurate, its significance for this article is that it closely parallels an important critique of sociology of law.

From the beginnings of modern sociology of law, its pioneers argued that law had to be studied as part of society; hence Eugen Ehrlich's famous claim in 1913 that the centre of gravity of legal development lies not in courts or legislators but 'in society itself'.[13] Nevertheless, much of sociology of law – however deep its commitment to a view of law as somehow embedded in society – can be criticized for failing to analyse *the idea of law itself* sociologically; for failing to 'get inside' legal ideas and doctrines and reinterpret them sociologically, so as to understand how and why they have taken particular forms and developed in certain directions rather than others[14] and how they embody particular understandings of the nature of social life and exclude others.

It may be that 'embeddedness-thinking' in both legal and economic sociology risks putting so much emphasis on what these phenomena (markets, law) might be embedded in that it leaves aside the task of asking how the phenomena themselves are structured as social entities. This is problematic because 'the market' and 'the law' should be understood sociologically as ways of referring to or expressing social relations. As such they are within the province of sociological inquiry. Without such inquiry there is little possibility of challenging in any fundamental way economists' and lawyers' thought-ways, showing, for example, how tied they are to the particular and contingent cultural contexts in which they develop. Without such an approach, economic sociology and sociology of law can only be parallel (perhaps always subordinate) studies alongside the dominant discourses of economics and jurisprudence. So, *what* is embedded (law and economy) must be explained by sociological inquiry.

The idea of embeddedness gives rise to different problems in Karl Polanyi's famous study of the idea and practice of the 'self-regulating market', as presented in his book, *The Great Transformation*.[15] The term embeddedness is only occasionally used in the text, but the book's overall message is clearly about the dangers and instability of trying to 'disembed'

---

11 This kind of separation, with a corresponding need to find means of 'structural coupling' between the separated elements, is also typical of modern systems theory. For a reinterpretation of embeddedness in systems-theory terms, see P.F. Kjaer, 'The Structural Transformation of Embeddedness' in Joerges and Falke (eds.), op. cit., n. 7.
12 Compare K. Gemici, 'Karl Polanyi and the Antinomies of Embeddedness' (2008) 6 *Socio-Economic Rev.* 5–33, at 26, linking this problem also to Karl Polanyi's work.
13 E. Ehrlich, *Fundamental Principles of the Sociology of Law* (2002) lix, 390.
14 R. Cotterrell, *Law, Culture and Society: Legal Ideas in the Mirror of Social Theory* (2006) 45–63.
15 Polanyi, op. cit., n. 5.

52

the market from its vital socio-political settings and supports – to treat it as if it has no dependence on a wider social context.

As many writers have noted, however, different interpretations of Polanyi's arguments are possible. On one view, the book presents a 'theoretical proposition'[16] about the emergence, pathology, and collapse of the idea and practice of a self-regulating market – an autonomous, self-organizing market economy free of political and social controls – in the period from the early nineteenth century to the time when Polanyi wrote during the Second World War. The claim is that, in specific historical conditions, the economy became disembedded from political controls and social responsibility, but was perhaps *inevitably* unable to maintain this unstable and 'utopian' condition.

A contrasting interpretation treats Polanyi as claiming that the economy is 'always embedded';[17] it cannot be otherwise, and attempts to argue for a self-regulating market free of political and social oversight are misguided, reckless, and utopian (in the sense of seeking something unrealizable). On this view, any worthwhile study of the economy must see it as inseparable from its socio-political context and explore how political processes and social conditions shape, structure or define it; this is a 'methodological principle'[18] suggesting what economic inquiry has to encompass if it is to confront reality.

I think a further interpretation is possible which has special significance for the prospects of legally regulating some powerful sectors of economic life. Could it be that the economy (or very significant parts of it) can, indeed, become disembedded, but that the historical trajectory detailed by Polanyi does not yield a *general* 'theoretical proposition' about this? In other words, a politico-social reaction (called by Polanyi a 'double movement'), exposing and cancelling the 'dangerous fantasy'[19] of the self-regulating economy, is *not bound to occur* – at least not without disaster overtaking social and political life first. On this view, Polanyi's book is a work of interpretive history rather than social theory,[20] and presents few *universal* claims about the possibility or otherwise of any 'stable' disembedding of the economy.

The imprecision of ideas of 'embedding' or 'disembedding' suggests why it is hard to build social theory on them. The problem of understanding *what* is embedded – the need to analyse law, markets, and so on, as social phenomena – was noted earlier. But Polanyi's book suggests a further deep ambiguity. *In what* is the economy or market embedded? Is it embedded in

16 Gemici, op. cit., n. 12.
17 Block, op. cit., n. 5, and F. Block, 'Karl Polanyi and the Writing of *The Great Transformation*' (2003) 32 *Theory and Society* 275–306; Perry-Kessaris, op. cit., n. 8.
18 Gemici, op. cit, n. 12.
19 Block, op. cit., n. 5, p. xxxiv.
20 Christian Joerges and Josef Falke ('Introduction' in Joerges and Falke (eds.), op. cit, n. 7, pp. 1–2) see Polanyi's work as 'within the tradition of grand theories of society' but they discuss Polanyian themes in a context of post-Polanyian social theory.

political institutions, legal controls, state policy or social conditions? If the answer is all of these (as it sometimes seems to be in *The Great Transformation*), the idea of embeddedness lacks theoretical specificity. Yet, if this idea is discarded, Polanyi's book can still be read as a disturbing lesson from history: whether or not the catastrophic consequences of an economy beyond socio-political control occur will depend on: (i) how far political movements and authorities have the opportunity and determination to prevent this through democratic processes, and (ii) how far economic regulation (both public and private) can be designed and implemented with sufficient insight, power, and sophistication to provide necessary controls. Viewed in this way Polanyi's analyses imply the absolute centrality of sociological studies of law and politics in addressing issues of economic organization.

ECONOMIC NETWORKS OF COMMUNITY

How might a focus on networks of community provide a foundation for these sociological studies? The idea of social networks is familiar in sociology, and the concept of community has been invoked in recent literature analysing how economic relations can be structured and how they produce forms of governance. The concepts of network and community are sometimes distinguished on the grounds that the latter suggests a common culture of some kind, while networks are strings of (often instrumental) links between individuals, not necessarily suggesting any wider sense of belonging to a collectivity;[21] the concept of community, by contrast, imports some such sense.

The danger, however, into which much social analysis has fallen, is to think of 'community' as a 'thing', an 'object', a distinct social phenomenon. So the talk is of 'communities' and it becomes easy for critics to say that communities as cohesive, integrated entities rarely exist in contemporary life and, where they do, their boundaries usually cannot be defined clearly. Thus, the very idea of a community is at odds with the fluid nature of contemporary life in which individuals form relatively transient bonds with others, and belong at various times to many different kinds of overlapping, interpenetrating groupings that form and reform, emerge, alter, and disappear. The notion of 'the community' (for instance, village community, local community) seems too static, vague or anachronistic; in any case, it is entirely peripheral to the main flow of contemporary individualized, atomistic social life.

21 R. Mayntz, 'Global structures: markets, organizations, networks – and communities?' in *Transnational Communities: Shaping Global Economic Governance*, eds. M.-L. Djelic and S. Quack (2010) 48; M.-L. Djelic and S. Quack, 'Transnational communities and their impact on the governance of business and economic activity', id., ch. 16, p. 384.

I argue that the idea of 'a community' as a distinct social phenomenon should be abandoned. Instead the focus should be on *social relations of community* of various contrasting types. Community refers to a *quality* of social relationships. It suggests a *degree* of stability and permanence in them – but not necessarily very much. For example, a contractual relationship, on this understanding, embodies a relationship of community that may last only as long as the contract. The stability of relations of community comes from *mutual interpersonal trust* between the participants in them. But it is vital to stress that trusting relationships can be (and usually are) also power relationships. Community in no way implies an absence of power or domination. Mutual trust can exist between individuals very unequal in power. Trusting relations do not replace, but may co-exist with and stabilize power relations. And the key to making the idea of community useful for legal inquiries is to recognize that relations of community can be of radically different types having different typical regulatory problems and possibilities – some of these easily seen as within the province of state law, others less so.

Thus, relations of community can be based (i) on a convergence of the participants' projects (*instrumental* community) which may be economic in nature; or (ii) on shared customs, traditions, physical environment or linguistic or historical heritage (*traditional* community) or (iii) on shared fundamental convictions (community of *belief or values*), or (iv) on essentially emotional attractions or rejections, likes or dislikes, loves or hatreds towards others (*affective* community). In theory, some of these types of communal relations lend themselves readily to well-defined legal regulation (for example, commercial, contract, and other law governing economic relations). Others present difficult practical problems for law (often the case with emotional bonds and rejections) or they present dangers of intense controversy (as in legal regulation touching on fundamental beliefs). Basic neighbourly coexistence in traditional community is often the focus of criminal, tort, and public order law. But setting conditions of coexistence can be legally controversial, as in protecting natural or cultural environments, languages or historical memory. Each type of communal relationship seems to present different clusters of regulatory problems and needs.

In social life these four pure (ideal) types of relations of community are almost always mixed together in complex patterns. Individuals have many different communal relations with others. Particular social groups or networks of social relations that have a degree of stability (even if their shape and membership changes continually) consist of combinations of these types of community. So, 'community' is never a social 'object'. It is a *way of thinking* about social relations based on mutual interpersonal trust – relations that overlap, interpenetrate, and conflict in networks. These can be called *networks of community* or communal networks. In this way, the ideas of network and community are linked together to focus attention on regulatory settings and issues. In this approach, it becomes possible to stress both (i) the fluidity and complexity of social relations – the atomistic, free-flowing

55

character of contemporary life – and (ii) the reality of ideas of belonging often associated with community.[22]

How should the idea of *economic networks of community* be understood? Communal networks are often dominated by one particular type of interpersonal bond (for example, shared belief, as of a religious group, or common or convergent economic projects, as of a business network). But where networks exist on any significant scale they are unlikely to be exclusively based on one type of communal relation. They will combine different types, even where, as in commercial or financial networks, one type (such as the bond of common or convergent economic projects) may dominate. Seen through a 'community lens',[23] the key failing of orthodox economic analysis is that it rarely emphasizes this complex interplay, in market networks, of instrumental (economic) relations with relations based on affect (emotional allegiances or rejections), tradition (for instance, customary practices existing in shared work environments) and beliefs or ultimate values (like those relating to the nature and purposes of economic networks and their place in wider society).

So, the community approach supports economic sociology and 'a sociological analysis of the role of law in economic life' as a realistic recognition of the nature of economic networks. It insists on the importance of studying 'non-economic' components of economic networks, as well as the economic aspects of networks of community that are not apparently organized to serve primarily economic aims.

Other recent approaches to the sociological study of economic regulation that have used some notion of community have certain commonalities with ideas set out above, even if almost always they treat 'community' as a thing, a social object,[24] in a way that this article rejects. So, for Marie-Laure Djelic and Sigrid Quack, generalizing from the findings of diverse empirical studies, 'communities' (I would say networks of community) are 'fluid and not rigid' and built on individuals' personal interactions; people can simultaneously be members of many such communities, which are internally diverse, 'time-bound, non-essential and non-permanent', with transient, fluctuating memberships (members being 'free to come and go'). Finally, in sharp contrast to older, romanticized images of community, Djelic's and Quack's observed communities 'are ... rife with conflict and power struggles'.[25]

22 The ideas in the above three paragraphs are elaborated and applied in many legal contexts in Cotterrell, op. cit., n. 14; and R. Cotterrell, *Living Law: Studies in Legal and Social Theory* (2008) 17–28 and Part 4.
23 Perry-Kessaris, op. cit., n. 8.
24 See, for example, Mayntz, op. cit., n. 21; B. Engelen, 'Beyond Markets and States: The Importance of Communities' (2010) 61 *International Social Science J.* 489–500.
25 M.-L. Djelic and S. Quack, 'Transnational communities and governance' in Djelic and Quack (eds.), op. cit., n. 21, ch. 1, pp. 26, 27; Djelic and Quack, 'Transnational communities and their impact', id., ch. 16, pp. 377, 380, 383, 386, 387.

Most of these formulations are consistent with this article's approach. But a focus on communities, rather than relations of community, leads to rigidity. Thus, 'a community' is seen by Djelic and Quack as having 'a common culture'[26] ('culture' also being seen by them as a thing, a social object). From the viewpoint of this article, however, it would be better to see disparate *elements* of culture – beliefs, values, material interests, emotional dispositions, habits and customs – interacting (sometimes reinforcing each other, sometimes conflicting) in the social relations of communal networks. The point is to avoid thinking of 'communities' or 'cultures' as bounded, discrete entities, and to emphasize changeability and shifting diversity, at least as much as stability, in community and culture. In the interplay of communal relations in networks, power will operate in many different ways and conflict may or may not be 'rife'. But it seems important to stress that conflict may arise at least as easily *between* communal networks as within them, a matter that poses special responsibilities for regulating economic networks in their relations with wider social networks.

The networks of community approach avoids problems of the embeddedness approach to economic sociology because it does not separate 'economy' and 'society' and it clarifies the nature of the social for regulatory purposes. It treats the economic as a part of the social which is itself made up of communal networks. Some such networks are dominated by economic objectives (though their communal character is unlikely to be exclusively economic). Regulating them will have to take into account the mixes of different types of communal relations that they may exhibit. Sociology of law, informed by this approach, is a study of *the means and effects of regulating networks of community*. That involves analysing and assessing their 'internally' generated governance structures as well as the problems of harmonizing and stabilizing relations between networks.

POLANYI AND WEBER ON LAW AND ECONOMY

The networks of community approach can be tested and sharpened against key insights from classical socio-legal theory. Although I suggested that Polanyi's *Great Transformation* is not mainly a work of social theory, it would be wrong to put it aside having considered only the problems it poses for the concept of embeddedness. Most importantly, Polanyi shows that, as a matter of history, the practice of the self-regulating market did not emerge as a natural phenomenon. In so far as it could have some semblance of stability, it had to be created and maintained determinedly and forcefully by state power and law; by contrast, counter-movements against the effects of market self-regulation, which economic liberals still often see as ideologically-

26 id. (ch. 16), p. 384.

motivated interference, were pragmatic responses to the social problems this practice created, responses often promoted by free-marketeers themselves.[27] The idea that markets do not need powerful legal frameworks and state support is thus entirely 'utopian'[28] – *ideological thinking* resistant to all evidence (though Polanyi avoids the term ideology, perhaps because of its association with Marxism).

The dependence of modern markets on the state and state law is clearly indicated also in Max Weber's social theory, which has been treated as a primary basis for a new economic sociology of law.[29] For Weber:

> an economic system, especially of the modern type, could not exist without a legal order with very special features which could not develop except in the framework of a public legal order ... The tempo of modern business communications requires a promptly and predictably functioning legal system, i.e. one which is guaranteed by the strongest coercive power;

market society requires *calculable* law working through rational rules.[30] While law does not, in Weber's view, necessarily need to be guaranteed in all societies *by a state*, the 'constant expansion of the market' in modern societies has promoted a monopoly of law by '*one* universalist coercive institution'; the pervasiveness of market relations has led to their legal regulation being concentrated in the state.[31] Thus, the modern state and its law are vital to the market society.

Weber's views, however, are very nuanced. Economic change, he notes, can often occur without any legal changes and, conversely, variations in legal doctrine may be economically irrelevant if law's practical effects are the same.[32] Most crucially, he emphasizes that legal coercion can have only *limited effects* in the economic sphere, and the power of law over economic conduct has *weakened* in modern times; efforts to change customary economic practices are always difficult and often counter-productive, and while economic actors tend to honour agreements because of self-interest, they usually avoid invoking law. Fundamentally, economic interests are often stronger than the forces supporting legal regulation, and circumventions of law can frequently be disguised in economic practices. Those working continuously in a market are often able to distort the meaning of legal rules

---

27 Polanyi, op. cit., n. 5, pp. 146–8, 154–6.
28 id., pp. 31, 157, 187, 258, 266. For a richly documented polemical account of the recent use of state coercion to impose 'free markets' on reluctant populations in many parts of the world, see N. Klein, *The Shock Doctrine* (2007).
29 Swedberg, op. cit., n. 1; R. Swedberg, 'Max Weber's Contribution to the Economic Sociology of Law' (2006) 2 *Annual Rev. of Law and Social Science* 61–81; M. Coutu and T. Kirat, 'John R. Commons and Max Weber: The Foundations of an Economic Sociology of Law' (2011) 38 *J. of Law and Society* 469–95.
30 M. Weber, *Economy and Society: An Outline of Interpretive Sociology* (1968) 336–7, 667, 847; Swedberg, id. (2006), pp. 69–70.
31 Weber, id., p. 337 (emphasis in original).
32 id., pp. 333–4.

in practice, and typically they have much greater expert knowledge of that market than do legislators and law enforcers.[33] The cards are strongly stacked against effective state regulation of economic life, at least in some very important respects.

So, Weber's position might be summarized by saying that modern market economies rely on state law for support but, as far as possible, the market takes law's interventions strictly on its own terms, for its own purposes. What Polanyi called the self-regulating market is, for Weber, never free of law and state power. Yet, while it takes the benefits of these, it subordinates them – through secrecy, monopoly of expertise, opportunism, and collusion – to its own regulatory priorities geared to the production of profit in self-integrated economic networks. These ideas suggest almost paradoxical ways in which economic networks of community shape their 'internal' self-regulation: as simultaneously *entirely parasitic on* and yet also *significantly autonomous of* state legal controls, which are, of course, aimed not merely at regulating economic life but at regulating the coexistence of innumerable networks of community in the national society whether or not these networks are focused on economic relations.

Weber's thinking points to issues that are relevant to any study of law's role in economic networks of community. Yet it might be asked how far, in the light of contemporary experience, his emphases need adjustment. One major issue has to be left aside entirely here. It is not possible to address in this article the vast literature on the changing role of the state, faced with globalization and the growth of transnational economic regulation,[34] which might raise questions about what Weber sees as the modern state's central place in coercively guaranteeing legal authority.

However, his claims about the importance of certainty and calculability of the effects of transactions, as a basic bridge between economy and law,[35] may also need some updating. Enforceability of contracts is surely crucial, but the resources for securing this are often provided in economic networks themselves, as sociology of law has long recognized,[36] irrespective of state law. It has often been suggested that in the larger and wealthier economic networks and organizations, state law's guarantees are, indeed, important and often indispensable. Yet, even here, circumstances can be envisaged where law becomes only an ultimate very distant guarantee, hard to relate to extremely complex transactions that, by their nature, evolve and change their

33 id., pp. 328, 334, 335, 336.
34 See, for example, A. Perry-Kessaris (ed.), *Socio-Legal Approaches to International Economic Law: Text, Context, Subtext* (2012); R. Cotterrell, 'What is Transnational Law?' (2012) 37 *Law & Social Inquiry* 500–24.
35 Weber, op. cit., n. 30, p. 667.
36 See, for example, Ehrlich, op. cit., n. 13, pp. 64–7; S. Macaulay, 'Non-Contractual Relations in Business: A Preliminary Study' (1963) 28 *Am. Sociological Rev.* 55–67; L. Bernstein, 'Opting Out of the Legal System: Extralegal Contractual Relations in the Diamond Industry' (1992) 21 *J. of Legal Studies* 115–57.

form and significance very rapidly, only loosely addressed by relatively static legal doctrine. In such cases calculable law may seem subordinate to far more significant everyday guarantees of transactions in major economic networks.

Law can seem outpaced by trading conditions in such arenas.[37] In some kinds of financial markets, traders need to assess extremely quickly ever-changing levels of risk and likelihoods of profit in strings of transactions based on a vast array of shifting valuations and conditions. Where information is processed automatically through computer programmes to achieve great speed in transactions, legal considerations (whatever their degrees of calculability) may be just elements in a complex mix. An IT consultant for banks is reported as noting that in:

> High Frequency Trading [the use of sophisticated computer programs to trade securities] ... [t]he banks recruit post-doctoral mathematicians every year to work on their trading algorithms ... I think about HFT ... as a sea of money slowly washing back and forward ... computers trading with other computers, taking advantage of minute variations in markets, very small discrepancies ... In HFT you don't even get a snapshot of what the computers are doing. More like a vague idea. But who knows and who cares?[38]

Technology thus replaces known law in giving security to or assessing risk in transactions.

Even if such financial arenas are far from typical as economic networks, they are hugely significant. Transactions may depend *ultimately* on law (if disputes arise or market failures occur) but, in everyday terms, economic activity depends on personal contacts, 'cultural' understandings in the network of community, and ever more sophisticated computer systems. The calculability of law may be a minor matter compared to the many types of (often automated) 'momentary' calculability on which some major modern markets depend.

On the other hand, Weber's suggestion that state law is fated to be relatively powerless in *shaping* (as contrasted with supporting) economic relations might be questioned in the light of a century of experience since he wrote. Polanyi showed historically the role of the state in moulding Euro-

---

37 For example, the trading of derivatives in financial markets, outside the framework of regulated exchanges, developed in the United States in the 1980s and 1990s in a situation of complete uncertainty as to whether such contracts were legally enforceable. Traders sought legal certainty in this vastly lucrative business which, having become established, expanded greatly when the legal position was clarified in favour of enforceability. See G. Morgan, 'Legitimacy in Financial Markets: Credit Default Swaps in the Current Crisis' (2010) 8 *Socio-Economic Rev.* 17–45, at 23–24. On the impact of the speed of transactions on considerations of legality, see W.E. Scheuerman, 'Global Law in Our High Speed Economy' in *Rules and Networks: The Legal Culture of Business Transactions*, eds. R.P. Appelbaum, W.L.F. Felstiner, and V. Gessner (2001).

38 J. Luyendijk, 'Banking Blog: Voices of Finance: IT Consultant and Developer' (12 December 2011) (anonymous interview), at <http://www.guardian.co.uk/commentisfree/2011/dec/12/voices-of-finance-it-consultant-developer>.

60

pean economies. That this active role has sometimes been harmful or unpredictable in its effects, or has simply not been developed with sufficiently sophisticated knowledge of regulatory possibilities (a matter for economics and sociology of law to address in combination) should not mean that state law is unavailable as a powerful resource for directing economic networks of community.

Some insightful sociological studies of law and economy emphasize that law can operate to influence economic relations and organizations not only as an 'exogenous shock' (an intrusion from outside, imposing change) but through 'mutual endogeneity' – that is, an ongoing reciprocal influence of legal and economic rationalities and practices.[39] Reinterpreting that claim in this article's terms, law should be seen as a means of influencing *elements* of culture (values, customary practices, patterns of material interests, collective allegiances, and so on) within economic networks of community, as well as being influenced in its turn by its interaction with them.

In at least one important respect Weber does see law as more than just supportive of economic relations and as able positively to *promote* them in specific directions: it can create new devices and instruments that can be applied to (and greatly develop) economic purposes.[40] Contracts in various forms, negotiable instruments, agency and corporate personality are all legal devices of this nature. In this way, more recent scholars have affirmed, law can *constitute* economic relations.[41] Historically, this was surely very significant. Yet it might be said that now it is accountants, financiers inventing new 'products', mathematicians and IT specialists who are creating the most important (in terms of the wealth they represent) instruments and devices of economic life. Here too, Weber may need updating.

SOLIDARITY, CULTURE, ECONOMIC REGULATION

There is a striking contrast between Weber's usually dispassionate 'scientific' prose and the obvious moral anger that animates *The Great Transformation*'s claims about the market's 'perils' to – even 'demolition' of – society; its 'unheard-of wealth' built on 'unheard-of poverty', and the 'determination to renounce human solidarity' that 'gained the dignity of a secular religion' in free-market thinking.[42] Polanyi wrote explicitly to pro-

39 L.B. Edelman and R. Stryker, 'A Sociological Approach to Law and the Economy' in *Handbook of Economic Sociology*, eds. N.J. Smelser and R. Swedberg (2005, 2nd edn.); L.B. Edelman, 'Legality and the Endogeneity of Law' in *Legality and Community: On the Intellectual Legacy of Philip Selznick*, eds. R.A. Kagan, M. Krygier, and K. Winston (2002).
40 Weber, op. cit., n. 30, p. 687.
41 R. Stryker, 'Mind the Gap: Law, Institutional Analysis and Socioeconomics' (2003) 1 *Socio-Economic Rev.* 335–67; Edelman and Stryker, op. cit., n. 39.
42 Polanyi, op. cit., n. 5, pp. 75, 76, 106, 107.

voke change but Weber insists on 'value-free' sociology. Richard Swedberg, advocating a Weberian economic sociology of law, declares: 'Whereas economics is normative, sociology is not.'[43] Yet, if part of the impetus for promoting economic sociology has been to challenge the perspectives of mainstream economics – which have powerful political and moral consequences when they shape policy – this can hardly be a disinterested intellectual inquiry. Fred Block states, in very Polanyian terms, that 'it is market society's guilty secret that it is fundamentally dependent on a moral order'.[44] A sociology of law and economy surely has to explore and assess these moral foundations.

Analysis in terms of regulating networks of community makes this possible. The sense of belonging which, as noted earlier, is associated with community can also be referred to, in Durkheimian terms, as a sense of solidarity or moral cohesion. Durkheim saw solidarity in modern societies as founded on interdependence and, in doing so, he was thinking especially – though never exclusively – of instrumental and economic relations of community, of the functional division of labour that produces ever-greater specialization of roles in complex modern life.[45] From this article's perspective, however, modern bonds of community are not just those of functional interdependence. They are based on affect (emotional allegiances or rejections), tradition (common heritage or environment), or ultimate values and convictions, as well as on common or convergent projects.

In this perspective, morality can be thought of as the basis of the mutual interpersonal trust (MIT) that each distinct type of communal relations depends on, and so it will be different in each type: for example, courtesy, civility, neighbourliness in traditional community; empathy, sympathy, and altruistic care in affective community; fellowship and respect for others' integrity in belief-based community; and honesty, fair dealing and performance (meeting obligations undertaken) in instrumental community. While the last of these might seem most relevant to economic networks of community, the fact that these networks are unlikely to be built solely on instrumental relations makes the other moral bases of MIT relevant too. Again, economic networks exist in relation to other networks of community in the social at large, so they have moral as well as legal relations with these other networks (including the umbrella network of the national political society as a whole).

Much of this moral mosaic is clearly not within the purview of law, but it indicates the wider, complex moral domain within which the regulation of economic networks of community can be considered in sociology of law. And moral precepts, at the limit, often become legal demands. For

43 Swedberg, op. cit. (2006), n. 29, p. 72.
44 In Krippner et al., op. cit., n. 3, p. 118.
45 E. Durkheim, *The Division of Labour in Society* (1984).

example: neighbourliness turns into a requirement not to harm others whom one encounters, or to disrupt shared basic conditions of coexistence; care and empathy turn into a need to control unlimited selfishness and recklessness as regards others' interests; respect for integrity turns into legal proscription of actions that deliberately or thoughtlessly degrade or dehumanize others.

Some socio-legal scholars may be uneasy with a moral focus. Sociology of law, if it is to deserve the label 'science', surely cannot transform itself into moral or political advocacy. Nevertheless, as Durkheim showed, sociology can reveal empirically and theoretically the social structures and conditions in which moral ideas become meaningful for people in particular times and places, and in which moral arguments become urgent.[46] It can also identify conditions that foster solidarity, and those that threaten its existence. This is not to say that solidarity – the maintenance of a certain degree of social cohesiveness and an experience of collective belonging – is approved by sociology as *valuable*. It is only to say that if it is thought valuable and the aim is to promote and defend it, social science can explain conditions that facilitate or hamper this. It can identify the forms of solidarity that are possible in certain types of society. And it can indicate the part that legal and other regulation can play in setting the conditions for solidarity.[47]

The solidarity of some communal networks can exist *at the expense of* wider social solidarity in society. This can be considered in relation to what has been seen as a distinct culture of some financial markets.[48] An analytically useful concept of culture treats it as a mix of common and convergent interests, customary practices, allegiances, beliefs, and values expressed in relations of community.[49] Accounts of the culture of some financial networks indicate how the displacement inside them of moral assumptions widely made outside can be seemingly normal: '[E]xecutives blabbed criminal conspiracies on the telephone even though they knew they were being recorded by their own company'; others 'wantonly fixed bond auctions' with such knowledge; 'bid rigging was so incredibly common the defendants simply forgot to be ashamed of it'.[50] In the view of a senior Financial Services Authority regulator:

---

46 R. Cotterrell, 'Justice, Dignity, Torture, Headscarves: Can Durkheim's Sociology Clarify Legal Values?' (2011) 20 *Social & Legal Studies* 3–20.
47 id.
48 See, for example, editorial: 'Shaming the Banks into Better Ways' *Financial Times*, 29 June 2012 (many references to banking culture).
49 Cotterrell, op. cit., n. 14.
50 M. Taibbi, 'The Scam Wall Street Learned from the Mafia' *Rolling Stone* (Politics), 21 June 2012, at <http://www.rollingstone.com/politics/news/the-scam-wall-street-learned-from-the-mafia-20120620>.

63

Banks are fundamentally amoral places ... morality simply has no part in the decision-making process ... It's not the people who are bad: it's the culture that builds up all these material expectations ... You get intoxicated and over time you get trapped.[51]

But, in fact, no communal networks can be 'amoral' if morality is seen sociologically as the currency of mutual interpersonal trust on which relations of community depend. Some financial networks merely have (if the reports quoted above are to be believed) moral currencies *radically different* from those of many other communal networks in society. Elements of culture existing within them, which may be normal bases of their everyday solidarity, can appear utterly scandalous, even incomprehensible, when viewed from the moral perspectives of other networks in the wider society whose solidarity is structured in other ways.

Sociology thus has to insist on reinserting 'culture' (in the specific sense used in this article) as an essential element in the study of economic relations. While culture is usually a complex, fluid mix of diverse elements, in some circumstances all or most of the elements can become overlaid, closely linked, and mutually reinforcing so that one can speak of 'cultures' *as if* they were distinct, bounded social objects, wholly separated from other cultures.[52] In such circumstances they can seem alien, threatening or incomprehensible to those outside the networks of community in which they exist. Their solidarity can appear as a problem for the solidarity of larger networks of community (such as that of the national political society) which requires their integration within it. If this larger solidarity is seen as valuable, one task of state law will be strongly to defend and promote it, regulating networks of community to influence their 'internal' culture for this purpose, while recognizing that solidarity in society at large depends significantly on the solidarity of its component communal networks and promotion of open communication and interaction between them.

This approach seems consistent with claims, noted earlier, that while law can operate as an 'external' directing and controlling force (an 'exogenous shock') on economic networks and institutions it can also operate on them 'internally', seeping into the rationality that surrounds economic relations.[53] Robin Stryker writes that 'law provides tools that help actors attribute meaning, existence, desirability or undesirability to their economic activities and environment' and 'legal schema help provide symbolic representation of who or what economic actors are, of how these actors

---

51 J. Luyendijk, 'Banking Blog: Senior FSA Regulator: "Can You Say No to Four or Five Times Your Salary?"' (25 June 2012) (anonymous interview), at <http://www.guardian.co.uk/commentisfree/joris-luyendijk-banking-blog/2012/jun/25/senior-fsa-regulator>.

52 R. Cotterrell, 'The Struggle for Law: Some Dilemmas of Cultural Legality' (2009) 4 *International J. of Law in Context* 373–84, especially at 377–8.

53 Edelman and Stryker, op. cit., n. 39.

64

would like to be viewed by others, and of how they would like to view themselves'.[54]

But this idea of law as constituting culture in economic relations should not be overemphasized. To some extent it may reflect a particularly American view of the great cultural power of law. What is surely important is to recognize that economic rationality is not culture-free;[55] that the content of economists' favoured concept – rational choice – is *always* culturally shaped. Hence law's relation to economy is not, as for example Weber's sociology (and more recent systems theory) tends to suggest, fundamentally a confrontation between distinct legal and economic rationalities or discourses, but a negotiation of the many forms of regulation possible in communal networks in which legal and moral supports of mutual interpersonal trust of different kinds interact with great complexity.

CONCLUSION

This article has attempted to apply a community lens to current debates about the new economic sociology and about its extension to legal research. It suggests that some main aims that have inspired the use of the concept of embeddedness might be fulfilled by seeing law's involvement with economic relations as that of regulating networks of community. Much of the regulation of these networks is *internally* generated by the need to support mutual interpersonal trust in communal relations within them. And even in specifically economic networks it is reasonable to suppose that not all such relations are economic in character. Hence a range of regulatory issues arise that go beyond what much of the literature has seen narrowly as the policing or promoting of economic rationality.

Other regulation of networks of community, however, comes from sources *external* to them (in larger networks of which they are a part, or in parallel networks). Thus state law, having the task of regulating the national political society as a communal network, imposes regulation on other networks within this society. Sociology of law has to explore the complexity of this task in relation to economic networks – recognizing their legitimate needs for autonomy and solidarity as well as the imperative of integrating them in and reinforcing their value for society as a whole.

These considerations can give sociology of law a normative orientation. As science, it does not prescribe solidarity as an aim but it can explore

54 Stryker, op. cit., n. 41, p. 349. See, also, C. Parker, 'Meta-Regulation: Legal Account-ability for Corporate Social Responsibility' in *The New Corporate Accountability: Corporate Social Responsibility and the Law*, ed. D. McBarnet, A. Voiculescu, and T. Campbell (2007) (analysing problems as well as possibilities of using law to shape the social outlook and value systems of corporate economic actors).

55 Compare L.B. Edelman, 'Rivers of Law and Contested Terrain: A Law and Society Approach to Economic Rationality' (2004) 38 *Law and Society Rev.* 181–97.

65

empirically and theoretically the conditions necessary to pursue that aim. And it can show when and why such an aim seems meaningful. To do these things and adopt these approaches would supplement and challenge dominant perspectives in economic analysis of law and also encourage sociology of law to address directly many current moral and political concerns about the workings of markets and the nature of contemporary capitalism.

Ultimately the agenda of such a study of law and economy would include asking how far regulation can control major economic networks in a way that promotes solidarity *beyond* them, prevents their cultural *isolation* from wider society, and ensures their social *utility*. This is partly a question about regulatory design but also partly about regulatory opportunity and political determination. In this way legal and political sociology are necessarily closely linked.

Polanyi identified the idea of the self-regulating market as utopian. But the myth of state law's relative powerlessness, redundancy or harmfulness in economic life has long survived the period in which Polanyi saw it as fundamentally shaken by historical developments. This myth has found support not just in influential currents of economic theory but in much legal sociology. Analyses of the pathologies of 'juridification',[56] empirical research on the use of law to bring about planned social change, and the arguments of Luhmannian systems theory have suggested that law is often ineffective to achieve chosen regulatory ends, that courts and legislature are often too out of touch with social (including economic) conditions to provide relevant regulation, that law's effects are often destructive in social life, or that law cannot influence but only create 'interference' in the economy, with the latter determining on its own terms how, if at all, legal communications are read within it.

All of this literature is important in balancing over-optimistic claims about law's capabilities in economic regulation. But the lesson to be learned should be *positive*: that the creation and enforcement of legal regulation of economic life are often extremely difficult and require much juristic, economic, and sociological expertise; and that this implies challenging but welcome agendas for sociology of law. The main message taken from this literature today – in a world faced with recurring economic crises – cannot be relentlessly negative; it certainly cannot be the counterproductive and unwarranted message that efforts to shape law to control economic networks of community to ensure that they serve wider social needs are fundamentally misdirected.

Sociological analysis of the role of law in economic life should be concerned with legal aspects of and contributions to the internal culture of networks of community. It should be concerned also with the ways law can

---

56 See, for example, G. Teubner (ed.), *Juridification of Social Spheres: A Comparative Analysis in the Areas of Labour, Corporate, Antitrust and Social Welfare Law* (1987).

66

coordinate these networks to support both solidarity *within* them and solidarity *amongst* them in the complex balances required, if promoting social cohesion is seen as a main task of legal regulation. And its studies will surely be relevant for those concerned with designing legal and other regulation to enhance the *calculability* of economic relations. It seems necessary, however, to recognize that the security and guarantee of these relations may now be a more complex matter than it was when Weber put calculability centre-stage in his theorization of the relations of law and economy.

67

JOURNAL OF LAW AND SOCIETY
VOLUME 40, NUMBER 1, MARCH 2013
ISSN: 0263-323X, pp. 68–91

Anemos-ity, *Apatheia*, *Enthousiasmos*: An Economic Sociology of Law and Wind Farm Development in Cyprus

AMANDA PERRY-KESSARIS*

This piece sketches 'an' economic sociology of law: one possible approach, in relation to one case study of wind farm development in Cyprus. Carbon emissions are a global threat to which wind farms may offer something of a solution. But wind farms can also pose local threats. So they tend to produce conflicts on different levels of social life: action, interaction, regime, and rationality. As such they are ill-suited to exploration through law or economics, and ideally suited to exploration through economic sociology of law. The approach set out in this article enables social life of all levels, intensities, and types (including the economic) to be placed on the same analytical page. What emerges is a most human story of animosity, apathy, and enthusiasm in which law acts variously as means, obstacle, and irrelevance.

PRELUDE

Leave the Nicosia-Larnaca highway at the Kalo Chorio roundabout. Skirt the rolling hills crowned with unhurried blades. Proceed on crunching foot up the steepening slope, past the olive tree-shaded foxhole and the cobbled-together fence. Scramble up the bright white, gravely path, dotted with scented crawlers, thistles, and grasses dancing in the quickening breeze. Allow the inductive, robotic hum to draw you in. Detach, turn around and drink in the view. Descend in turmoil: animosity, apathy, enthusiasm?

* *SOAS, University of London, Thornhaugh Street, Russell Square, London WC1H 0XG, England*
a.perry-kessaris@soas.ac.uk

Thanks to Diamond Ashiagbor, Sabine Frerichs, Terry Halliday, Prabha Kotiswaran, Martin Krygier, and Joanne Scott for insightful comments; and to Helen Perry for taking me here, there, and everywhere.

68

The title of this piece promises 'an' economic sociology of law – it sketches but one possible approach, and showcases it in relation to a single case study: wind farm development in Cyprus.[1] 'At first sight the environmental benefits of generating energy from wind farms would seem to be overwhelming.'[2] Carbon emissions are a global threat – economic, emotional, and environmental – to which wind farms may offer something of a solution. But wind farms can also pose local threats – economic, emotional, and environmental. So they tend to produce conflicts on 'different scales' of social life.[3] As such they are ill-suited to exploration through law or economics, and ideally suited to exploration through economic sociology of law.

A legal approach entails the 'rationalisation of and speculation on the rules, principles, concepts and legal values considered to be explicitly or implicitly *present in* legal doctrine.'[4] From this perspective, 'law comes first and is the substantive focus. There is no need to look any further.'[5] An economic approach might be said to be similarly constrained, entailing 'rationalizations' and 'speculations' regarding rules, principles, concepts, and economic values thought to be present in human nature, and their impact on production, consumption, and distribution.

By contrast, and in keeping with its sociological roots, an economic sociology of law is outward looking. It conceptualizes both the 'legal' and the 'economic' as social phenomena occurring on all, interconnected, levels of social life: 'individual actors and their *actions*', '*interactions* between actors'; 'the institutions of social *regimes*' into which interactions 'aggregate'; and the '*rationalities*' that 'underlie and direct social regimes'.[6] These levels are analytically liberating because they elide boundaries imposed within the disciplines of economics (such as state, firm, household) and law (such as private or public, local or international), allowing us more effectively to capture messy reality. They are presented together, in stylized form, in Figure 1.

---

1 Interviews and site visits were conducted in Cyprus in April 2012. Interviews are referred to by code, or not at all, to protect identity. Areas under Turkish occupation are not covered.
2 S. Jackson, 'Wind Power: The Legal and Environmental Issues' (2005) *ELFline* at 4.
3 J. Holder and M. Lee, *Environmental Protection, Law and Policy* (2007, 2nd edn.) 698.
4 R. Cotterrell, *The Sociology of Law: An Introduction* (1992, 2nd edn.) 3.
5 A. Perry-Kessaris, 'What does it mean to take a socio-legal approach to international economic law?' in *Socio-Legal Approaches to International Economic Law: Text, Context, Subtext*, ed. A. Perry-Kessaris (2012) 4.
6 S. Frerichs, 'Re-embedding neo-liberal constitutionalism: a Polanyian case for the economic sociology of law' in *Karl Polanyi, Globalisation and the Potential of Law in Transnational Markets*, eds. C. Joerges and J. Falke (2011) at 68. Emphasis added. See, also, A. Perry-Kessaris, 'Reading the story of law and embeddedness through a community lens: a Polanyi-meets-Cotterrell economic sociology of law?' (2011) 62 *Northern Ireland Legal Q.* 401, at 402.

69

Figure 1. Actions, Interactions, Regimes, and Rationalities[7]

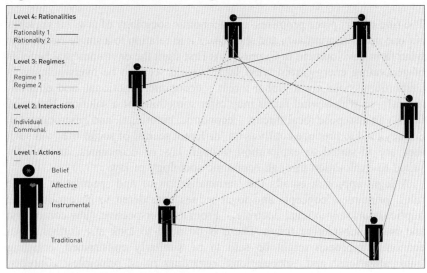

© Amanda Perry-Kessaris. Designer Sarah Schrauwen.

Social actions centre on widely divergent values and interests. This observation is illustrated in Figure 1 by reference to the human body using the Weberian typology of affective (heart), belief (head), traditional (foot), and instrumental (hand). Most importantly for economic sociology of law, this image reminds us that economic activities (production, distribution and consumption) are just one sub-type of instrumental social action, intimately interconnected, through multi-layered and multi-tasking human beings, with other forms of social action (instrumental and otherwise).[8]

Social interactions cover the full range of Weberian actions, and can be conceptualized as occurring at different intensities. This observation is captured in the lines that connect the actors in Figure 1. Broken lines indicate individualistic, superficial, impersonal interactions; solid lines indicate deep, stable, and trusting relationships that Roger Cotterrell has termed 'communal networks'.[9] The dominant motivation, or underlying values and interests, of

---

7 The diagram does not allude to the possibilities that parties perceive their relationship differently; or that interactions might be affected by no, or multiple, regimes.
8 As Fred Block, citing Viviana Zelizer's notion of 'relational work' notes, people have 'the capacity ... to build and maintain powerful affective and reciprocal relations with each other even when commercial relationships and the rhetoric of self-interest are dominant.' F. Block in this volume, p. 40, citing V. Zelizer, *The Purchase of Intimacy* (2006).
9 R. Cotterrell, *Law, Culture and Society: Legal Ideas in the Mirror of Social Theory* (2006) 162–3 and in this volume, pp. 54–7. See, also, G. Walker, 'The role for "community" in carbon governance' (2011) 2 *Wiley Interdisciplinary Revs.: Climate Change* 777.

70

the interaction is suggested by the section of the body to which the line connects.

Laws and other regimes are of sociological interest because they are part – created, used, abused, avoided, and destroyed in the course – of social life. So they appear in Figure 1 as part of social interactions: in the colouring of the lines that connect actors (black for Regime 1, grey for Regime 2). Law can trigger, facilitate or hinder all kinds of action and interaction, from individualistic to communal networks, in particular by supporting (or not) mutual inter-personal trust. It does this by expressing (or not) and coordinating between (or not) the often competing values and interests that are central to different social actions and interactions, and by facilitating and encouraging (or not) participation in social life. It is also possible for law to undermine such networks.[10]

Rationalities or 'shared ways of apprehending the world'[11] are of socio-legal interest to the extent that they influence and are influenced by socio-legal phenomena such as the creation, use, abuse, avoidance, and destruction of laws. So they appear in Figure 1 as an overlay on regimes – black for Rationality 1 which is associated with Regime 1, grey for Rationality 2 which is associated with Regime 2.[12]

What are the implications of the unique capacity of economic sociology of law to integrate multiple social levels and perspectives in this way? The following sections set out in turn some of the econo-socio-legal phenomena that become visible when actors, rationalities, and regimes, and interactions surrounding Cypriot wind farm development are placed on the same page. For the purposes of the present confined space, special attention is paid to interplays between those levels of social life. What emerges is a most human story of animosity, apathy, and enthusiasm in which law acts variously as means, obstacle, and irrelevance.

ACTORS

This article focuses on four sets of actors: developers, government actors, project-affected residents, and civil society actors. All of these actors engage in instrumental interactions – resisting, assisting or acceding to the development of wind farms. But, as Figure 2 intimates, they are also likely to be acting on a combination of other motivations, centred on divergent values and interests. A developer might wonder: will I maximize the return on my investment if I locate my wind turbine here? For the resident the questions could be: will the market value of my (or our) land fall (instrumental); and

---

10 See A. Perry-Kessaris, *Global Business, Local Law: The Indian Legal System as a Communal Resource in Foreign Investment Relations* (2008).

11 J.A. Dryzek, *The Politics of the Earth: Environmental Discourses* (2005) 9 and Part 3.

12 For complications arising when rationalities shift, see Perry-Kessaris, op. cit., n. 6.

71

Figure 2. Hala Sultan Tekke and the Alexigros Wind Farm

© Amanda Perry-Kessaris. Photo: Nicos Kessaris.

will my (or our) beloved view be ruined (affective)? A civil society actor might ask: am I (or we) ethically bound to encourage residents to accept the turbine in order to protect others from the effects of climate change (belief)? A government actor might ponder the cultural implications of a wind farm towering over an eighteenth-century mosque, built on the 649 burial site of the aunt of the Prophet Muhammad (traditional). Of these actors in Cyprus only project-affected residents can be said to be engaged in stable, trusting 'communal' networks. Relations between developers, government actors, and civil society actors are characterized by instability and distrust.

The government of Cyprus is, as one interviewee put it, akin to a small business: its executives are constrained by impossible demands for multi-tasking and by the ego-bloating concentration of responsibilities. Most regulatory decisions on wind farms are taken by central government bodies, in particular the Ministry of Agriculture, Natural Resources and Environment (MARE) and the Ministry of the Interior in the construction licensing phase; the Cyprus Energy Regulatory Authority (CERA/*PAEK*) and the Transmission System Operator (TSO) in the production licensing and subsidy phase;[13] and the Ministry of Commerce, Industry and Tourism

---

13 Established under Law 122(1)/2003 on Regulating the Electricity Market, implementing Directive 2003/54/EC on common rules for the internal EU electricity market.

72

(MCIT) for energy strategy. Relations within and between different levels and branches of government are often fractious: 'It is a mess, it's a mess ... There are a lot of voices.'[14] Local governance falls into two categories: 23 municipalities, including the major towns; and 355 community councils.[15] Their input into wind farm development is constrained primarily to planning issues arising during the construction licensing phase.[16] Lines of communication between the local and central government are notoriously bad.[17]

The wind farm developers of Cyprus are a motley crew. For some, their wind farm is simply the latest in several decades of experiences in large-scale infrastructure development. For others it is a first foray beyond a career in retail or finance. Between 2003 and mid-2012 CERA received 51 applications for a license to construct wind farms and granted 35, of which 23 remain live.[18] Developers were left to identify sites with the necessary amount of wind, obtain permits related to construction (including planning, environmental, and a long list of others) and operation (from CERA and the CEA), all in time for the, narrowly advertised and brief, opening of the application window for the Renewable Energy Sources (RES) Fund (should they wish to apply for it) described below.[19] One developer reported in an interview that:

> If you ask me whether I would have done it again, no, never, no way. [You keep going because] you're so much into it that you lost so much time and so much money you think well ... and then at the end you feel like a fool.

Another said 'I didn't know where I was going and whether I would succeed in the end or, you know, or I would get to the end of it ... I felt I was just throwing money away.' In the beginning, the developers formed a 'very tight' and 'very vocal' Cyprus Wind Energy Association.[20] 'We all had the same interest' and there was a degree of 'solidarity'. Today 'everybody is pursuing his own interests'. And when 'some people choose the easy way ...

---

14 Interview F23Y. For example, the MARE refused to take part in an energy policy review initiated by the MCIT: TUV Rheinland Immissionsschutz und Energiesysteme GmbH and BGP Engineers B.V. (hereinafter TUV and BGP), *Inception Report Provision of services for the preparation of a government strategy and action plan for exploiting the opportunities offered by the Clean Development Mechanism (CDM) and European Emissions Trading Scheme (or others) for the periods 2008–2012 and 2013–2020* (2009) 11. In another case, the Games Department objected that a wind farm application would interfere with bird flight – in fact they 'didn't want [the area] to be withdrawn from their territories': interview K26C.
15 See Union of Cyprus Municipalities, at <http://www.ucm.org.cy> and Union of Cyprus Communities, at <http://www.ekk.org.cy>.
16 Governed by the Town and Country Planning Act of 1972, Law No. 90/72 as well as Local Plans and Area Schemes.
17 Interviews T23C and A27C.
18 Email communication with CERA Energy Officer, 12 July 2012.
19 TUV and BGP, op. cit., n. 14, p. 60. Interviews K23M and T23C.
20 Interview T23C.

73

without care of environmental … or other issues … it is damaging for the rest.'[21]

Cypriot civil society is 'very young and very unprofessional', but 'getting stronger and more professional'.[22] The term civil society has 'only recently' come to be used by media and politicians in Cyprus, and then often inaccurately – for example, to refer to the general electorate. Volunteer service-provision and labour association has a long history, but 'advocacy, dialogue and human rights groups' are few, 'nascent', and generally 'poor' at 'influencing' and enforcing public policy. The camaraderie and independence of civil society are threatened by their reliance on EU/United States/government of Cyprus patronage. Most civil society actors in Cyprus choose to conduct their advocacy activities through 'clientelistic' relations with political parties.[23] This may be because the government has a history of systematically internalizing private and civil society actors by, for example, co-opting them onto committees.[24] For those who are not so internalized, 'the Government does not know what consultation means, or take it seriously.' One civil society actor remarked that is 'only with the EU that they have introduced this constant jargon' of consultation – 'they have to say they are doing this.' But least 'it gives us a space' and 'is moving the right direction – I say this very cautiously.'[25] Also noteworthy is the Environment Commissioner, who creates an unusual bridge between government and governed by independently investigating and reporting on environmental matters to the President, while maintaining a daily blog and engaging in public protests.[26]

21 Interviews K26C and F23Y.
22 Interview D26J.
23 M. Vasilara and G. Piaton, 'The Role of Civil Society in Cyprus' (2007) 19(2) *Cyprus Rev.* 107, at 108, 112, 116–17. A 2005 survey revealed 44 organizations covering environmental matters on the (un-occupied section of the) island: Bicommunal Development Programme, *Cyprus Environmental Directory* (2005), at <http://mirror.undp.org/cyprus/endir/EnvDir_En_2005.pdf>.
24 For example, the Federation of Environmental and Ecological Organizations is an umbrella group of 18 NGOs covering consumption, chemistry, mountain climbing, and wildlife and is on environmental committees. See <http://www.oikologiafeeo.org> and Cyprus Department of Environment, MARE, Republic of Cyprus *National Implementation Report on Aarhus Convention* (2011), generated at <http:// apps.unece.org/ehlm/pp/NIR/index.asp> on 3 April 2012.
25 Interview P25S. For example, it was reported that when developing priorities for the EU Structural Fund, the government only consulted the Pan-Cyprian Volunteerism Coordinative Council – 'service providers who know nothing of activism' which is founded by statute and government-funded: interview P25S. Law 61(1)/2006 on the Pancyprian Volunteerism Coordinative Council.
26 For the blog, see <http://theopemptou.blogspot.com>. For public protest, see <http:// youtu.be/ogSzvx3TKb8>.

Two international regimes, and their associated rationalities, are implicated in the development of wind farms in Cyprus: the Kyoto climate change regime and the Aarhus participation regime. In order to understand their origin and interaction it is necessary to understand the island as, among other things, a post-colony many times over, occupied most recently by the Ottoman and then British empires, and now Turkey.[27] It is only the third largest island in the Mediterranean, and it is divided into three spheres of governance. The northern third has been occupied by Turkey since 1974 and is governed by executive, legislative, and judicial institutions under the title of the Turkish Republic of Northern Cyprus. The Sovereign Base Areas of Dhekelia on the southwest coast and Akrotiri to the southeast remain British Overseas Territories governed by a military-civil administration. Most of the island is under the control of the Republic of Cyprus, including a President and Council of Ministers, an elected House of Representatives, and a judiciary.

After its 1960 independence from Britain, the developmental state of Cyprus was in many ways highly effective, shepherding in the 'Cyprus Miracle' of 'extraordinary' recovery and growth following the invasion of 'the more productive part' of the island.[28] Cyprus also immediately embarked on a journey of Europeanization, becoming a member of the EU in 2004. Political scientists have referred to processes by which regimes (and rationalities) are transmitted between (candidate and member) states and the EU as 'downloading' (from the EU to states), 'cross-loading' (between states), and 'uploading' (from states to the EU). This terminology is echoed in Niall Ferguson's nattily branded 'six killer apps of western civilization'.[29] The sociological elephant in the room is that these 'apps' are socially constructed, inherently open source and, as such, subject to what Halliday and Carruthers have called 'recursive cycles' of national and international social and legal change.[30] So they get used, abused, and avoided; to positive, negative, and no effect; as part of the actions and interactions of social life. That is the stuff of economic sociology of law.

The prevailing direction, accuracy, speed, and so on of Europeanization in a given state is governed by what Sepos terms 'territorial' and 'temporal' attributes. Cyprus can be categorized as 'territorially' small, southern, and peripheral. On the 'temporal' dimension, Cyprus is a late joiner to the EU; like other predominantly agrarian, orthodox, and Catholic societies,

27 See W. Mallinson, *Cyprus: A Modern History* (2009).
28 D. Christodoulou, *Inside the Cyprus Miracle: The Labours of an Embattled Mini-Economy* (1992) and interview A27C.
29 N. Ferguson, *Civilization: The Six Killer Apps of Western Power* (2012).
30 T.C. Halliday and B.G. Carruthers, *Bankrupt: Global Lawmaking and Systemic Financial Crisis* (2009).

relatively slow to 'reform its traditions'; and like many other post-colonial states, 'bears the imprint and legacy' of its Ottoman and British colonizers, and has suffered from 'ethnic conflict, civil war, political turmoil and divisions'.[31]

Like other post-colonial, small, southern, peripheral states, Cyprus is 'characterized by anticipatory, adaptive and "downloading" Europeaniza-tion'. It tends to 'policy-taker' not 'maker'.[32] Social anthropologist Vassos Argyrou has directly linked this tendency to the dominance of a post-colonial rationality, proposing that post-independence Cyprus has been 'ruled' by 'the idea of Europe'. As a post-colony, 'the best [it] could ever hope for was to modernise' – in this case, to 'de-Ottomanise' and to 'become *like* Europe – similar, but never quite the same'. He mocks the idea of the so-called 'decision' of Cyprus to join the EU: neither was Europe sure it wanted Cyprus, nor was there serious debate as to whether Cyprus wanted Europe, especially as compared to any other team. So there was no hesitation or debate when Cyprus was asked to drop involvement in the Third Worldly Non-Aligned Movement, of which it was a founding member, as a condition of entry to the First Worldly EU. The downloading of European regimes has, aside from religious objections to homosexual civil marriage, been fairly automatic. What citizens elsewhere in Europe 'experience as an imposition', Cypriots 'experience as natural and necessary', so much so that 'the most effective way to legitimise new legislation' is to suggest that the EU requires it.[33] Accordingly, in a 2011 Eurobarometer survey of Cyprus, 95 per cent of interviewees agreed that EU law 'is necessary' to protect the environment in Cyprus, and 81 per cent that the government should make environmental decisions jointly with the EU.[34]

Two regimes downloaded by Europeanizing Cyprus are central to the development of wind farms on the island: the Clean Development Mech-anism of the Kyoto climate change regime and, to a lesser extent, the Aarhus Convention participation regime. In his highly influential taxonomy of the *Politics of the Earth,* John Dryzek identified three 'environmental discourses' or rationalities that dominate 'environmental problem solving' regimes. They are all 'prosaic and reformist' (operating within the confines of industrial market society), not revolutionary. Dryzek dubs them 'admini-strative rationalism', which privileges 'experts' and produces expert-based regimes; 'economic rationalism', which privileges 'markets' and produces

31 A. Sepos, *The Europeanization of Cyprus* (2008) 6–14.
32 id., pp. 9, 10.
33 V. Argyrou, 'Independent Cyprus? Postcoloniality and the spectre of Europe' (2010) 22(2) *Cyprus Rev.* 39, at 41–3. This is a phenomenon widely observed: see P.M. Hass, 'Compliance with EU directives: insights from international relations and comparative politics' (1998) 5 *J. of European Public Policy* 17.
34 European Commission, *Eurobarometer Survey: Attitudes of European Citizens Towards the Environment, Cyprus Factsheet* (2011).

76

market-based regimes; and 'democratic pragmatism', which privileges 'people' and produces participation-based regimes.[35] Elements of each of these rationality-regimes have played a part in wind farm development in Cyprus.

KYOTO: ADMINISTRATIVE RATIONALISM

Under the 1998 Kyoto Protocol to the 1992 UN Framework Convention on Climate Change (UNCCC), richer parties (listed in Annex I) are allocated an emissions target in the form of tradable Assigned Amount Units (AAUs).[36] In addition, developers of emissions-reducing projects, such as wind farms, that are hosted in poorer ('non-Annex I') states and are registered under the UNCCC Clean Development Mechanism (CDM) can earn tradable Certificates of Emissions Reduction (CERs or 'project offsets' or 'carbon credits') each representing 1 tonne of CO_2 emissions avoided. So parties can produce emissions to the level of their assigned (and any purchased) Amount Units and CERs.[37] In the taxonomy developed by Dryzek, the carbon market element of the Kyoto regime can be described as market-based, grounded in economic rationalism.

The Protocol was downloaded into EU law in 2002.[38] EU member states committed from the outset jointly to fulfil their Kyoto obligations, and the Treaties under which Cyprus and others joined the EU in 2004 included national targets for production from renewable energy sources to ensure those obligations were realized.[39] Instead of targets, the EU caps emissions from member states, power stations, and plants across the EU. It allows under-shooters to trade certified emissions reductions to over-shooters. The Emissions Trading Scheme (ETC) is 'largely parasitic upon' the global carbon market created by Kyoto because it recognizes the CERs derived from CDM projects.[40]

In Dryzek's taxonomy, the CDM project registration element of the Protocol regime (upon which this article focuses) can be described as expert-based, grounded in administrative rationalism. It relies heavily on 'a certain idea of bureaucracy' and on 'assumptions' that 'at each step of the process' success will be achieved by 'appropriate ordering'. Applying the lens of Actor Network Theory, Emilie Cloatre has described the CDM as 'hybrid

---

35 Dryzek, op. cit., n. 11, p. 9 and Part 3.
36 Kyoto Protocol, Articles 10 and 2.2.
37 id., Article 12.
38 Council Decision 2002/358/EC.
39 Initially 6 per cent by 2010: Directive 2009/28/EC on the promotion of the use of energy from renewable sources.
40 J. Scott, 'In legal limbo: post-legislative guidance as a challenge for European administrative law' (2011) 48 *Common Market Law Rev.* 329, at 332. See Directive 2004/101 OJ (2004) L 338/61.

socio-legal and technical solution' produced by lawyers, state negotiators, and UN officials ('administrator-sociologists') in partial fulfilment of the 'actor-world' (vision of the type of society into which the CDM solution would fit) that they generated at Kyoto. That world was to include developers and engineers with project design documents (PDDs) detailing how CDM registration will enable the production of new 'clean' energy ('additionality') and contribute to 'sustainable development'. Projects would be approved by the Designated National Authority (a government body), validated by a UN-approved commercial auditing company (Designated Operational Entity (DOE)), registered by the CDM Executive Board in Bonn, implemented (including technology transfer, capacity building, and sustainable development) by engineers, monitored by validators, and con-verted into CERs.[41] Significantly, the CDM actor world did not explicitly include project-affected residents or civil society.

For reasons unclear, but resonating with post-coloniality, Cyprus was originally listed as a non-Annex I Party, eligible to host CDM projects. It was not agreed until 2011 that it might join the rest of the EU in Annex I – and then not because Cyprus could no longer pretend to be a developing country, but in order to put it on the 'same legal footing as other Member States'; and not before 2013, so as to ensure 'smooth transition' and 'avoid implications' for issuing CERs for CDM project reductions achieved to that point.[42] The EU recognizes the problem, and is beginning to upload a number of quality controls to the CDM regime, starting with a campaign to limit CDM projects to least developed countries (LDCs) – that is, not Cyprus, Brazil, China, and India; and a refusal to allow to be traded on the ETS any CERs emanating from non-LDC CDM projects that are registered after 2013, in the absence of a specific agreement.[43] Meanwhile, six Cypriot wind projects have obtained CDM registration: Alexigros, Orites, Agia Anna, Kambi, Klavdia, and Mari, of which the first three are operational.

The following sections explore three mismatches between, on the one hand, the actor-world envisaged during the construction of the Kyoto rationality-regime and, on the other hand, actors and interactions in Cyprus. The first two mismatches relate primarily to the 'additionality' requirement, the third relates to the 'sustainable development' requirement.

41 E. Cloatre, 'A Socio-Legal Analysis of an Actor-World: The Case of Carbon Trading and the Clean Development Mechanism' (2012) 39 *J. of Law and Society* 76, at 77–8, 82.

42 Secretariat of the UN Framework Convention on Climate Change (2011) Document DBO/JBU/smb/Log 11-2075, at <http://unfccc.int/resource/docs/2011/cop17/eng/03.pdf>.

43 J. Scott and L. Rajamani, 'EU climate change unilateralism' (2012) 23 *European J. of International Law* 469, at 471. See, also, European Commission (2011), 'Questions and answers on the use of international credits in the third trading phase of the EU ETS', at <http://ec.europa.eu/clima/news/articles/news_2011111401_en.htm>.

1. *Apathy and in-expertise*

The Kyoto rationality-regime relies on the existence of enthusiastic experts who are largely absent in Cyprus. As one developer put it, the government 'was the most important factor regarding the success' of wind farms but they 'didn't know what they were doing' and 'were expecting us to do it for them … It was very confusing.' Another observed 'a lack of willingness to take a decision – you would rather that they just say no – or yes.'[44] This gap between international theory and local reality has two important effects.

First, in Cyprus as elsewhere, the Clean Development Mechanism appears to have inadvertently supported projects that would, thanks to local government support, have been financially viable without it.[45] The government has twice (in 2003 and 2009) committed to support a limited amount of wind energy by guaranteeing to pay a particular 'feed-in tariff' per unit of electricity supplied by a limited number of wind farms for a specified period.[46] That tariff is made up of the price normally paid by the Electricity Authority of Cyprus (EAC) for non-renewable energy (determined by global energy prices),[47] supplemented with a contribution from the consumer-funded RES Fund.[48] The 2003 tariff was low, so the credibility and CER revenue offered by CDM registration were crucial to convincing investors of the financial viability of the project: CDM registration would indeed result in the production of 'additional' clean energy. When EU renewable energy targets were raised in 2009 (to 13 per cent by 2020) clean energy 'became important for the government' and the government responded with a generous rise in the feed-in tariff.[49] Several projects were thereby rendered 'economically viable' so that 'additionality' could 'most probably no longer [be] proven.' Nevertheless they were CDM-validated and registered, prompting several developers to query the expertise of validators in Cyprus: they 'had no idea, but they were licensed for it.'[50] And 'the thing is that at the United Nations, once there is a stamp from a validator …'.[51]

---

44 Interviews K26C, T25S, and F23Y.
45 Cloatre, op. cit., n. 41, p. 88.
46 Law 33(I)/2003 on energy conservation and the promotion of renewable energy sources, implementing Directive 2001/77/EC on the promotion of electricity produced from Renewable Energy Sources in the internal electricity market.
47 At the time of writing, about 0.1542 Euros/kwh.
48 A levy of 0.22 Euro-cent/kWh is charged on all electricity consumption under Law 33(I)/2003.
49 Interviews T25S and K26C. Directive 2009/28/EC. The feed-in tariff was raised by 26 per cent in 2009 as compared to 2003.
50 Interview T26S, and TUV and BGP, op. cit., n. 14. The feed-in tariff was 0.092 Euros/KWH in 2003, rising to 0.166 Euros/KWH in 2009.
51 Cyprus report under Directive 2009/28/EC on progress in the use and promotion of energy from renewable sources (2011), at <http://ec.europa.eu/energy/renewables/reports/2011_en.htm>.

79

The second effect of the lack of expertise on the island is that the void where public sector expertise ought to be has been filled by market 'expertise'. So a rationality-regime grounded in administrative rationalism is in fact being guided by economic rationalism. Developers of any project applying for CDM registration are responsible for commissioning the validation of their project by an approved private company (DOE). That system has been found to be open to abuse by validators and the developers who employ them.[52]

In Cyprus, the involvement of economic rationality went much further as, due to government apathy and in-expertise, developers were allowed to co-create the overarching regulatory framework, in addition to commissioning and paying for the environmental impact assessments and public consultations associated with their individual projects. The first Cypriot project to apply for CDM registration, and to navigate the Cypriot regulatory system, was the Mari project in Larnaca – a Cypriot–German joint venture initiated in 1996. The developers '[n]ot only lobbied' but 'trained the whole of the Town Planning Board', funding their 1999–2000 tour of German wind farms and planning departments, providing bespoke translations of German regulations. The 'very specific reason' was to prevent the transplantation of the 'absolutely atrocious ... very, very strict' English regulations on wind farm location. In other cases residents were taken to Germany, and officials were taken to Greece: these were, in the words of one developer 'a huge investment of time and money.' This piece of the wind farm legislative puzzle – the desired 'German philosophy in common law drafting' – was finally implemented in 2006.[53] Similarly, an environmental adviser working for developers reported that he 'started from scratch':

> The rules were created along the way ... Having done the first one and improved the second one then more or less our table of contents became a standard ... I remember meetings with the town planning people [in central government] who were asking us for information and references so that they could come up with certain guidelines for future investors.

As he delights in reminding regulators, they have neither the skill nor the inclination to verify what they are being told by those applying for licenses. But if the borrowers, the lenders, and the Executive Board of the CDM 'have satisfied themselves that it will work ... why should anybody else be worried?'[54] Apparently those who ought to be are not.

---

52 Cloatre, op. cit., n. 41, pp. 86–7.
53 Interview TP25S. See, also, RES Planning Law 162(1)/2006.
54 Interview F23Y. Likewise, a Belgian firm was hired as a consultant MCIT after acting as co-participant in a CDM application: Kambi Project Design Document (PDD) 23, at <http://cdm.unfccc.int>.

2. *Animosity*

Relations between wind farm developers and government actors have been very much '"them" and "us"'.[55] This is sociologically significant because it has contributed to the above-noted frustration and fractiousness among developers, and because it constitutes a further warping of the actor-world envisaged at Kyoto. In a further twist, the CDM registration process treats animosity from governments (and the general population) as evidence of additionality: without the credibility of the CDM, the project (and resulting clean energy) with not materialize.

There is evidence of government animosity towards wind farm developers generally. In 2009 the CERA undermined the worth of CDM registration by including a clause in RES Fund contracts to say that income derived by RES-funded producers from CERS 'without approval of the Fund shall be deducted from the Subsidy Payments to be made to the producer.'[56] One developer retorted that the clause was arbitrary and 'illegal' so that the 'government will be in … big trouble if any of us go to court'.[57] Some developers have responded by diverting CER rights to special-purpose companies[58] or third parties. Moreover 'it is too much hassle and expense to go through the monitoring (or the initial validation process) with the Cyprus authorities to get them to issue the CERs.' So some have not bothered to apply, and are in breach of their obligations to the third parties, to whom they are paying compensation.[59]

There has also been a degree of animosity in the implementation of provisions designed to ensure that developers offer benefits to project-effected residents.[60] Following a tradition built up in relation to quarries, 2 per cent of revenue for electricity generated by a project is automatically withheld from developers for distribution to the community hosting it. This can work out to a sizeable amount, about 200,000 euros per year for a large wind farm, upon which the community or municipality can then draw as seed funding for other development projects. 'But the Government has yet to establish a mechanism for dispersing the funds' – whether because they 'are trying to avoid' giving money to local communities where 'there is no

---

55 Interview F23Y.
56 TUV and BGP, op. cit., n. 14, p. 11.
57 id., p. 58.
58 Orites PDD 3, and interview P26C.
59 Interview TS27.
60 Such provisions have been found to have positive socio-psychological effects on project-affected residents in other countries: C.R. Warren and M. McFadyen 'Does community ownership affect public attitudes to wind energy? A case study from south-west Scotland' (2010) 27 *Land Use Policy* 204. But some regard them as bribes: N. Cass et al., 'Good neighbours, public relations and bribes: The politics and perceptions of community benefit provision in renewable energy development in the UK' (2010) 12 *J. of Environmental Policy and Planning* 255, at 269.

81

transparency and everything works in a very sort of funny sort of way', or because they simply 'don't know how to divide it'.[61] Significantly, the government does not seek to correct the impression in the press that it is the developers who are at fault. One developer is working together with the local community leader to press the government to release the funds.[62]

Finally there are reports of animosity towards particular developers – of applications for construction licenses being rejected, only to be passed when presented by another developer. Some also suggested that life is harder for foreign developers: 'There is no way' that a foreign company can invest in Cyprus 'on their own'. 'It's one of these places in order to do anything you need to have someone from that – from the country to, sort of, lead you by the hand.'[63]

The CDM regime does much to reward applicant developers for finding fault with local (public and private) expertise and attitudes. Developers are invited to identify in their project design documents any 'barriers' that would 'prevent' the implementation of the proposed project activity in the absence of CDM registration. Developers gladly accept, often quoting each other verbatim. Exhibit A is the fact that 'Cyprus is not very famous for its winds'[64] which are 'not that favourable' and lead to projects of 'limited efficiency',[65] that are 'financially unattractive to investors'.[66] To be clear, that is treated as a point in favour of registration. Exhibit B is the 'void' where local Cypriot wind energy technological expertise ought to be.[67] Maximum emphasis is placed on Exhibit C: the failures of the government of Cyprus to implement 'regulation and process definitions'. Construction phase laws were 'not enacted', available only as 'guiding principles', and required 'more than 30 licenses'. The 'lack of experience' among government actors 'in dealing with wind farm applications and preparing contracts imposed additional delays.'[68] Detailed timelines are presented revealing years of delays between costly license applications being made and approvals being given.[69]

Returning to the theme of expertise, developers are being prompted to draw on their market expertise to turn the absence of expertise on which administrative-rationality regimes rely into an economic advantage.

---

61 Interviews PC25 and KM25.
62 Developers pay a construction fee that goes to local communities for use in projects, such as a school: interview K26C.
63 Interviews T25S and P25C.
64 Interview K26C.
65 Klavdia PDD 29, 30; Kambi, op. cit., n. 54, p. 23.
66 Agia Anna PDD 13, at <http://cdm.unfccc.int>.
67 For example, Kambi, op. cit., n. 54, p. 22.
68 Alexigros PDD 9, Orites PDD 16, and Klavdia, op. cit., n. 65, p. 19, at <http://cdm.unfccc.int>.
69 Klavdia, id., pp. 19–20.

82

3. Sustainable development

CDM registration will not be given unless the host country is willing to 'confirm that it will contribute to "sustainable development"'. This wrongly implies that this term bears some sort of globally-shared technical meaning.[70] Worse still, the CDM regime makes no enquiry into whether such an understanding has been arrived at locally in relation to a given project, for example, by requiring proof of substantive public participation in the awarding of planning approval. So the CDM excludes almost entirely the expertise of project-affected residents.

Yet it is at the local level that multiple interpretations of 'sustainable development' – as economic growth with emissions reduction, as conservation, and/or as improvement to the lives of the relatively poor – come into conflict. The CDM regime simply black-boxes participation, accepting the word of validator and the government in question that it has occurred, was comprehensive, and resulted in any necessary change. A typical validation document reads:

> Relevant stakeholders have been informed five times (one time during the EIA process, two times during the town planning permit process, two times during the licencing process by the [CERA]) by newspaper announcements; further on the [involved community] has been directly addressed. No negative comments have been received. All meetings are documented.

When specific concerns are raised in local proceedings, the project design document will assert, for example, that 'the issues of aesthetics and noise have been dealt with' in the environmental impact assessment commissioned by the developer 'and the conclusion can be extracted that no negative consequences exist.'[71] As the next section reveals, that is never quite all there is to it.

AARHUS: DEMOCRATIC PRAGMATISM

The second relevant regime downloaded by Europeanizing Cyprus is the Aarhus Convention on Access to Information, Public Participation in Decision-Making and Access to Justice in Environmental Matters of 1998.

---

70 On the many meanings of sustainable development, see S. Bell and D. McGillivary, *Environmental Law* (2008, 7th edn.) ch. 3. In a 2008 opinion survey in Cyprus, about a third (35 per cent) of interviewees reported never having heard of the term 'sustainable development': RAI Consultants, *Report on a Quantitative Survey on Perceptions on Sustainable Development and Climate Change in Cyprus* (2008), prepared for AKTI and CESF in cooperation with UNDP. Available at <http://akti.org.cy/turkish/AKTI_report_2008(f).ppt>.

71 Orites CDM PDD 32, at <http://cdm.unfccc.int>. But see <http://www.youtube.com/watch?v=DKtmAWvSxpU>.

The concept of 'participation has a very strong pull on environmental policy making, but its meaning and aims are rarely made clear.' At an international level, the idea of public participation – that is, evaluation, comment, and influence in relation to regulatory decisions on policies or projects[72] – rose to prominence with Principle 10 of the 1992 Rio Declaration on the Environment and Development. It was then elaborated in the three pillars of the Aarhus regime.

Cypriot law has been in formal compliance with the first Aarhus pillar – access to environmental information – since 2004, and the second Aarhus pillar – public participation in decisions on projects, plans, and programmes – since 2005.[73] Ex ante public participation occurs as part of the planning application process. In theory, any concerns raised at such meetings must be addressed before a license will be given.[74] 'Every single department is present' – about 15 to 20 voices – even though they have already expressed their views to the planning authority, and 'if somebody objects then it has to be reviewed again.'[75] The EU has not yet downloaded the third pillar, namely, access to environmental justice, which is directed primarily towards ex-post facto solutions, but Cyprus appears to be formally compliant, thanks in large part to a judicial review gateway via Article 146 of the Constitution which allows complaints to the Supreme Court against an administrative act or omission alleged to be unconstitutional, illegal or an abuse of powers; and directly and adversely affecting legitimate interests of the complainant 'as a person or as a member of a Community'.[76] This is not quite a gateway to the kind of 'quintessentially communal' public interest litigation enjoyed in India[77] because Article 2 specifies that the term 'Community' which threads through the Constitution of Cyprus refers specifically to the Greek Cypriot or Turkish Cypriot Community of which Cypriots are a member by birth or

72 M. Lee and C. Abbott, 'The usual suspects: Public participation under the Aarhus Convention' (2003) 66 *Modern Law Rev.* 80, at 82, 86.
73 Law 125(I)/2000 on Free Public Access to Information Relating to Environmental Issues; Law 119(I)/2004 on Public Access to Environmental Information implementing Directive 2003/04/EC; Law 140(I)/2005 on the Assessment of the Impacts on the Environment from Certain Projects; and Law 102(I)/2005 on the Assessment of the Impacts on the Environment from Certain Plans and Programmes. Member states decide whether to require an EIA for wind farms (Directive 85/337/EEC Article 4(2) and Annex II) and Cyprus requires one for projects of more than 1 MW: Environmental Impact Assessment of Certain Works, Law 140(I)/2005 (as amended by Law 42(1)/2007) Article 31, Appendix I.
74 One project allegedly obtained an environmental permit without the agreement of the local community. The matter is being heard in court. Interview K26C.
75 Interviews K25M and F23Y.
76 Any 'directly affected' person or organization may complain to the Ombudsman that an administrative decision 'violates human rights' or the law of 'proper administration'. But one civil society actor observed that 'it takes too long' and is pointless as it 'is not binding': interview P25S. See s. 5(1)(a) and s. 6 Commissioner for Administration Law 3/1991 and <http://www.ombudsman.gov.cy>.
77 Perry-Kessaris, op. cit. n. 10, pp. 112–13.

84

later choice. Legal persons 'created with the purpose of promoting environ-mental protection' are, since 2005, 'considered to have sufficient interests that may be affected by a decision' and therefore entitled to launch a judicial review.[78] But as we shall see below, that entitlement has not been exercised.

Each of these pillars (two of which were downloaded into EU Directives) might be seen as a 'hybrid socio-legal and technical solution', akin to the CDM, in partial fulfilment of the 'actor world' generated at Aarhus. In Dryzek's taxonomy, the Aarhus regime can be described as primarily people-based, grounded in democratic pragmatism. So the actor world was imagined to include individuals and civil society actors with an interest in information, participation, and justice.[79]

1. *Apathy*

'[P]erhaps the most significant innovation' of the Aarhus regime and the actor world it generated is 'the distinct role' envisaged for civil society actors[80] – that is, 'non-state actors whose aims are neither to generate profits nor to seek governing power'; and who 'unite people to advance shared goals and interests.'[81] In particular, where (as seems to be the case in Cyprus) gateways to participation are generally unknown, misunderstood, and even undesired, civil society is key to the success of democratic-rationality regimes. So the emphasis on civil society actors raises all sorts of concerns about their representativeness and independence,[82] as well as their abilities.

As might be expected, there has been some government apathy towards the first Aarhus pillar, access to environmental information: 'Trying to get [information] out of the Government is like getting the proverbial blood out of a stone.'[83] More remarkable are the demand-side constraints.

First, in relation to access to information, the Department of Environment reported in 2011 that '[m]ost' information requests are made by consultants and students. Members of the public only becoming 'involved ... when they are directly affected' by a project, not as civil society actors.[84]

---

78 Law 140(I)/2005. Department of Environment (2011).
79 It is also expert-based, grounded in administrative rationalism, imagined to be populated by judicial and bureaucratic actors with the necessary expertise to facilitate (or not obstruct) them.
80 Lee and Abbot, op. cit. n. 72, p. 87.
81 UNDP, 'UNDP and Civil Society Organisations: A policy of engagement' (2001), at <http://www.undp.org/content/undp/en/home/ourwork/partners/civil_society_organizations>.
82 Lee and Abbot, op. cit., n. 72, p. 87.
83 For example, the Cyprus Council of Ministers has had specifically to direct local authorities to make information available for a reasonable fee, not to treat planning applications as private, not to insist that members of the public themselves identify plot numbers: interview T28C.
84 European Commission, op. cit., n. 34.

85

In relation to the second Aarhus pillar, public participation, it is revealing that only 36 per cent of interviewees in a 2008 opinion survey in Cyprus were aware of a law protecting citizens' participation in environmental decision-making processes; and most (60 per cent) reported that citizens are not usually consulted in the decision-making process on environmental matters. Moreover, there was only limited enthusiasm for the idea that decisions regarding environmental sustainability should be taken by the local community (11 per cent of interviewees) rather than at EU (29 per cent) or state (38 per cent) level.[85] Perhaps as a result, proceedings including an element of public participation are reportedly dominated by developers and government actors.

The CDM project design documents of some Cyprus wind projects refer to 'public hearings' and 'public consultation'[86] but developers and their advisers in Cyprus were adamant:

> It's not a public hearing. It's not a public hearing. They just gather these different government departments in one meeting room, and they discuss, everybody says their opinion, basically. If you know somebody you can influence you, you know ... And depending on this, you know ... [For some bigger projects they hire a room in a hotel. But in others it is] only the closed sort of, dark room with about 10 people around [the developer] ... It's crazy, I mean, it is not a very transparent way of doing things.[87]

By all accounts proceedings are commonly dominated by central government and developers – others in attendances are usually one-shot players without experience.[88] A major missing factor is civil society.

In relation to the third pillar of access to justice, civil society actors have not availed themselves of the judicial review gateway offered by Article 142 of the Constitution, perhaps because they reportedly have 'no faith in the courts at all. Zero.' They feel they 'will not get justice there'.[89]

2. Animosity

Social-psychological studies have shown that residents can form 'positive emotional' – in Weberian terms, affective and traditional – 'links' with a location. These links may be 'disrupted' by wind farm (and other) developments, resulting in feelings of 'anxiety and even grief' both for the direct loss of the loved location, and for the consequential loss of any 'sense

---

85 RAI Consultants, op. cit., n. 70.
86 Alexigros PDD 24, Kambi PDD 36, Klavdia PDD 48, at <http://cdm.unfccc.int>.
87 Interview K26C.
88 Interview F23Y.
89 Interview P25S. Developers also claim reason to be wary, but one has reportedly filed a 146 claim against the Paphos District Officer in relation to a permitting error: interviews KM25 and PC25.

of self or identity' bound up in the location.[90] It is true that 100 per cent of interviewees in a 2011 Eurobarometer survey of Cyprus agreed that 'protecting the environment' was 'important' to them 'personally', and half included 'climate change' as one of the 'five main environmental issues' they 'worried about'.[91] There are also those who find wind farms 'quite attractive ... fascinating ... as a piece of modern art'.[92] Some developers have been able to identify residents who are naturally apathetic, or even enthusiastic, about having a wind farm nearby.[93] One developer remarked on the fact that many wind farms have been built on 'refugee' land – formerly Turkish Cypriot villages now inhabited by Greek Cypriot refugees from the North. 'They were very, let's say, calm in their approach.' They were 'the most sceptical' but 'did not raise a lot of objections'.[94] Likewise, residents of 'remote' locations with little pre-existing economic activity reacted 'positively' because they saw the value of their land increasing or because they enjoyed the fact that 'suddenly people started going and coming, they showed interest.'[95] But behind every wind farm in Cyprus lie the wrecks of proposals foiled by the animosity of project-affected residents.[96]

Equally, buried beneath every existing wind farm are the remains of animosity that has been manipulated – marketed – away. One developer reported picking off residents one by one, getting them to rent their land to the project, and then relying on them to 'lobby' their neighbours: 'So they will be working on our side.' The planning approval process is then less of a 'bother' because owners have already consented.[97] Another reported making surreptitious payments to just one of several affected communities so that the project as a whole might proceed.

The lack of an active civil society through which to pool energy, ideas, and information, also means that discussion is limited, disjointed, unsophisticated, and muted. Animosity (and enthusiasm) remain largely individual experiences. Developers are left as the only repeat players, able to dismiss or quash objections, and to define the terms of the debate. Residents, just like the government:

---

90 N. Cass and G. Walker, 'Emotion and rationality: The characterization and evaluation of opposition to renewable energy projects' (2009) 2 *Emotion, Space and Society* 62, at 63.

91 European Commission, op. cit., n. 34.

92 Interview A27C.

93 Interviews A27C and K26C. Other have built on government land, or bought land. There has been no compulsory purchase.

94 In Mari, residents invited an independent specialist and a Member of Parliament to 'adjudicate'. Mari PDD 23, at <http://cdm.unfccc.int>, and interview K25M.

95 Interview K26C.

96 England and Wales reportedly have a 60 per cent refusal rate for onshore windfarm applications: Cass et al., op. cit., n. 60.

97 Interview F23Y.

87

depended, mostly, on the effort [developers] made to inform them ... If I make the effort and come and find you and explain ... the rationale behind why I want to promote this, and nobody else came to tell you the other side of the story, then you would be influenced by my way of presenting things or ideas. And ... there was no [other] serious approach. It's sad, to be honest, in many ways, because you would expect that, you know, in the government and the civil side, they would be approaching the thing more maturely.[98]

One environmental expert noted an interplay between public fear and government lack of expertise, suggesting that 'fear of windfarms' exists in part because people don't trust the authorities – and with 'good reason'. 'There is a small paragraph' in environmental assessments 'which nobody reads: "provided all the rules and regulations are followed".' Environmental inspectors are too few and poorly qualified 'to check that the terms of the licence are actually adhered to.'[99] In short, the experts are the market.

3. *Expertise and 'expertise'*

Expert-based regimes, such as the CDM registration process, tend to privilege 'expertise based in scientific and economic rationalities' that are most closely associated with instrumental values and interests. They tend to leave little or no space for 'intangible and aesthetic values' such as 'loss and grief', which can generate just as much animosity as any economic, or other instrumental, motivation.[100] Space for 'loss and grief', and the resulting responses of animosity, ought to be found in regimes based on democratic pragmatism. But even here, non-instrumental (affective, belief, and traditional) values and interests are all too often silenced by the dominant economic and administrative rationalism.

One way of dealing with animosity that is grounded in non-instrumental values and interests is to dismiss it as misinformed. In the United Kingdom, developers frame their interactions with the public using an 'information deficit model', preferring to engage with the public through 'exhibitions' rather than 'public meetings'.[101] It is assumed that most, if not all opposition can be dispelled by a programme of myth-busting. The constant presentation by policy makers and developers of 'not-in-my backyard – NIMBYs' as deviant minorities[102] is, some argue, unsubstantiated and deliberately designed to render them something to be 'overcome', in particular, by

---

98 Interview K26C.
99 Interview F23Y. It is reported that one civil society actor, having failed to rouse enthusiasm in Cyprus, is complaining to Brussels about the breach of conditions by one developer to protect birdlife: interview K26C.
100 Cass and Walker, op. cit., n. 90, p. 64.
101 id., p. 67.
102 J. Swofford and M. Slattery, 'Public attitudes to wind energy in Texas: Local communities in close proximity to wind farms and their effect on decision-making' (2010) 38 *Energy Policy* 2508.

improving levels of 'trust' in developers.[103] Likewise the only information available on the website of the Cyprus Wind Energy Association is a leaflet on the 'myths' and 'truths' about wind farms, and developers referred to holding 'a public presentation' with 'maps, photographs, examples of other places'. 'We have to explain to people, although sometimes people are not ready to understand.' 'It doesn't cost them anything to say all the nonsense in the world. They don't have to prove it.' 'All these monsters that people are dreaming of, they don't exist.'[104]

A second method of dealing with animosity grounded in non-instrumental values and interest is to dismiss it as irrational and, therefore, irrelevant to the participation-based regime in question. Developers in the United Kingdom have been found refer to animosity among project-affected residents as 'gut', 'visceral', 'passionate' or 'angry' and, therefore, irrelevant.[105] In Cyprus, developers reported that it is time consuming but bearable when government actors object to a project during the construction license phase – it is to be dealt with 'on the statutory level'. But the objections of local communities are uniquely infuriating because they are just 'a question of opinion' and 'then the whole thing stops.' Other typical comments in this vein include: 'At [Location X] they were throwing stones at us' and 'That mayor [at location Y] was shouting like a mad thing'.

Thirdly, developers and their advisors in Cyprus regularly dismissed animosity expressed in the course of participation-based regimes as a, somehow illegitimate, cover for instrumental concerns about the value of land or other assets. For example, 'people will bring out environmental objections in order to cover their real fears. Their real fear is the value of the land.'

> It's unbelievable what nonsense we heard about the objections [in Location Z], even that wind farms will affect the ground water ... They were hiding behind the environmental things but they were afraid that they will lose a very lucrative illegal trade of these small birds, *ambelopoulia*.

Likewise, when anemometers set up by developers in 2007 to measure wind speeds in Agios Theodoros were torn down – some say by 'just ordinary people', others say by property developers or competitors – developers agreed it was because of 'fear'.[106] One developer present at the scene asked reporters to focus on the fact that 'something like this shows that Cyprus is a country full of risks for wind farms' (thereby scoring another potential point towards CDM registration). A second developer reportedly observed that locals were: 'simply delaying the inevitable. We are acting perfectly legally, we have all the necessary permits and will not be undone. We have done too

---

103 M. Aitken, 'Why we still don't understand the social aspects of wind power: A critique of key assumptions within the literature' (2010) 38 *Energy Policy* 1834.
104 Interviews PC25 and F23Y. For the leaflet, see <http://cwea.org.cy>.
105 Cass and Walker, op. cit., n. 90, p. 65.
106 Interviews A27C, F23Y, PC25, and KM25.

much and spent too much money to stop now.'[107] Implicit in these reports is the idea that economic or other instrumental concerns were somehow of less weight or relevance when held by residents, than when held by developers.

CONCLUSION

The approach that I have set out in this article enables social life of all levels, intensities, and types (including the economic) to be placed on the same analytical page. Empirically, it works from interviews and site visits backed up with secondary sources. Analytically, it connects actions and interactions, with regimes and rationalities – or as Roger Cotterrell puts it elsewhere in this volume, it connects 'what is embedded' with 'in what it is embedded'. Normatively, this approach seeks to given equal consideration to the perspectives of each set of actors. In so doing it offers a unique combination of insights.

It highlights the rationalities that dominate a given regime – in this case economic rationalism and administrative rationalism in Kyoto, and demo-cratic pragmatism and administrative rationalism in Aarhus. It also high-lights mismatches between, on the one hand, the actor worlds envisaged by administrator-sociologist regime creators, in this case at Kyoto and Aarhus, and, on the other hand, real-life actions and interactions – in this case occurring among developers (markets), engineers and regulators (experts), project-affected persons and civil society actors (people) in Cyprus.

So we see that expertise is at the heart of the Kyoto rationality regime, but it is lacking among government actors in Cyprus, that the differently-expert views of project-affected residents are excluded, and that the void is filled by the expertise of developers.

We see that civic participation is at the heart of the Aarhus rationality regime, and government enthusiasm is at the heart of the Kyoto rationality regime. But *apatheia* (απάθεια) – in the original meaning of detachment – was cherished by the Stoics, and one might be forgiven for wondering whether it is so valued by civil society and government actors today.

We see that wind, *anemos* (άηεμος), is in short supply in Cyprus, but wind farms are rather plentiful, thanks in part to *enthousiasmos* (ενθουσιασμός) – in each of its evolving meanings, originally ecstasy arising from possession by God, then over-confidence arising from the delusion that one is inspired by God, then extremism and finally, plain old positive feelings – emanating from carbon-market creators in Brussels and Bonn.

---

107 *Cyprus Mail*, 27 February 2007, reposted at <http://www.wind-watch.org/newsarchive/2007/02/27/we-have-spent-too-much-money-to-stop-now>. See, also, TUV and BGP, op. cit., n. 14, p. 55.

The concerns of residents affected by wind farms are mere frippery as compared to the threats of flooding and famine that are faced by others elsewhere and that are ascribed to the use of fossil fuels. But this observation does not dull the significance of the insights set out in this article. For the extent to which carbon avoidance and sustainable development result from CDM registered projects, whose local support and approval are intended to be aided by the international imprimatur of the UN, is also wide open to scientific question.[108] So the balancing of local values and interests remains an honourable and reasonable task, and one well suited to exploration through an economic sociology of law.

108 See K. Holm Olsen and J. Fenham, 'Sustainable development benefits of clean development mechanism projects: A new methodology for sustainability assessment based on text analysis of the project design documents submitted for validation' (2008) 36 *Energy Policy* 2819.

JOURNAL OF LAW AND SOCIETY
VOLUME 40, NUMBER 1, MARCH 2013
ISSN: 0263-323X, pp. 92–114

Maine (and Weber) Against the Grain:
Towards a Postcolonial Genealogy of the Corporate Person

RITU BIRLA*

This essay forges ties between postcolonial methodologies and the economic sociology of law, emphasizing the history, legal production, and governmental habitus of that modern abstraction called 'the economy'. It pursues three interrelated sites to do so: the categories of government and economy, via Weber and Foucault; classical legal discourse on corporate or group life and its temporizing from status to contract; and the relationship between the legal subject and homo economicus, investigated and telescoped through the figure of the corporate person. Empirically, focusing on India as a lens to highlight a colonial genealogy of neoliberal modernity, the analysis animates these themes via the history of colonial market governance, its relationship to the 'embedded' practices of vernacular capitalism, and emergent forms of economic citizenship today, seen through Indian case law on the corporate person and corporate veil-piercing.

Let me begin with a note of thanks to the editors for posing the challenging and compelling task of articulating (if not comprehensively, then provocatively) a postcolonial approach to the economic sociology of law. At its ground, a postcolonial deployment of the economic sociology of law would examine the legal regimes and the political economies of modern colonialisms and colonized societies. It should do so, I would like to argue, not *only* as an empirical project, to 'fill in' the big historical picture of law's role in economic life with new global case studies and translations of culture; it should also seek to chart colonial genealogies of contemporary forms of governing more broadly, which direct flows of capital, from fictive and speculative, to material and human. 'Postcolonial' is therefore posed here as a method of reading the present, one that highlights, through an historical engagement with the techniques and limits of modern colonial governance,

* *Department of History and the Centre for South Asian Studies, University of Toronto, Toronto, Ontario M5S 3G3, Canada*
r.birla@utoronto.ca

the necessity for loosening the borders of law and economy studies. This would mean addressing socialities that do not neatly fit into the classic binaries of modern political and economic liberalism – public/private, state/ civil society, and state/market – and at the same time, detailing the generative power of both legal and economic fictions. There is an extensive and diverse archive of nineteenth- and twentieth-century colonial histories to mine for such a project. Here, my analysis is informed by the study of late colonial India, a site that opens a genealogy from colonial liberalism (both political and economic) to contemporary neoliberalism, one that may help to problematize a world where markets govern and governments market the nation as a brand. Colonial genealogies of modernity must at once consider discourses invested in the velocity of free trade alongside the constraints and weight of the new security state, a project ripe for critical approaches to law and economy.

What can histories of colonial governmentality bring to the study of law and economy? Motivated by this question, this essay foregrounds three interrelated sites for mapping postcolonial approaches to the economic sociology of law: the category and practice of government; the problem of corporate or group life and its temporizing; and the relationship between the legal subject and *homo economicus*, investigated and telescoped here through the figure of the corporate person. To begin, I emphasize that the thing we call 'the economy' has a history, and that colonial formations expose its production as an abstract object of governance and indeed as a legitimating origin of sovereignty. This way in to the study of law and economy, and indeed of the staging of sovereignty *as* economy, highlights colonial contexts for key insights on contemporary neoliberal reflexes, most broadly, the consistent deployment of 'the economy' as a stand-in for 'the public', a process evident foremost in nineteenth- and twentieth-century colonial contexts, where governance managed subjects, not citizens.[1]

Colonial histories demand that we unpack the complicated historical-philosophical nexus of law, agency/instrumentality, and subjecthood/subjection and so call for a robust reading of law and governmentality. They also grapple with the temporalities and spatialities of what Karl Polanyi called embeddedness, a term which points to socialities that are not fully captured by the modern abstraction of social relations as exchange-relations, the recoding and flattening of deep layers of social meaning into exchange-values.[2] Said differently, the economic sociology of law, informed by

1 For more on law and sovereignty *as* economy, see R. Birla, 'Law as Economy: Convention, Corporation, Currency' (2011) 1 *UC Irvine Law Rev.* 1015–37. On historicizing 'the economy' and the colonial displacement of the public as market, see R. Birla, *Stages of Capital: Law, Culture and Market Governance in Late Colonial India* (2009).

2 K. Polanyi, *The Great Transformation* (1957/1944). To describe embedded social relations, Polanyi's reading evokes a nostalgia for a pre-industrial *gemeinschaft*, and deserves a critical eye on that account, for his temporal politics affirm master

© 2013 The Author. Journal of Law and Society © 2013 Cardiff University Law School

colonial/postcolonial studies, may offer new paths for challenging one-dimensional accounts in which law operates on the one hand as simply a tool for political and economic actors, or on the other, the unmediated voice of sovereignty. Too often in economic histories, for example, law appears as the instrument of economic actors, a mechanism through which their intentionality, historical agency, and political choice can be read, mapped, and fixed.[3] Posed in this way as a barometer and thermometer for reading economic climates, law in its full range of performative power – its generative fictions, its artificial realities, its incarnations from juridicial logic to customary practice – and so the dynamic social text of law and economic life that concerns the economic sociology of law, remains unaddressed.

Certainly two decades of postcolonial research writing in the spirit of Upendra Baxi's now much-cited analysis of the flattening, narrowing, and monopolizing of law in its colonial étatization, in partnership with feminist methods, has broadened not only the geographical, but also the ethico-political terrain of legal studies.[4] This work has grappled with the janus-faced characterization of law as merely a tool of authority, and as its voice, the sovereign speech-act. Still, in contrast with the more frequently investi-gated domains of law and culture, law and gender, or law and community

narratives of modernization (status to contract, *gemeinschaft* to *gesellschaft*) that have been successfully challenged by scholars working on the economic history of global capitalism, as well as those addressing postcolonial capitalist modernities. See, for example, D. Chakrabarty, *Provincializing Europe: Postcolonial Thought and Historical Difference* (2000); P. Chatterjee, *Lineages of Political Society* (2011); and J. Comaroff and J. Comaroff, *Ethnicity Inc.* (2009). Still, the term 'embedding' does point to the multiplicities of negotiations that are hidden, if not erased when the market, as an abstraction, moves to monopolize our conception of social – even as this monopoly is never complete – and so remains a useful term.

3 For an excellent overview of the debates among legal scholars, economists, and economic historians, and a comparison of the range of approaches in economic history from neoclassical, law and economics to new institutional economics, see R. Harris, 'The Encounters of Economic History and Legal History' (2003) 21 *Law and History Rev.* 297. Harris maps different stages of economic theory and history since the late nineteenth century, and the growth of interest in law (most especially property rights and contracts) with the rise of institutional economics. He emphasizes what he calls 'Historical Institutional Economics' and its overlaps with the interests of legal historians, including not only a focus on institutions, but also 'context sensitivity, accounting for noneconomic factors, and on a multiplicity of outcomes and factors' (p. 345). Such a conversation across economic and legal history approaches may be furthered by greater attention to the mechanics of instrumentality and agency at stake in both legal and economic histories. For the classic elaboration of the analytical moves which address the double meanings of the terms subject (philosophical Subject of History versus the subject of authority) and agent (the philosophical Agent of History versus agent-instrument of another), see the work of G.C. Spivak, especially *The Critique of Postcolonial Reason: Toward A History of the Vanishing Present* (1998).

4 U. Baxi, 'The State's Emissary: The Place of Law in Subaltern Studies' in *Subaltern Studies VII*, eds. P. Chatterjee and G. Pandey (1992).

94

rights, postcolonial analyses of law and economic life remain sparse. Building critical approaches to law and economy would significantly fortify the challenge to scripts of law as pure agency (the unmediated voice of sovereignty, whether that of the state or 'the economy'), or as pure instrumentality (as a tool of unmediated economic or political or historical actors). Said differently, the textured habitus of law, also referred to as 'embeddedness,' would be better accessed through a careful attention to the ways in which economy and law are folded into, or complicit with, each other: to the ways in which norms, rules, directions are folded into practices, material arrangements, and world-views always in the making.[5] Here, it is productive to remember that the classical Greek origin of our term economy, *oikonomia*, has a concept of law folded into it: *oikonomia* refers to the *nomos*, or the law/conventions that regulate the *oikos*, or household.

The project of animating the social text of law and economy has many entry points. Here, I elaborate on my empirical research on late colonial India, a moment when legal fictions – like the trust and limited liability – enabled, indeed fuelled, the unprecedented global reach of finance capital and its speculative logics.[6] Informed by this history, the analysis here resists the 'law and its outside' presuppositions of classic functionalist formulations: that is, formulations that pose law and economy as distinct, a priori arenas that work either with or against each other to enable or disable economic development. Transformative critical approaches – legal realism, law and society, critical legal studies – have certainly tempered such functionalist framings. But even amid rich accounts of the law's dynamism in economic life, the functionalist residues of a state versus market binary can reappear. The study of the relationship between state and market, each conceived as always already established spheres, structures social science approaches to political economy, as well as the field of law and economics. To supplement critical approaches in legal studies, I read economy as a legal performative, as a script and stage for governing.[7] In the process, I seek to

---

5 For the foundational theorizing of habitus, see P. Bourdieu, *Outline of a Theory of Practice* (1977). The robust reading of law (as norm, disposition, habit, practice) in Bourdieu's concept of habitus is not unfamiliar to legal scholars. For an early and influential articulation of law in this vein as world-making, see R. Cover, 'The Supreme Court 1984 Term – Foreword: Nomos and Narrative' (1983) 97 *Harvard Law Rev.* 4. I am extending Cover's foundational critical legal studies articulation by considering economy as a discourse of governing, and so always a legal project. On the epistemology of the fold (the verb in French, *plier*) and complicity, see G. Deleuze, *The Fold: Leibnitz and the Baroque* (1992).

6 See Birla, op. cit. (2009), n. 1.

7 Here, I am elaborating on Judith Butler's theory of performativity, which does not simply refer to performance by an already constituted actor but, rather, focuses on the generative possibilities of the performative act and its citational plays. See J. Butler, *Excitable Speech: A Politics of the Performative* (1997) and R. Birla, 'Performativity Between Logos and Nomos: Law, Temporality and the Non-Economic Analysis of Power' (2012) 21 *Columbia J. of Gender and Law* 90.

draw attention to colonial genealogies of contemporary governmental modes, most especially, the *recoding of political democracy as market freedom*. So today, as public space is colonized by market motives, as philanthropy becomes more forcefully than ever the enabling co-dependent partner of market logic, the critical impetus of the economic sociology of law might be furthered via studies of colonial formations of power, in order to fine-tune its established convictions: that is, that law is constitutive of economic life, and that economy is embedded in social relations, and so irreducible to the agency of either individual rational choice or social structure.[8]

To elaborate, this essay foregrounds the figure of the corporate person, posed as a condensed site of the histories, politics, and contradictions of market governance. The corporate person is, on the one hand, the apex of modernized, disembedded market abstraction, a leviathan-like artificial person manifest as *homo economicus*, constituted by individual contracting actors.[9] On the other, this is arguably the very mechanism that enables, par excellence, the reproduction of *gemeinschaft* personalized relations – the boardroom boy's club, the endogamy of the top 1 per cent. The corporate person, in other words, seems to embody at once the abstracting mechanisms and legal formalities of the 'modern' as well as the personalized socialities of the 'feudal'. It is exactly the dilemmas of such temporal collapse and condensation, the textured layering of temporalities into complicated spatialities (beyond, perhaps, the analytical boundaries of uneven development) that motivates critical postcolonial approaches to history and capital.[10] More broadly, this essay also channels the expansive nineteenth century socio-legal discussion of the corporate in its classical sense as group life, with its corresponding legal jungle of associative forms that marked 'the teeming life' of 'ever new species and genera of persons,' in F.W. Maitland's words.[11] I engage this broad notion of the corporate, reading it against the grain of the status-to-contract temporizing in which it is usually staged, to foreground the problem of the legal translation and mistranslation of economic embeddedness. Highlighting master narratives of legal

---

8 For the classic argument, see M. Granovetter, 'Economic Action and Social Structure: The Problem of Embeddedness' (1985) 91 *Am. J. of Sociology* 481.

9 The links between Thomas Hobbes's *Leviathan* (an artificial person) and the corporate person were much contemplated in the late nineteenth and early twentieth centuries, and indeed the subject of debate. See F.W. Maitland, translator's introduction to O. von Gierke, *Political Theories of the Middle Age* (1922, 3rd edn.); J. Dewey, 'The Historic Background of Corporate Legal Personality' (1926) 35 *Yale Law J.* 655; W.M. Geldhart, 'Legal Personality' (1911) 27 *Law Q. Rev.* 90; R. Harris, 'The Transplantation of the Legal Discourse on Corporate Personality Theories' (2006) 63 *Washington and Lee Law Rev.* 1421.

10 The foundational text in this mode is Chakrabarty, op. cit., n. 2.

11 F.W. Maitland, *State, Trust and Corporation*, eds. D. Runciman and M. Ryan (2003) 69.

modernization in the contexts of market governance in colonial and independent India, I consider the discourse of corporate life through the management of vernacular Indian capitalism, which was famously embedded in kinship and caste, recognized as crucial for the colonial economy, and at the same time coded legally as an ancient and anachronistic cultural formation.

The analysis follows three key lines of inquiry. First, it emphasizes an attention to economy as a discourse of governing, to work against the analysis of law and economy as distinct spheres; second, an engagement with the temporal and civilizational scales articulated in nineteenth century *gemeinschaft* to *gesellschaft*, status-to-contract narratives which structured colonial market governance and that haunt even Polanyi's classic coding of embeddedness; and third, the making of the legal subject as Economic Man.[12] After an initial overview of colonial market governance in India, I identify a theoretical ground for thinking law, economy, and governmentality at once, briefly placing Weber alongside Foucault on the topic of 'government', a term linked to the concept of economy, implicitly in Weber and explicitly in Foucault. Then, drawing attention to colonial anxieties about kinship and clan-based economic activity, the paper turns to the government of corporate life.[13] Highlighting the shift in legal thought from corporate life to the corporate person, I then launch a postcolonial genealogy of the corporate person, a figure fortified in law at the beginning of the twentieth century.[14] As a key example of the contemporary relevance of a postcolonial economic sociology of law, I consider the fate of the corporate

12 Though Polanyi's goal is clearly to highlight embeddedness as a counterpoint to the logic of market society, and though he poses a re-embedded future, the concept of embeddedness itself relies on a temporal staging, one that poses 'embedded' and 'disembedded' as distinct space-times. It is interesting to note here that Polanyi's narrative gets mapped onto distinct cultural/racial differences that distinguish modern Western societies from ancient and anachronistic ones. For example, and prominently, it is important to note that Louis Dumont, the iconic orientalist sociologist of caste who theorizes India as a society of *Homo Hierarchicus*, wrote the introduction to the third edition of Polanyi's text. Dumont followed *Homo Hierarchicus*, with his text *Homo Aequalis: From Mandeville to Marx*, a story of the emergence of economic man of the West; the counterpoint to the figure of *Homo Hierarchicus*. Dumont writes in his introduction to the third edition of Polanyi's *Great Transformation* that it was Polanyi who inspired him: in Dumont, Polanyi's temporal staging of embedded becomes mapped spatially, as hierarchical East and egalitarian West. See L. Dumont, *Homo Aequalis: From Mandeville to Marx* (1977).
13 Influential texts like Henry Maine's *Ancient Law* (1931), first published in 1860, and his *Village Communities in East and West,* which followed in 1871, were historical-ethnographic narratives motivated by governing the range of indigenous communities, customary practices, and local forms of governance that British administrators confronted in India and other colonies.
14 Corporate personhood has been posed as a key site of investigation in recent articulations of the economic sociology of law. See, for example, R. Swedburg, 'The Case for an Economic Sociology of Law' (2003) 32 *Theory and Society* 1.

97

person in independent India, highlighting how 'embedded' economic practices are enabled by the modern legal regime of contract, and how the postcolonial Indian state, more than its neoliberal counterparts in the United States and the United Kingdom, seeks to challenge such re-embedding. At the same time, I also emphasize that India's colonial history enables a new kind of coding of the corporate person, one that marks emerging economic discourses of the citizen and of sovereignty. The corporate person thus becomes a site for unpacking legal narratives of economic modernization, for exposing modern legal techniques of enchantment, and for investigating forms of neoliberal market governance produced by the postcolonial state.

COLONIAL MARKET GOVERNANCE IN INDIA: THE CULTURAL POLITICS OF DISEMBEDDING

In the period from about 1870–1930 in India, colonial legislators and jurists sought actively to promote economic development in the face of declining agricultural productivity, exacerbated by a decline in the value of India's silver currency. New policies sought to standardize market practice and installed a new object of sovereign management, a thing called 'the market'. As I mentioned, this was a supra-local space that stood in for 'the public' in a political formation of subjects, rather than citizens. New legislation and jurisprudence negotiated the situated conventions and practices that structured indigenous (or what I call vernacular) capitalism, that operated through norms of kinship, extended family, clan and caste. As I've argued more extensively elsewhere, colonial legislation and jurisprudence installed 'the market' as an abstract model for all social relations and as terrain for the making of modern subjects.[15] My term 'market governance' therefore refers to both the production of 'the economy' as an object of governance, as well as the enforcement of 'the market' as an ethico-political sovereign with a monopoly over the very imagining of the social. Colonial policy in India, which sought to distinguish legally between the domains of economy and culture, and so to distinguish between commercial firm and family, is one key example of such a process.

A tidal wave of new measures directed at the free circulation of capital were introduced in this period, measures that ranged from the law on companies, to negotiable instruments, to income tax, trusts, and charitable endowments, as well as futures trading and government securities, among others. A key story in the global standardization of contract law in the nineteenth century, this accelerated colonial process installed new forms of group association grounded in contractual relations of individual subjects. Reflecting the broader discussion of corporate life and the modern shift from

15 Birla, op. cit. (2009), n. 1.

98

status to contract among legal thinkers of the nineteenth and twentieth centuries, most famously, Henry Sumner Maine, but also others like Otto von Gierke and F.W. Maitland, legislators and judges grappled with forms of embedded social life, perhaps no more exhaustively than in the discourse on indigenous mercantile norms emerging as colonialism's economic development regime took shape.

Vernacular practitioners of capitalism, operating through norms of kinship, were universally acknowledged engines of credit, production, and consumption; they confronted the establishment of contract as a universal instrument for market exchange. The confrontation exposes the difficulties in translating the embedded worlds of local market conventions.[16] These were characterized by what I have called an *extensive negotiability* between the symbolic capital of kinship and the capital flows of commerce and finance; this world-view sat uncomfortably with that of colonial jurists and legislators, for whom legitimate market exchange was distinguished by legal procedures of contract and the ubiquitously reiterated criterion of 'general public utility'. (Indeed, all new measures were enacted with this call.) Political liberalism's categories of public and private infiltrated commercial and financial law in India in the nineteenth century, distinguishing between two general forms of group life, a colonial 'public' of modern market actors, and a so-called 'private' world of ancient indigenous culture and religion, which was to be regulated by the Hindu and Muslim personal laws that had also been largely standardized by the 1860s. Colonial liberal pluralist ideologies, burgeoning after the 1857 rebellion, articulated non-interference in indigenous 'culture,' even as culture itself was reified and classified for efficient governance, most prominently in personal law. Thus, though they were key actors in the colonial economy, vernacular 'family firms' were made subject first and foremost to personal law. Colonial market governance did not summarily prohibit vernacular market practices but, rather, delegitimized them; it established new parameters for proper economic activity as distinct from the domain of culture, and so restaged vernacular market practices both temporally, as backward, and spatially, as private.[17]

As such, the public/private distinction sat asymmetrically over the 'embedded' world of the bazaar, run by indigenous firms whose extensive kinship networks were as public in their import as they were private in their selective constitution. The disembedding dreams of legal modernization thus operated through an economy/culture distinction: as economically influential vernacular actors were governed as agents of an ancient culture, the texture of their embedded social relations were written over by colonial scripts about

16 For a key comparison, and important account of the problems in translating kinship-based commercial forms in the case of modern Chinese 'clan' corporations, see T. Ruskola, 'Conceptualizing Corporations and Kinship: Comparative Law and Development Theory in a Chinese Perspective' (2000) 52 *Stanford Law Rev.* 1599.
17 These arguments are elaborated in detail throughout Birla, op. cit. (2009), n. 1.

99

the stasis of native cultural norms. It is important to emphasize here that vernacular capitalism's embedded market practices were exploitative, commanding labour through the usurious control of rural credit, and by about 1920, in industrial production. Moreover, the extended kinship that was so central to vernacular market norms and their community identities was grounded in strict control over women and their exchange in marriage. It was colonial law's translation of vernacular market practices as protected *cultural* practices first and foremost that reinforced these hegemonies.

ARTFUL ECONOMY: GOVERNMENT AND ADMINISTRATION

In what ways can our familiarity with this colonial process – its liberal techniques of governance, in which new rules of the market game are enacted through the dissimulation of non-interference, through a rewriting of complex layers of embeddedness in legal translations and scripts of 'culture' – inform new approaches to the study of law and economic life? One important theoretical path is to re-engage Weber via the concept of government. As we know, Weber's foundational discussion of the legal order and the economic order in volume 1 of *Economy and Society* investigates economy as a problem *of* law. Implicitly, Weber evokes the classical concept of economy or *oikonomia*, the convention(s) (*nomos*/law) that govern the arrangement, distribution, and management of the household (*oikos*).[18] He does not pose 'the economy' as a problem *for* law, or economics as a problem *for* law, but speaks rather of 'the economic order,' a term that has a distinct resonance with the classical concept of economy, for it emphasizes the 'power of disposition' and distribution, and so economy as a practice.[19] Economy, that is, practices of managing and governing, are posed as a problem of law – addressed in its full range as conduct, convention, custom, and juridical code. It is important to remember that Weber's formal definition of convention – conduct without any coercion – posits an elusive theoretical limit and so poses questions about formal legal translations of the norms and currencies of conduct.[20] This Weberian project, attentive to legal mistranslation, is at the heart of a critical economic sociology of law. It

---

18 For the most influential classical definition of *oikonomia*, see Aristotle, *The Politics*, Book 1, tr. T.A. Sinclair (1983).
19 M. Weber, *Economy and Society*, volume 1, eds. G. Roth and C. Wittich (1978) 312.
20 For Weber's definition of convention, see id., p. 319:

> Convention ... shall be said to exist wherever a certain conduct is sought to be induced without, however, any coercion, physical or psychological, and at least under normal circumstances, without any direct reaction other than the expression of approval or disapproval on the part of those persons who constitute the environment of the actor.

Weber thus imagines convention as a ground without coercion in order to explore the coercive character of law.

100

opens questions about the mechanics of ethico-political agency within systems of valuation and relations of community, group or corporate life not fully incorporable into either formal juridical logics or the logic of the value-system of the free market. Said differently, Weber calls us to investigate economic embeddedness through the process of translating across formal juridical logics and the robustness of what he calls 'the legal order', or 'the complex of actual determinants ... of human conduct.'[21]

At the same time, Weber's very telling discussion of government and administration at the beginning of his chapter mapping the sociology of law (entitled 'Economy and Law') in the second volume of *Economy and Society* also opens the study of law, economy, and governmentality. Here, Weber considers how practices of governing that are manifest as *administration* can exceed formal law and rights claims. Economy, in its classical sense of arranging and managing, undergirds the analysis and the characteristic Weberian elaboration of the force of law. The chapter opens with an analysis of the modern distinction between public and private law. In Weber's words, public law marks the 'total body of those norms which regulate state-oriented action', while private law refers to 'the totality of those norms, which while issuing from the state, regulate conduct other that state-oriented conduct.'[22] His method reads public and private law through the same lens – the regulation of conduct – and so emphasizes their blurry boundaries, most especially in an explanation of the ways in which rights and claim-norms established by the state may operate as 'reflexes' of 'reglementations' of conduct, in both public and private law. Still, he does offer a novel distinction between these two categories of law: 'private law might be contrasted with public law as the law of coordination as distinguished from that of subordination.'[23] Private law operates, in other words, *as a practice of economy*, via managing or coordinating; public law, by the exercise of subordinating. Weber nevertheless characteristically reminds us that these categories are slippery and can overlap. If we are interested in a colonial genealogy of contemporary neoliberal governance, we must consider the overlap, or the ways in which subordination, or making subordinate, is dissimulated by coordinating and managing.

What follows in this section of *Economy and Society* is an account of how subordination may be exercised in what appears to be benign fashion, when discourses of efficient *administration* dominate over the protection of rights claims. Administration, according to Weber:

> is not a concept of public law exclusively ... [W]e must recognize the existence of private administration, as in the case of a household or a business enterprise, alongside the kind of administration carried on either by the state or by other public institutions.[24]

---

21 id., p. 312.
22 M. Weber, *Economy and Society,* volume 2, eds. G. Roth and C. Wittich (1978) 641.
23 id., p. 642.
24 id., p. 644.

Indeed, he states, the 'primeval form of administration' has its roots in 'patriarchal power, ie the rule of the household. In its primitive form, the authority of the master of the household is unlimited.'[25] Here, Weber draws a link between the origins of administration and economy or *oikonomia* – in the distribution and management of the household by its master. (In classical Greek, the term for the master of the household is *despotes*, tied etymologically to the English word 'despot'). Administration, in other words, aligns the paternal authority of the household and the authority of the state – realms that are necessarily distinct in liberal political theory – and allows us to read them on a continuum. Moreover, states Weber, in the public domain:

> the expression 'public administrations' includes not only legislation and adjudication but also other residuary activities which we here want to call 'government'. 'Government' can be bound by legal norms and limited by vested rights. In these respects it resembles legislation and adjudication.[26]

But at the same time, Weber emphasizes:

> one specific characteristic of government ... resides in the fact that it aims not only at acknowledging and enforcing the law simply because the law exists and constitutes the basis of vested rights, *but also in that it pursues other concrete objectives of a political, ethical, utilitarian, or some other kind*. To the government, the individual and his interests *are in the legal sense objects* rather than bearers of rights [emphasis mine].[27]

Weber focuses here on the ways in which rights, and what Foucault will call juridical sovereignty, are overridden by practices of government, which are directed, like the colonial state, at governing subjects, rather than protecting and enabling citizens, or bearers of rights. Indeed, Weber continues his analysis by identifying the ways in which forms of patrimonial authority sustain forms of kinship-based arbitration, which are melded into British parliamentary procedure, and modern adjudication.[28] Foucault's debt to Weber is clear here, especially if we consider the intellectual grounding of his term 'governmentality' and his interest especially in the genealogy of liberal governmentality. A term that draws analytical focus on the mentalities and practices of governing, the directing or conducting of conduct, or what Foucault calls the 'conduct of conduct' (an elaboration, we might argue, of Weber's interests in the 'reflexes' of 'reglementation'), governmentality as a historical formation refers specifically to the rationalities of governing that have developed since the emergence of the discipline of political economy in the late eighteenth century. In his 1978–79 lectures at the Collège de France, Foucault poses a genealogy of political economy, addressing its wide range of schools from the late eighteenth century. For Foucault, political economy is a

---

25 id., p. 645.
26 id., p. 644.
27 id., pp. 644–5.
28 id., pp. 645–7.

potent and powerful modern arrangement of power directed at managing political subjects as bodies and populations, even as juridical discourses of sovereignty begin to recode absolute sovereign right as social contract, as the sovereignty of 'the people', and citizenship rights are established and celebrated.[29] Unfortunately, he does not address colonial formations, especially colonial liberalism manifest as the improving mission of British utilitarians, which lay bare political economy's modern political rationalities, and the power of free market ideology.

Foucault's 1978–79 lectures, one of which is the well-known essay 'Governmentality,' detail the ways in which 'economy' comes to dominate as a discourse of governing, especially with the modern emergence of political economy. Tracing the many meanings of 'government' in Western tracts, the lectures address it not just as the administration of state, but also as techniques of controlling the self, guiding the family, managing the household (*oikonomia*), and as the art of governing political subjects.[30] For Foucault, modern liberal forms of governance evoke economy in its classical sense. The ancient Greek concept of economy as arranging and managing is revitalized with the emergence of political economy as a knowledge form, which marks a shift from 'imposing law on men' to 'disposing things' (Weber's focus on the power of *disposition* in his definition of the economic order resonates strongly here) and using 'laws themselves as tactics to arrange things in such a way that ... such and such ends may be achieved.'[31] So, as Foucault now famously puts it, forms of governing introduced by political economy, isolate 'the economy as a specific sector of reality' and also becomes the 'science and the technique of intervention ... in that field of reality.'[32] It is in this vein that Foucault contemplates modern 'civil society as an arrangement of economic men,' or what he calls '*la technologie de la gouvernmentalité libérale* [the technology of liberal governmentality].'[33] British colonialism, spanning utilitarian philosophies of governance and methods of political economy from the Physiocrats, to Smith, J.S. Mill, and Keynes, all the while articulating cultural pluralism and

29 For the definition of governmentality as a historical formation, see M. Foucault, 'Govermentality' in *The Foucault Effect*, eds. G. Burchell, C. Gordon, and P. Miller (1991). This essay is one of Foucault's lectures at the Collège de France in 1978–79: see M. Foucault, *The Birth of Biopolitics: Lectures at the Collège de France 1978–79*, tr. G. Burchell (2008) in which he elaborates on the conduct of conduct. For the definition of conduct, see M. Foucault, *Security, Territory, Population: Lectures at the Collège de France 1977–78*, tr. G. Burchell (2007).
30 See id. (2008).
31 id. (1991), p. 95.
32 id., p. 102.
33 'Civil society as an arrangement of economic men' is a translation of a section of Foucault's lecture at the Collège de France, 1 April 1979 by C. Gordon: see 'Governmental Rationality' in Burchell et al. (eds.), op. cit., n. 29, p. 23. For the discussion of *la gouvernmentalité libérale*, see the original French version of Foucault, op. cit. (2008), n. 29, *La Naissance de la Biopolitique* (2004) at 300.

103

non-interference in indigenous culture, offers a deep historical archive for mapping forms of liberal governmentality, especially, I would like to emphasize, techniques that institute the social imaginaries of economic liberalism through the language of political liberalism.

MAKING ABSTRACT ECONOMIC MAN: FROM CORPORATE LIFE TO THE CORPORATE PERSON

In India, civil society – a public of subjects – was indeed staged in modernizing law as an arrangement of economic men. Nevertheless the very economic actors upon which the colonial state relied – vernacular capitalists – were not coded as economic men but, rather, as cultural actors, for their embedded socialities were thought to restrict the free circulation of capital. At stake in the civilizing mission which distinguished between a modern and public domain of economy and an ancient and 'private' domain of native culture, was a spatial implementation of the temporal stages of corporate life that structured British and European legal theory and jurisprudence.

When we think of the corporation, we immediately associate it with the joint-stock limited liability company, regulated by formal legal processes and distinguished by the mystical, even theological concept of legal personality. Still, it is important to remember that the modern idea of the corporation overrode a much more extensive notion of 'corporate' or 'group life'. Legal thinkers and social theorists from Maine to Weber evince the nineteenth-century obsession with a broad category of forms of collective social organization that ranged from the family to the clan to the guild, and beyond. That prominent voices deliberated on 'corporate life' in its most expansive conceptualization was actually a sign that these older, embedded forms of economic and social life were being aggressively recoded through a significant global legal formation: the standardization of principles and procedures for contract (The Indian Contract Act dates from 1872). As economic development became a focus for colonial policy in the late nineteenth century, vernacular capitalism's kinship, clan, and caste-based networks challenged a developing liberal governmentality intent on producing a civil society that would be an arrangement of economic men conceived as individual legal subjects.

As we know from Maine's *Ancient Law*, the problem of corporate life – forms of collective association or what Max Weber called 'consociation' – constituted the dominant lens through which to understand the forward march of economy and society. *Ancient Law* marked the kind of temporizing that enforced the modern authority of contract, and the standardization of the distinction between public and private law, both of which presupposed the individual person as legal subject.[34] Influenced by Maine, colonial jurists

---

34 Maine, op. cit. (1931/1860), n. 13, p. 174.

understood extended or "joint" family organization in nineteenth-century India as a leftover, ancient form of corporation. (The joint family form, in both the Hindu systems of *Mitakshara* and *Dhayabaga*, was a collective association that did not even presuppose individual shares of property, but that was nevertheless translated legally as a 'coparcenary'.) The difficulty with the joint family, as with other such ancient forms in medieval Europe, was that, in Maine's words, 'corporations never die': they have a perpetual life, an extensive temporal negotiability that renders it impossible to know when they begin and when they end.[35] The commercial joint family firm in India, identified in the colonial personal law by the term 'Hindu Undivided Family', challenged British legislators and jurists in this way, posing a problem of extensive temporal negotiability in which ownership and debt could be passed on through generations, a significant effect of the extensive negotiability between kinship and capital.[36] This extensive negotiability was a marker of forms and conventions of 'embedded' social life that we can only understand as *gemeinschaft* (community), after *gesellschaft* (society grounded in contract), and law's processes of 'disembedding' have been initiated. I draw attention to this nineteenth-century discourse on the range of forms of corporate life, and the temporizing of many worlds of 'consociation' as evidence of the growing modern monopoly of the joint-stock company over the very concept of the corporate, understood through contractual models and as either market-based (as in the limited liability corporation, and even more colloquially, via the logo 'inc.') or state-based (as in municipal corporation).

THE CORPORATE PERSON, VIA 'PIERCING THE CORPORATE VEIL'

While the East India Company is perhaps the world's most famous example of corporate personhood in the form of the limited liability joint-stock, the concept of generalized limited liability, that is, the ability to incorporate without royal charter, was introduced into India via early forms of Companies legislation in 1866, and then more extensively in the first Indian Companies Act of 1882 (revised 1913, then 1956). It is important to remember that at this time when the limited liability company was estab-lished as a formal legal person, so too was the colonial legal category of the 'Hindu Undivided Family' or HUF. The former was coded as an economic actor, and the latter, a cultural one. As I mentioned, in this way, the dynamic and embedded kinship-based activities of the family firm (which was read as an HUF) was abstracted into a master culturalist logic that both enabled the reproduction of embedded kinship-based economic practices and at once delegitimized them as primarily agents of ancient culture, thus legitimizing

35 id., p. 135.
36 For more detail, see 'Introduction' in Birla, op. cit. (2009), n. 1.

their exploitative activities under the protection of personal law. As contractual procedures began to settle into Indian economic relations in the post-independence period, vernacular market actors began to recode themselves through the formal logic of contract and formal legal incorporation. But even still, and even among the actors who now inhabit the world of legal contract, kinship-based, embedded market practices have not diminished. In fact, the story merits a robust reading of law and economic life.

I can give just a slice of this rich legal archive here, through two sets of cases. These cases are intimately tied to the legal history of the evocatively-named corporate law doctrine, 'piercing the corporate veil'. 'Piercing the veil' refers to a range of conditions under which the 'veil' of the corporate personality can be challenged so that directors and shareholders can be made responsible for the debts, damages, and other obligations of the corporation. A recent comparison of the doctrine in the United Kingdom and the United States emphasizes three phases: the first was a period from the landmark British case of *Salomon* v. *Salomon* in 1897, which I will touch upon here, to about the Second World War; the second period went from approximately the end of the war to 1978, which saw the 'heyday' of the doctrine; and then the period from 1978 to the present, when the deployment of the doctrine has, at least in the United Kingdom and United States, been on the decline, predictably with the rise of neoliberal economic philosophies and policies.[37]

In India, the doctrine of piercing the veil has been deployed more liberally than in the United States and United Kingdom, and among practicing lawyers, the sense is that since independence, the Supreme Court has been expanding the conditions under which the veil can be lifted.[38] It is clear from recent and contemporary cases of corporate veil-piercing that they continue to echo questions in colonial history that concern vernacular market practices: the problem of the legitimacy of the HUF as an economic entity, the discourse around *benami* transactions (transactions in the name of third parties or fictitious parties), and the problem of kinship-based business networks. To emphasize that scholars must navigate the oscillation between the introduction of abstract legal fictions and their reappropriation within embedded economic forms, I offer here summaries of two sets of cases about corporate veil-piercing. I present these stories to telescope key themes in the evolution of the corporate person in India, part of a larger project and anti-reading of Maine's teleology of corporate life. Said differently, to highlight the peculiarities of a postcolonial genealogy of the corporate person, I'd like to address corporate personhood through a consideration of the conditions under which the corporate person may be *dismantled*.

37 T. Cheng, 'The Corporate Veil Doctrine Revisited: A Comparative Study of the English and US Corporate Veil Doctrines' (2011) 34 *Boston College International and Comparative Law Rev.* 329, at 334.
38 See, for example, P. Jain, 'Is There a Perpetual Solution in Resolving the Corporate Veil Issue?', at <http://www.jainkinkar.com/article3.pdf>.

106

My first example contrasts the landmark British decision in *Salomon* with an Indian Supreme Court Case of 1998 that relies on this 1897 decision, but comes to a very different conclusion. The contrast tells us about the weight of the concept of family business in India, for better or for worse. The second set of cases consider the corporate person through the problem of the multi-national company, and they evince the radical shift from India's immediate post-independence understanding of the corporation as compared with its current globalizing enthusiasms.

RECODING EMBEDDED BUSINESS: *SALOMON* v. *SALOMON* AND *CALCUTTA CHROMOTYPE* v. *COLLECTOR OF CENTRAL EXCISE*

Salomon is a foundational case adjudicated at the highest level in the British House of Lords.[39] It clarified the meaning of corporate personhood, and also opened the question as to the conditions under which the authority of the corporate person could be challenged. Aaron Salomon, a leading merchant in East London, operated a sole-proprietor business, and in 1892, his son wished to join the business. As companies law at the time required a minimum of seven people to incorporate, the man Salomon created the company Salomon with this wife, daughter, and four sons, two of whom were also made managing directors. Salomon owned 20,001 of the company's 20,007 shares; the remaining six were distributed among his family members, with each member owning one share. The story so far evokes practices of joint family businesses as well the family structuring of corporate shareholding of the kind that still dominates the structure of Indian companies and stock markets. Salomon sold his business to the new corporation for £39,000, of which £10,000 was debt to him; he was the company's principal shareholder as well its main creditor. But soon after the company was formed, it met with serious economic trouble, and it was forced to seek debentures as security for its debt. When soon thereafter liquidators sought to recover those loans, they argued that Salomon had created the company solely to transfer his business to it and that he was personally responsible for paying off the debt. In cases in the High Court as well as the Court of Appeal that preceded the final decision, the judges found in favour of the liquidators. Judgments at these levels variously argued that the corporation was mere myth, and that the scheme of incorporation only enabled fraud on Salomon's part; that he had incorporated his business only to be able to attract debentures and limit his liability. But when the case finally reached the House of Lords, a fantastic legal turn ensued, perhaps as fantastic as the Bombay High Court decision that had recently preceded it in 1887 and which confirmed that the

39 *Salomon* v. *Salomon and Co.*, House of Lords [1897] A.C. 22.

107

Hindu deity was a juristic entity.[40] The House of Lords overturned the lower courts' decisions and ruled that the company could not be considered simply an agent of shareholders or directors. The company, they asserted, was a distinct and separate person, and not merely a legal or economic instrument for its shareholders. Said differently, the court forcefully affirmed the principle of corporate personhood to establish that shareholders could neither benefit personally from incorporation, nor be liable personally for the company's obligations.[41]

Salomon is a foundational example of the deployment of the force of legal fiction to recode informal kinship-based economic relations into the formalities of law, even in the face of lower courts posing a common-sense reading of incorporation as simply an instrument to protect personalized and possibly fraudulent dealings. It is for this reason that the doctrine of piercing the corporate veil was elaborated actively in the case law and jurisprudence following *Salomon*: 'piercing' would become the logical exception to the general rule about the corporation as legal person, and not just as a servant to its shareholders, but as a sovereign sahib.

Let us now compare *Salomon* with an Indian Supreme Court case from 1998, *Calcutta Chromotype* vs. *Collector of Central Excise*.[42] In short, the case concerned a manufacturer and sole distributor of playing cards. The manufacturer, Ganga Saran and Sons Pvt. Ltd, consisted of shareholders that were members of the G.S. Sharma family. The sole distributor of the playing cards, or the 'buyer company' was a separate company that also consisted of members of that same family. Advocates for the Collector of Central Excise argued that Ganga Saran and Sons would have to pay a higher rate of excise (as per section 4(4) of the Central Excises and Salt Act 1944) because the company that was its sole distributor consisted of 'related' persons with an 'identity of interest' that affected each others' businesses directly or indirectly; that, indeed, the Director of Ganga Saran and Sons was also the Director of the distributing company; and that Ganga Saran and Sons had been accorded favourable treatment by being charged a low price for distribution. The lawyers for Ganga Saran and Sons, in contrast, argued in the spirit of *Salomon* that the manufacturer and distributor were distinct companies and therefore separate legal entities, and should not be subject to the higher rate.

Citing specific High Court precedents addressing these questions from the 1980s, which speak of an active fine-tuning of the concept of 'related persons' (a feature of both the Companies Acts of 1913 and 1956) in this

---

40 *Manohar Ganesh Tambekar* v. *Lakhimram Govindram* (1887) I.L.R. 12 B. 247. For more on this, see Birla, op. cit. (2009), n. 1, pp. 67–102, which places this decision in the context of market governance.
41 For a summary of the judgment, see A.G. Forji, 'The Veil Doctrine in Company Law' (September 2007), at <http://www.llrx.com/features/veildoctrine.htm#_ftnref23>.
42 *Calcutta Chromotype* v. *Collector of Central Excise* (1998) 3 SCC 691.

period, the Indian Supreme Court judgment returned to a foundational Indian case of 1964, *Tata Engineering and Locomotive* v. *State of Bihar*[43] to open the question of veil-piercing:

> The principle that a company under the Companies Act, 1956 is a separate entity and therefore ... [two distinct companies] cannot be 'related persons' ... has travelled quite a bit after the decision of the House of Lords in Salomon v. Salomon.... [I]n Tata Engineering and Locomotive v. State of Bihar [the court stated that] ... : 'The corporation in law is equal to a natural person and has a legal entity of its own. The entity of the corporation is entirely separate from that of its shareholders; it bears its own name and has a seal of its own. ... *However, in the course of time, the doctrine that the corporation or a company has a legal and separate entity of its own has been subjected to certain exceptions by the application of the fiction that the veil of the corporation can be lifted and its face examined in substance.... As a result of the impact of the complexity of economic factors, judicial decisions have sometimes recognized exceptions to the rule about the juristic personality of the corporation. It may be that in the course of time these exceptions may grow in number and to meet the requirements of different economic problems, the theory about the personality of the corporation may be confined more and more*' [emphasis mine].[44]

With this reasoning, the Indian Supreme Court ruled that in certain cases in which there was enough evidence to show that business between companies was linked to ties of 'related persons', the corporate veil could indeed be pierced to investigate the nature of the relations and their effect on the business, and it was in this case.

Calcutta Chromotype is one among many cases since the 1980s that evince the ways in which the Indian legal system as well as vernacular economic actors have negotiated the categories of kinship and relation within formal legal procedures.[45] In India, it seems that colonial anxieties about vernacular market actors have produced the sophisticated deployment of veil piercing by legal authorities. At the same time, jurisprudence has had to engage with the persistence of kinship as a model for market organization, and indeed even the possibility that abstract corporate persons can be related, weaving 'embedded' economic relations into the 'disembedded' world of law.

In closing, I shall turn briefly to two cases that consider the corporate veil through the problem of the multinational company. They pose provocative questions about the relationship between capital flows and political citizenship today – among capital personified in the corporation, governed

43 *Tata Engineering and Locomotive* v. *State of Bihar* (1964) 6 SCR 885.
44 Judgment, *Calcutta Chromotype*, op. cit., n. 42, at <http://indiankanoon.org/doc/995583> 10–12.
45 There are many cases since this one that develop the conditions under which the veil can be lifted. Another key case from this period is *State of UP and Ors* v. *Renusagar Power Co. and Others* (1988) AIR 1737 and (1988) SCR Supl. (1) 627. See Jain, op. cit., n. 38, pp. 8–9 and judgment at <http://indiankanoon.org/doc/1901448/>.

human bodies, and legal persons who constitute juridical sovereignty. They also highlight the robust deployment of concepts of kinship and 'related persons' on the part of the Indian state in order to virtually extend its borders in the post-liberalization era. The cases, I would like to argue, foreground a shift in the social imaginaries that are protected by veil-piercing gestures – from the nation, a kind of juridical kinship, to a transnational kinship that is as abstract and virtual, and as deeply embodied, as capital itself.

THE CORPORATE PERSON: CITIZEN OR ECONOMIC MIGRANT?

As we know, in the United States, the corporate person has been slowly appropriating the features of juridical citizenship, most prominently in the recent case of *Citizens United* v. *Federal Election Commission*, which acknowledged the corporation's right to free speech, expressed as finance.[46] This would be consistent with the country's retreat from veil piercing in the past three decades. In India, as may be suspected, the history of corporate veil piercing has charted another trajectory. India's legal path marks a different, postcolonial neoliberalism, one perhaps even more adept than its Western counterparts at restaging the world as market, and able to do so by actively recoding kinship as an economic performative. In a tax case that was brought to the Indian Supreme Court in 1961 entitled *State Trading Corporation* v. *Commercial Tax Officer*, the corporate person sought to achieve new status as a *citizen*.[47] The court addressed the question of whether (i) the State Trading Corporation could be understood as a citizen of India under Article 19 of the constitution, and (ii) whether it could enforce the fundamental rights of persons against the state as articulated in Article 12, Part III of the Constitution (most specifically, the right to 'acquire, hold and dispose of property' as well as the right to 'to carry on any occupation, trade or business'). In this case, the State Trading Corporation sought relief from various agencies of the state for the sales tax assessed against it. The Corporation filed petitions under Article 32 of the Constitution of India, which empowers the Supreme Court to 'issue orders or directions or writs ... appropriate for the enforcement of fundamental rights.'[48] The Justices asserted clearly in a 7 to 2 decision that the corporation *is not a citizen*, and that therefore neither of the petitioners' claims could be enforced. The key feature of the majority opinions was a veil-piercing gesture, for they asked questions about the citizenship of shareholders, and therefore expressed early post-independence concerns about foreign capital infiltrating the new nation-state. As the Chief Justice speaking for the majority explained, 'the rights of

46 *Citizens United* v. *Federal Election Commission* 558 U.S. 50 (2010).
47 'Note on *State Trading Corporation* v. *Commercial Tax Officer*' 3 ILM 119 (1964), at <http://heinonline.org>.
48 id., at p. 119.

110

citizenship and the rights flowing from the nationality or domicile of a corporation are not coterminous.'[49] Said differently, corporations have legal domicile, but not citizenship rights: the ruling thus distinguished between the citizen who inhabits the domain of the state, as opposed to the corporation, a kind of economic migrant, profitably engaged in the domain of economy but devoid of the rights and claims of citizenship.[50] So, in India's first post-independence decade, the corporate person sought juridical citizenship, but the developmentalist nation-state, fortified by its anti-colonial triumphs and the centralized authority of its colonial ancestry, rejected any such claims to changing the character of its sovereign constituents.[51]

This landmark case can be contrasted with another later much-cited one, *Life Insurance Corporation of India* v. *Escorts Ltd*, decided by the Supreme Court in December 1985, which marks an early shift towards India's liberalization policies.[52] At this time, the government of India, in need of foreign exchange, sought to attract 'non-resident individuals of Indian nationality or origin [NRIs] to invest in shares of Indian companies' and thus formulated a 'Portfolio Investment Scheme' to provide incentives to these NRIs.[53] In this case, a group of non-resident Indians in the United Kingdom had wished to invest in Escorts Ltd, an Indian company, but the directors of Escorts Ltd sought to prevent such investment.[54] One of the shareholders in Escorts Ltd was the Life Insurance Corporation of India, a state company and so an arm of the state. It contested the resistance of Escorts Ltd to non-resident Indian investors and so called an 'extraordinary meeting' of the shareholders to overturn the anti-NRI investor policy and to remove nine of the part-time directors of Escorts Ltd. Escorts Ltd petitioned, stating that the

49 id., at p. 120.
50 Dissenting opinions, in contrast, supported trends in twentieth-century United States law that had also used corporate veil-lifting, in this case actually to affirm that the corporation had some form of citizenship rights: United States cases had given corporations the rights of the residents of a state if it was shown that the corporation consisted of shareholders of that state.
51 This is indicative of the kind of market governance that emerged with the post-independence developmentalist state, in which sovereignty was exercised as state authority over market relations, and the territory of the nation was mapped as a bounded economy. At the same time, the post-independence developmentalist decades were also dominated by a marriage of state and an industrial capitalist elite that had funded the nationalist movement. As Partha Chatterjee has argued, the developmentalist state was characterized by the dominance of a few 'monopoly houses from traditional merchant backgrounds and protected by the license and import substitution regime.' P. Chatterjee, 'Democracy and Economic Transformation in India' *Economic and Political Weekly*, 19 April 2008, 56.
52 *Life Insurance Corporation* v. *Escorts Ltd* (1985), 1986 AIR 1370, and 1985 SCR Supl. (3) 909.
53 SCR Supl., id., at p. 910.
54 Despite its rather racy and evocative name, Escorts Ltd manufactures tractors, automotive and railway parts, and construction equipment.

111

Life Insurance Co of India did not have the right to call such a meeting. The judgment, perhaps not surprisingly, fell on the side of the state, arguing that as a shareholder in Escorts Ltd, the Life Insurance Co of India had every right to call an extraordinary meeting, indeed emphasizing that this was an essential exercise in 'corporate democracy' and in fact the only recourse that shareholders had (in contrast with the more extensive recourses of the citizen in a parliamentary democracy). It is important to note that this decision affirmed the policy of the Foreign Exchange Regulation Act of 1973, which relied fundamentally on the principle of lifting the corporate veil in order to identify foreign investors: the Act allowed for foreign companies to invest in Indian ones if the foreign companies consisted of at least 60 per cent of shareholders of Indian nationality.[55] In this case, the law affirmed this Act's veil-piercing logic in order to *enable* foreign investment/transnational corporate investment; two decades before, in the earlier case, veil piercing had been deployed to prevent such foreign investment. The shift marks an emergent new reading of the corporate person. In the Escorts Ltd case, the directors of Escorts Ltd had sought to enforce the tie between residency and citizenship, in which foreign capital, via the non-resident Indian, would be prevented from entering the nation-state. Here, it was *the corporation* that performed a claim to a narrow notion of citizenship, tied intimately to territory. Instead, the judgment affirmed the rights and authority of citizenship by *de-linking it* from territorial residency. As such, this 1985 judgment quite appropriately reflects its time, a liminal moment between the aggressive marking of territorial citizenship that marked the post-independence nation-state, and the virtual opening up of borders that motivated economic liberalization. The case marks a postcolonial refraction of the status to contract teleology, in which the modern world of contract-based market practice, and the legal universe of corporate persons, emulates the extensive negotiability of capital and kinship (as staged virtually in the figure of the NRI) that had characterized the 'embedded' market practices of the bazaar. This development, I would like to suggest, also marks a contemporary, neoliberal Indian recoding of the very concept of citizenship itself, *via the figure of the vernacular entrepreneur.*[56]

The history of the legal fiction of the corporate personality in India is

55 In addition to extending to the whole of India, the Act applied to 'all citizens of India outside India and to branches and agencies outside India of companies or bodies corporate, registered or incorporated in India': Foreign Exchange Regulation Act 1973, at <http://www.rbi.org.in/scripts/ECMUserView.aspx?Id=21&CatID=12>.
56 My argument here offers a legal story that follows Partha Chatterjee's powerful account of the transition from the India of the development decades to the current neoliberal mode. Chatterjee elaborates on the economist Kalyan Sanyal's analysis of primitive accumulation in postcolonial globalization. According to Sanyal, in post-colonial India, the capitalist process of primitive accumulation does not herald a forward transition through historical stages of capital; instead, those who are dispossessed of their means of production under primitive accumulation are also,

likely to tell us extensive stories about the wide range of habits and practices of its market actors, especially the persistence and legal performance of family and kinship-based value-systems in the postcolonial period. Indeed, judging by just a few key Supreme Court cases on veil piercing in the past three decades, the question of what constitutes a 'related person' in economic contexts poses itself as a master thematic for future analysis. Working against the grain of Maine (and Weber's *Gemeinschaft* to *Gesellschaft* narrative), a postcolonial project of thinking economy as an inhabiting of law would seek not only to unpack the scripts of market practice in India, it would also open to broader questions, such as the economic recoding of the very concept of citizenship today.

As an 'economic man', the modern corporate person heralds new forms of transnational economic citizenship which rely not only on the power of domicile over formal political citizenship, but at the same time, on an aggressive definition of ethnicity, descent, and national ties. We might even say that the corporate person is like a voluntary economic migrant, much like the NRIs and other diasporas whom the Indian Ministry of External Affairs are now courting and counting actively through new categories like the Overseas Citizen of India (OCI), which allows for the free movement of persons and investments, but not Indian passports; this alongside more rigorous visa procedures for foreign nationals of Indian descent. Said differently, the velocity of capital is matched, in this case, by an explosion of

according to the logic of new governmental technologies, given basic means of livelihood: K. Sanyal, *Rethinking Capitalist Development: Primitive Accumulation, Governmentality and Post-Colonial Capitalism* (2007); Chatterjee, op. cit, n. 51, p. 55; also Chatterjee, op. cit., n. 2. (Said differently, Sanyal's analysis brings a Foucauldian reading of the techniques of biopolitics – to make live and let die – to an analysis of postcolonial capital: see Foucault, op. cit. (2007), n. 29.) For Chatterjee, this insight is crucial for understanding the extension of the domain of capital in postcolonial globalization: the governmental process of trying to reverse the effects of primitive accumulation has resulted in the extension of market logic and interventions, directed at preserving the livelihoods of dispossessed surplus populations who have been rendered useless in the dominant sectors of the formal economy. This has made previously subsistence sectors integrated into the market economy, but with a key distinction between what Chatterjee calls 'corporate' and 'non-corporate' capital, marking the boundary between the formal corporate sector and the informal economy. For Chatterjee, 'civil society is where corporate capital is hegemonic' while 'non-corporate' capital marks the domain of what he calls 'political society,' outside the formal domain of bourgeois civil society. While corporate capital is defined by those interested in the reproduction of capital and the maximization of profit, non-corporate capital is dominated by the logic of 'providing livelihood to the workers in the units' which structures the politics of the governed. See Chatterjee, op. cit, n. 51, p. 58. The use of the term 'corporate' in this essay – channelling a broader nineteenth-century meaning – calls us to examine both the domains of civil and political society. Indeed, the legal story told here, by which the corporate person comes to monopolize a broader notion of the corporate as group life, supports Chatterjee's reading of the formal versus informal arrangements of capital in civil versus political society.

113

discourses of kin, both virtual and deeply embodied. In India, we have already witnessed an accelerated legal descent of economic man in which the Non-Resident Indian has given birth to the Person of Indian Origin (PIO) and the OCI. On the other side of the cosmopolitan itinerancy of the corporation and its embodied relatives, the NRI/PIO/OCI, are transnational flows of labour with little or no legal rights, for whom the formal language of citizenship, both political and economic, has failed. These governed bodies inhabit and make law in the robust sense that an economic sociology of law seeks to capture, posing a contrapuntal politics to the world of legal fictions. By examining the making of 'the economy' as a legal domain, as well as economy as a project and practice of governing, historians and theorists of law may read the connections across these moving trajectories of bodies, both literal and incorporated.[57]

---

57 The relationship between the legal fiction of virtual corporate body and legal claims made by governed surplus populations, exactly as bodies, may be one way that the economic sociology of law might address what Partha Chatterjee has called 'the politics of the governed'. See Chatterjee, op. cit., n. 51, and also P. Chatterjee, *The Politics of the Governed: Reflections on Popular Politics in Most of the World* (2006).

JOURNAL OF LAW AND SOCIETY
VOLUME 40, NUMBER 1, MARCH 2013
ISSN: 0263-323X, pp. 115–36

Do Feminists Need an Economic Sociology of Law?

Prabha Kotiswaran*

Feminist legal scholars have long exposed the mutually constitutive relationship between the market and the social sphere, particularly, of the family, as mediated by the state. A peculiar division of labour has emerged in American feminist legal theorizing on the market in the context of care work, on the one hand, and sex work on the other. Care is valorized, thus entrenching the family-market dichotomy while the sex-work debates view the market as a source of harm and violence and therefore to be eliminated from the social. This produces a problematic feminist understanding of the market and generates legal reforms that produce unintended consequences for women themselves. The article offers an economic sociology of law pursued in legal ethnographic terms as a way of revitalizing contemporary feminist legal thought on the market and, indeed, the economy, illustrating its use in the context of international anti-trafficking law and transnational surrogacy.

INTRODUCTION

Do feminism and feminist legal theory need an economic sociology of law (ESL), defined as 'a sociological analysis of the role of law in economic life'?[1] After all, despite the well-established canons of economic sociology of law,[2] feminists have typically played the role of the outsider in these debates. To illustrate, Richard Swedberg, in a call for developing the field of economic sociology of law, identifies its task as analysing the relationship of law and economy to 'other' spheres of society, including the private sphere

* Dickson Poon School of Law, King's College London, Strand, London WC2R 2LS, England
prabha.kotiswaran@kcl.ac.uk

1 R. Swedberg, 'The case for an economic sociology of law' (2003) 32 *Theory and Society* 1–37, 1.
2 R. Cotterrell, 'Rethinking "Embeddedness": Law, Economy, Community' in this volume, pp. 49–67.

115

of the family, suggesting that the family would not logically fall within the province of the market.[3] Yet at the other end of the spectrum of American legal scholarship, conventional law and economics scholars are known to justify the sexual division of labour as efficient. In this article, I map feminist responses to both these sets of formulations in the context of social reproduction[4] (and the labour it involves, namely, reproductive labour), the drawbacks of such interventions, and why an economic sociology of law holds prospects for revitalizing their critical insights.

Feminism in general, and feminist legal theory in particular, accommodate such a diversity of political projects, theoretical commitments, and inter-disciplinary impulses that it is impossible to generalize about them. Therefore, I will confine myself in this article mostly to American feminist legal theory, given its influence internationally. Feminist lawyers and experts are after all engaged in an increasingly transnational legal project[5] involving both substantive law reform and the formulation of soft-law mechanisms of governance that travel well. Some of us have identified this influential role of North American feminists as governance feminism.[6] I will start by delineating the strong critical legal roots of feminist theorizing of the market-family dichotomy. Although feminist legal theory is hardly limited to analyses of gender alone,[7] feminists in theorizing the market have gravitated towards the laws that structure social reproduction. Hence, I turn to the recent care-work debates and the cultural feminist impression it bears. Next I turn to feminist legal theorizing of reproductive labour performed in disaggregated ways in the market, using the sex-work debates to highlight its significant stumbling blocks. I then offer empirical legal research as a way to disrupt the stalemate produced by highly polarized ideological debates amongst feminists on issues of considerable policy significance. I demonstrate this in the context of the two emerging transnational legal arenas of trafficking and commercial surrogacy.

3 Swedberg, op. cit., n. 1.
4 By this, I mean processes involving the daily labour performed in bearing and raising children, maintaining households, and socially sustaining male labour; such labour is performed predominantly by women.
5 S. Merry, *Human Rights and Gender Violence: Translating International Law into Local Justice* (2005).
6 J. Halley, P. Kotiswaran, H. Shamir, and C. Thomas. 'From the International to the Local in Feminist Legal Responses to Rape, Prostitution/Sex Work, and Sex Trafficking: Four Studies in Contemporary Governance Feminism' (2006) 29 *Harvard J. of Law & Gender* 335–423.
7 See Martha McCluskey's contributions on WTO law and welfare reform in *Feminism Confronts Homo Economicus*, eds. M. Fineman and T. Dougherty (2005).

116

Economic sociologists as Zelizer points out, with some exceptions, tend to ignore 'quasi-economies' such as households, informal economies, and trust networks.[8] In ESL, the family, if at all mentioned, occupies an anomalous position, subsumed at times within the market or society, yet at other times, presented as being in opposition to the market and the state. Thus, although Swedberg refers to the modern economy as including the capitalist economy, the official economy of the state, and the 'private' economy of the household, the discursive terrain he sets out already assumes the dividing lines of the public and private. Feminists have always problematized this distinction. Genealogically speaking, initial feminist theorizations of the market and family were centrally associated with Marxist traditions. Where the contemporary point of critique for economic sociologists has been to demonstrate the always-embedded nature of the market in social life, feminists offered the family as the very glue that facilitated this embedding while managing to project a disembedded view. Thus in the domestic labour debates of the 1970s,[9] materialist feminists challenged the idea that domestic labour created simple use values within the family in an essentially pre-capitalist and pre-industrial mode of production without reaching the market.[10] They argued that more than simply benefiting the capitalist mode of production through the reproduction of labour power,[11] housewives were in fact exploited productive workers who through their reproductive labour produced *surplus value* for the capitalist mode of production,[12] rendering their labour the very foundation of surplus value production.

Yet, before long, feminists were disenchanted with Marxism. As the unhappy marriage between feminism and Marxism unravelled, radical feminism with its theory of sexual subordination as the sole cause of women's inequality soon took root. The fortunes of materialist feminism in the United States have remained poor, yet given the strength of leftist traditions elsewhere, materialist feminism flowered into transnational theorizations of women's conditions. Feminists in international political economy theorized female reproductive labour in the context of the large-scale migration of women for domestic work, care work, and sex work. Meanwhile, with the rise of neo-classical economics, feminist economists offered a critical intervention from

8 V. Zelizer, *Economic Lives: how culture shapes the economy* (2011) 8.
9 See P. Kotiswaran, *Dangerous Sex, Invisible Labor: Sex Work and the Law in India* (2011) 57–69.
10 L. Vogel, *Woman Questions: Essays for a Materialist Feminism* (1995) 54.
11 id., p. 55.
12 M. Mies, *Patriarchy and Accumulation on a World Scale: Women in the International Division of Labour* (1998); L. Fortunati, *The Arcane of Reproduction: Housework, Prostitution, Labor and Capital*, tr. H. Creek, ed. J. Fleming (1995); Vogel, id., pp. 56–7.

117

within the discipline. Institutionalized through journals like *Feminist Economics*, feminist economists challenged the predominance of rational choice theory, the paradigm of the rational, utility-maximizing individual agent, and the heavily mathematical nature of contemporary economic theory.[13] Thus, there have been waves of feminist theorizing about gender and the market/economy, leading Viviana Zelizer, the pioneering economic sociologist, to remark that it may take feminist theory to bring her key concept of 'relational work' into the predominantly male economic sociological territory.[14] I will draw on relational work later in this article.

Closer to home, in law schools, American legal feminists have had to mount an orchestrated critique of neo-classical economics given the influence of the law and economics movement in American legal academia and the attention that law and economics scholars have paid to the family under the influence of Gary Becker's new home economics, effectively justifying the sexual division of labour. Hence, the extensive 2005 volume, *Feminism Confronts Homo Economicus*.[15] This feminist legal engagement with economic issues is impressively multi-faceted. The feminist critique challenges the normative assumptions of mainstream economic thought, its legal doctrinal proposals in contract, tort, and family law as well as its suggestions for institutional reform (such as welfare reform). Mirroring prior materialist feminist traditions, feminist legal scholars like Fineman have demonstrated how particular visions of the world as 'just', 'efficient', 'natural', and so on rely on the consensus that the family is the institution primarily responsible for dependency, thereby masking the family's gendered form and the dependency of society on 'the uncompensated and unrecognized dependency work assigned to caretakers within the private family.'[16] The market and state in Fineman's critique are free-riders on the backs of care takers and families.[17]

A particularly lasting legacy of feminist legal theory as a field is the deconstruction of the public-private divide in the law.[18] In Frances Olsen's path-breaking article as far back as in 1983, she problematized the radical separation of the market and the family and related dichotomies of male/female and state/civil society.[19] In particular, she highlighted the constructed nature of both the market and the family and the justification for non-

13 A. Estin, 'Can Families Be Efficient? A Feminist Appraisal' in Fineman and Dougherty, op. cit., n. 7, p. 423.
14 V. Zelizer, 'How I Became a Relational Economic Sociologist and What Does That Mean?' (2012) 40 *Politics and Society* 150.
15 Fineman and Dougherty, op. cit., n. 7.
16 M. Fineman, 'Cracking the Foundational Myths: Independence, Autonomy, and Self-Sufficiency' in Fineman and Dougherty, id., p. 179.
17 id., p. 188.
18 M. Fineman and T. Dougherty, 'Introduction' in id., p. xii.
19 F. Olsen, 'The Family and the Market: A Study of Ideology and Legal Reform' (1983) 96 *Harvard Law Rev.* 1497–578.

118

intervention on the part of the state when in fact the state already heavily regulated both the market and the family.[20] These insights resonate with feminist legal scholars to date.[21] Building on this deconstruction of the market-family divide, Olsen offered further macro-level theses explaining the relationship between the market and the family. Viewing the market and family as being interdependent,[22] she showed how legal reforms to ameliorate women's unequal social status mobilized the market logic of self-interest vis-à-vis family relations while deploying the family ethic of altruism to infiltrate market relations. Olsen proposed a matrix whereby legal reforms could be understood as making the market more like the ideal market or more like the family, and the family more like the ideal family or more like the market. All four sets of reforms however assumed the market-family dichotomy according to her and hence could not transcend the drawbacks of either institution.[23] Path-breaking as it was, Olsen very much took the family-market dichotomy as the fundamental unit of feminist legal analysis thus effacing market locations such as the brothel, the surrogacy hostel, the old-age home or the lap-dance club where wifely labour is performed by non-wives or locations such as the informal economy from which non-wifely female labour is sourced for the household.

Unfortunately, this family-market dichotomy has been reproduced in the latest iteration of feminist legal theorizing on the family and the market, namely, the care-work or childcare debates.[24] While it is impossible to reproduce the specificities of these debates in any detail here, two camps have emerged occupied by care feminists (or cultural feminists) on the one hand, and those who are less sentimental about what Quinn labels 'family values orthodoxy' on the other.[25] They differ 'primarily over whether to seek monetary compensation for family work or to demand women's emancipation from the home and entry into the paid labour market.'[26] Both camps have offered proposals ranging from a reorientation of the state's institutional set-ups to better validate and provide for care, given that it is, as some feminists argue, a public value,[27] to increased equity within the

20 id., pp. 1508, 1511.
21 Fineman and Dougherty, op. cit., n. 7; M. McCluskey, 'Deconstructing the State-Market Divide: The Rhetoric of Regulation from Workers' Compensation to the World Trade Organization', id., pp. 147–8; J. Halley and K. Rittich, 'Critical Directions in Comparative Family Law: Genealogies and Contemporary Studies of Family Law Exceptionalism – Introduction to the Special Issue on Comparative Family Law' (2010) LVIII Am. J. of Comparative Law 755.
22 Olsen, op. cit., n. 19, p. 1524.
23 id., pp. 1529–30.
24 K. Quinn, 'Mommy Dearest: The Focus on the Family in Legal Feminism' (2002) 37 Harvard Civil Rights-Civil Liberties Law Rev. 447.
25 id., p. 450.
26 id., p. 451.
27 L. McClain, 'Care as a Public Value: Linking Responsibility, Resources, and Republicanism' (2001) 76 Chicago-Kent Law Rev.1673–731.

household through a joint property system or even a premarital security agreement.[28] Yet others who call for increased female participation in the paid labour market aim for less discrimination against working mothers and for a more equitable allocation of work within the household between men and women made possible through reduced working hours.[29] Despite the range of proposals thrown up by the care-work debates, they can be sorted through Olsen's conceptual matrix explaining why they have not been and are unlikely to be successful.

Feminists in the care-work debates have pointed to the telescoping and indeed normalization of a cascading set of categories and social practices like sex, gender, family, and reproduction[30] which feminism has consistently sought to untangle.[31] They claim that 'many legal feminists' ideas of household work as productive rely solely on an underlying moralization of the family, dependency, and women's roles in both.'[32] Family structures are taken as a given[33] and several feminist proposals centred round the middle-class heterosexual couple.[34] In other words, cultural feminist understandings have tended to dominate the care-work debates, setting the trend for both policy proposals and the very meaning of what it means to be a good feminist.[35] Thus the care-work debates have to a large extent ignored the subversive impulses of the feminist critique of marriage and are unable to justify the distributive and unintended consequences of their proposals for a range of stakeholders who fall outside the feminist prototype of the married middle-class mother co-habiting with her wage-earning husband, thus excluding childless women, poorer working families, and queer families.[36] In methodological terms, feminist proposals to remunerate household work

28 M. Ertman, 'Commercializing Marriage: A Proposal for Valuing Women's Work Through Premarital Security Agreements' (1998) 77 *Texas Law Rev.* 17–112.
29 V. Schultz, 'Life's Work' (2000) 100 *Columbia Law Rev.* 1881–964; N. Fraser, 'After the Family Wage: A Postindustrial Thought Experiment' in *Justice Interruptus: Critical Reflections on the 'Postsocialist' Condition* (1997) 41–66.
30 Quinn, op. cit., n. 24, p. 448.
31 Cooper identifies four problems with the valorization of care as 'normative care', namely, its normalization of 'endogenous' harms, conceptual slippage, discursive abstraction, cultural specificity, and the idealization of existing relationships: D. Cooper, '"Well, you go there to get off": Visiting feminist care ethics through a women's bathhouse' (2007) 8 *Feminist Theory* 243.
32 P. Tsoukala, 'Gary Becker, Legal Feminism, and the Costs of Moralizing Care' (2007) 16 *Columbia J. of Gender and Law* 357, at 383.
33 id., p. 363.
34 id., p. 404.
35 id.
36 K. Franke, 'Theorizing Yes: An Essay on Feminism, Law and Desire' (2001) 101 *Columbia Law Rev.* 181; M.A. Case, 'How High the Apple Pie? A Few Troubling Questions About Where, Why, and How the Burden of Care for Children Should be Shifted' (2001) 76 *Chicago-Kent Law Rev.* 1753–86; M. McCluskey, 'Caring for Workers' (2003) 55 *Maine Law Rev.* 314–33.

120

because of its productive but unpaid nature rely on 'an idea of household production that sounds in economics but ultimately borrows little from economics as an analytic method'.[37] There is thus a reluctance to engage with New Home Economics on its own terms, pointing instead to the problematic nature of the assumptions or normative goals of economic analysis.[38]

This discussion of the household economy primarily in terms of the family and the unpaid and non-valued labour of housewives vis-à-vis undertaking paid work in the market suggests an eerie re-instantiation of the private-public dichotomy and their accompanying logics, which Olsen had earlier sought to deconstruct. Some feminists have sought to problematize this slide. Martha McCluskey in *Caring for Workers*[39] brilliantly delineates the female reproductive labour needed to nurture male labourers who are market participants rather than focusing simply on childcare carried out within the private realm of the household. This allows a Class-Crit like McCluskey to produce a class-based critique of the law by suggesting that it subsidizes families with a high-wage earning husband and non-working wife. Similarly, feminist legal realists[40] like Halley and Rittich problematize the exceptional status of the family as a legal category, which does concrete distributional work through specific rules and the bounded concept of family law itself.[41] They instead propose the 'economic family' to put the nuclear family back into the 'context of the economically functioning household in which they live'.[42] Halley, in particular, shows how, historically speaking, both the terms 'economy' and 'family' originally referred to the household but became untethered from it through the era of modern liberal capitalism to now refer to the market and nuclear family respectively.[43] Not only that, the distinction between the market and family became further crystallized into an opposition.[44] Thus, where the term 'economy' in its Attic Greek version means household management, feminists have made considerable conceptual hay of this etymological nugget[45] by resisting the contemporary loss of reference of the 'economic' to the household.

Despite these efforts, the emphasis of much American feminist legal theory has been on a particular form of the family vis-à-vis the market rather

37 Tsoukala, op. cit., n. 32.
38 id., pp. 373–4.
39 McCluskey, op. cit., n. 36.
40 J. Halley, 'After Gender: Tools for Progressives in a Shift from Sexual Domination to the Economic Family' (2011) 31 *Pace Law Rev.* 887.
41 Halley and Rittich, op. cit., n. 21, p. 756.
42 id., p. 758. For a similar move, see R. Ellickson, *The Household: Informal Order Around the Hearth* (2008).
43 Halley, op. cit., n. 40.
44 id., pp. 894–5.
45 M. Ertman, 'The Business of Intimacy: Bridging the Private-Private Distinction' in Fineman and Dougherty, op. cit., n. 7, p. 467; Halley and Rittich, op. cit., n. 21, p. 758.

than on the household which sources reproductive labourers from the informal economy or alternate market settings where reproductive labour is purchased (such as the brothel or the surrogacy hostel). We can attribute this to a more fundamental academic division of labour within American feminist legal theory, between cultural feminists who are influential in the care-work debates and radical feminists who dominate debates around women's reproductive labour in the market understood under the banner of 'violence.' This division of labour has emerged against the backdrop of what Mariana Valverde calls 'a dual shift in theoretical scale' in feminist legal theory, at least one of which is significant for us, namely, a shift in geographical and jurisdictional focus away from the domestic to the transnational.[46] According to Valverde, the shift has had the unintended effect of burying or at the very least backgrounding the feminist critique of 'ordinary' marriage in the West.[47]

To elaborate in terms of the sex-work debates, where American radical feminists like Kathleen Barry and Catharine MacKinnon have had considerable traction internationally, the move that Valverde describes has the double effect of exceptionalizing bargains struck between men and women outside of marriage as necessarily violent and harmful while normalizing the heteropatriarchal family through the mode of what Halley calls family law exceptionalism. The larger effect is the glorification of the housewife and her work[48] and the victimization of the whore whose labour is denied. This division of labour amongst feminists is, interestingly, homologous with a substantive legal division of labour. Violence in the form of sex work and 'sex trafficking' belongs to the public, increasingly transnational sphere, needing the strongest form of state protection through criminal law. Care work meanwhile occupies the domestic legal space requiring some combination of family law and market-based devices to further women's claims to equality and redistribution, reflecting the legal eclecticism of cultural feminists when compared to their radical feminist counterparts.

The radical feminist reliance on criminal law in particular is perplexing, given its legal formalism and the assumption that state law can unilaterally suppress the market. This is not only at odds with the strong oppositional stance that women's movements have typically had against state power, but also with feminist legal scholarship, which has been anything but beholden to legal formalism. Feminist legal scholars have carried forth a range of legal realist and socio-legal insights into the functioning of the law. Indeed, a classic text in the socio-legal canon, 'Bargaining in the Shadow of the Law',

46 M. Valverde, 'The Re-Scaling of Feminist Analyses of Law and State Power: From (Domestic) Subjectivity to (Transnational) Governance Networks' (2013) 3 *UC Irvine Law Rev.* 1, at 2.
47 id., pp. 2, 4.
48 Tsoukala, op. cit., n. 32, p. 396.

122

was on divorce,[49] so feminists have always been attuned to the sociological insight that social norms operate alongside formal legal rules and that bargains are indeed struck in the shadow of formal state law. Feminists have also drawn on the central insights of legal realism, particularly, the significance of background legal rules, which influence the bargaining power of a social actor in any given situation. Hence the magisterial investigation by Katherine Silbaugh[50] of the plethora of legal rules that influence the valuation of household labour ranging from family law through to tort law, welfare law, bankruptcy law, tax law, and labour law. More recently, Halley and Rittich arguing against the exceptionalist legal treatment of the family through family law (FL) have backgrounded legal rules into several categories ranging from FL1, the subject matter of family law textbooks to FL2 (tax, immigration, bankruptcy laws), FL3 (tenancy law, employment rules, labour laws) and FL4 (incorporating norms around the household). Feminists have also been keenly attuned to the distributional consequences of specific rule changes and legal reforms.[51]

'ANTI-MARKET' FUNDAMENTALISM IN THE SEX-WORK DEBATES

Strong anti-commodification arguments have been a hallmark of feminist legal theorizing on the market. Debates on the sale of sex for money in particular mark the highpoint of commodification anxiety amongst feminists. The paradox is that where legal feminists have undertaken sophisticated analyses to render visible women's *unpaid* labour within the home, one would have thought naming a *paid* form of labour as such would have posed no major challenge. Yet, in the mid-1990s commodification anxiety extended even to household labour,[52] with scepticism about an exchange/ bargain model for understanding relations within the family, comparing production within the market and the family, and the commodification of family life.[53] This is a fear that has persisted in feminist legal scholarship.[54] The absolutist opposition of the radical feminists (also called abolitionists because they equate sex work with slavery) to the market is then hardly surprising. For them, 'sexual exploitation is a political condition, the foundation of women's subordination and the base from which discrimi-

49 R.H. Mnookin and L. Kornhauser, 'Bargaining in the Shadow of the Law: The Case of Divorce' (1979) 88 *Yale Law J.* 950–97.
50 K. Silbaugh, 'Turning Labor into Love: Housework and the Law' (1996) 91 *Northwestern University Law Rev.* 1–86.
51 Halley and Rittich, op. cit., n. 21; Case, op. cit., n 36; Franke, op. cit., n. 36.
52 Silbaugh, op. cit., n. 50.
53 Estin, op. cit., n. 13, p. 438.
54 Tsoukala, op. cit., n. 32, p. 383.

nation against women is constructed and enacted.'[55] Exploitation here is a *political* rather than an *economic* condition. Consistent with what Viviana Zelizer calls the 'Hostile Worlds' view,[56] where sex and the market may not intermingle, sex as an integral dimension of the human being[57] is 'a positive human experience'[58] *outside* of structured patriarchal power as such. Within the harm-centred narrative of sex work, the fact of commodification is the foundational harm that sex workers suffer.[59]

Interestingly, despite the influence of Margaret Radin's thoughtfully nuanced *Contested Commodities*[60] on feminists writing about the market, by 2005, they were warning that the 'Hamlet question of whether "to commodify or not to commodify" only serves to confuse'.[61] Indeed, even in the care-work debates, a legitimate feminist position now not only had to value women's household work but also had to remunerate it.[62] The parallel shift in the sex-work debates produced a keener appreciation for the role of the market but instead of reversing its anti-commodification stance, only intensified it. As I discuss elsewhere,[63] radical feminist abolitionists have of late trained their lens on the materiality of sex work, including, by addressing broad questions of political economy, pegging a country's development to the stage of its sex sector and by offering a theory that apparently deals with sexual *exploitation* instead of sexual *domination*. Their ultimate goal, however, is to de-commodify sex work by simply abolishing sex markets. I will focus here only on the regulatory dimension of the shift in the radical feminist position.

Radical feminists had for long opposed decriminalization and legalization in terms of deleterious economic outcomes, namely, a *domino effect* that would create a larger sex industry without any benefits for sex workers.[64]

---

55 K. Barry, *The Prostitution of Sexuality* (1995) 11.
56 In the 'Hostile Worlds' view, intermingling between intimate social relations and monetary transfers produces 'moral contamination and degradation': V. Zelizer, 'The Purchase of Intimacy' (2000) 25 *Law & Social Inquiry* 818. In the 'Nothing But' approach, the purchase of intimacy is reducible to a rationally conducted exchange or an expression of prevailing cultural values or coercion (id.) The 'Differentiated Ties' view is the only one to acknowledge the variety of social relations, each marked by a distinctive pattern of payment which mediate the purchase of intimacy (id., p. 819).
57 Barry, op. cit., n. 55, p. 33.
58 id., p. 57.
59 id., p. 112.
60 M. Radin, *Contested Commodities* (1996).
61 J. Williams and V. Zelizer, 'To Commodify or Not to Commodify: That Is *Not* the Question' in *Rethinking Commodification Cases and Readings in Law and Culture*, eds. M. Ertman and J. Williams (2005) 362, at 368.
62 Tsoukala, op. cit., n. 32, p. 395.
63 Kotiswaran, op. cit., n. 9.
64 M. Farley, '"Bad for the Body, Bad for the Heart": Prostitution Harms Women Even if Legalized or Decriminalized' (2004) 10 *Violence Against Women* 1087, at 1099; S. Jeffreys, *The Industrial Vagina: The Political Economy of the Global Sex Trade* (2009) 177.

124

The current radical feminist proposal to criminalize the demand for sexual services (customers) but not the supply (sex workers), however, explicitly relies on market logic. A confessional moment from one radical feminist reveals her reluctant embrace of such logic: 'This may be labelled simplistic, unnuanced, or conceptually impaired; however, a prostitution market without male consumers would go broke.'[65] Yet this very economic analysis is not carried through to assess if and how the costs of increased criminalization may well be ultimately borne by sex workers. In other words, the engagement with economic method is peripheral as the complex unintended consequences, economic or otherwise, flowing from policy options are ignored.

Paradoxically, despite the polar-opposite political motivations and regulatory agendas that distinguish radical feminists from mainstream economists and their law and economics counterparts, they all believe in the radical separability of and the disembedded relation between the market and the social sphere. While mainstream economists call on the state to desist from regulation, radical feminists call on the state to use all its powers to pry open the market from the social so as to de-commodify it. In the process, the legal realist emphasis on the importance of background rules disappears (except perhaps for the call to eliminate poverty) as well as socio-legal insights into the complex interaction between formal state law, informal social norms, and market structures. So, where scholars draw on legal realism as a way to counter the 'market fundamentalism' of neoclassical economics, that is, 'an exaggerated reverence for market self-regulation',[66] for radical feminists, their earlier legal realist impulses have morphed into 'anti-market' fundamentalism. This disembedded view of the market adds another dimension to the radical feminist complicity with conservative and neoliberal political agendas.[67]

REVISITING METHOD, OR A CALL FOR FEMINIST LEGAL ETHNOGRAPHY (AT LEAST SOME OF THE TIME)

From my short survey, discomfort with economic methodology seems to explain at least in part the problematic nature of feminist legal engagement with the market.[68] Beyond rejecting the 'economic man' of neoclassical

---

65 J. Raymond, 'Prostitution on Demand: Legalizing the Buyers as Sexual Consumers' (2004) 10 *Violence Against Women* 1156, at 1160.

66 Block, this volume, p. 28.

67 E. Bernstein, 'Militarized Humanitarianism Meets Carceral Feminism: The Politics of Sex, Rights, and Freedom in Contemporary Antitrafficking Campaigns' (2010) 36 *Signs: J. of Women in Culture and Society* 45–71.

68 Estin, op. cit., n. 13, p. 424; D. Kennedy, *Sexy Dressing: Essays on the Power and Politics of Cultural Identity* (1993); Tsoukala, op. cit., n. 32, p. 361.

125

economics, feminists disagree over whether to reject economic analysis within the law altogether or use it to challenge the gendered power dynamic within the law[69] or simply view it as occasionally interesting and useful.[70] Yet, in both the care-work debates and the sex-work debates, feminists have failed to engage with economic analysis on its own terms even while they draw on it in a limited way. This is a missed opportunity for feminist legal scholars because, although they are right to problematize the usefulness of neoclassical economic analysis, they could well counter it on its own terms as Tsoukala does[71] or draw on the emerging field of feminist economics.[72] However, the quest for feminist methodologies need not be restricted to the use of economic method alone. Indeed, one might pursue empirical study as an alternate path. Care-work feminists have so far tended to emphasize normative critique rather than empirical research, possibly given their pressing need to problematize the influence of law and economics writing on the family. Radical feminists on the other hand engage in little empirical work on sex sectors. Yet empirical work is particularly germane for the feminist study of economies of women's labour, whether within the household, the market or institutions like the informal economy, which glue these together.

The use of the empirical method is a significant aspect of ESL. While not all ESL scholars conduct empirical work, Swedberg identifies the field's task as the production of 'careful empirical studies of the role that law and regulations play in the economic sphere'[73] so as to understand not what the law proclaims but how it operates on an everyday basis.[74] Swedberg, in fact, identifies the lack of empirical research in both law and economics and the Marxist sociology of law as the basis for developing the field of ESL.[75] Interestingly, this call coincides with a resurgence of interest in empirical scholarship in the American legal academy from proponents of empirical legal studies as well as new legal realism. It would be safe to say that empirical work in ESL is likely to be aligned with new legal realism, with its 'methodological diversity, theoretical grounding, and sensitive translation', its interest in 'integrating research from cross-cultural and global arenas',[76] and an orientation towards the role of law in everyday life.[77] Importantly,

69 Fineman and Dougherty, op. cit., n. 7, p. xvi.
70 Estin, op. cit., n. 13, p. 439.
71 Tsoukala, op. cit., n. 32.
72 I offer a rather rudimentary analysis based on feminist economics for sex work: Kotiswaran, op. cit., n. 9, ch. 6.
73 Swedberg, op. cit., n. 1, pp. 2, 12.
74 id., p. 30.
75 id., p. 1.
76 M. Suchman and E. Mertz, 'Toward a New Legal Empiricism: Empirical Legal Studies and New Legal Realism' (2010) 6 *Annual Rev. of Law and Social Sci.* 555–79, at 564.
77 id., at p. 562.

any feminist turn to empirical legal work would be wary as new legal realists are, of an 'overinflated reliance on poor research' simply for the sake of empiricism.[78] Indeed, such an endeavour would benefit from an ethnographic sensibility or even the 1980s notion of 'feminist praxis' or action research if not a strictly ethnographic method requiring extended periods in the field, for which feminist legal scholars are anyway not trained.

I offer some caveats about the need for feminist legal scholars to do empirical work before highlighting possible benefits. We can certainly access the insights of empirical work without visiting the field by simply remaining porous to feminist disciplines that theorize the economy, such as international political economy (IPE). Recent examples include a special issue of *Signs* coedited by a political theorist and a law academic on feminist approaches to IPE, with hardly a reference to the angst of inter-disciplinary scholarship,[79] and Stewart's rich, synthetic account of feminist legal theory and IPE embodied in her idea of 'body work chains'.[80] We might filter into our legal analysis notions such as the 'care diamond,' where social reproduction is provided through the market, state, community, and the family[81] or the 'global household' as an economic actor and macroeconomic category.[82] I am also not suggesting that we look to empirical work to resolve or defer what are fundamentally ideological differences amongst feminists on issues of women's labour. Meanwhile, legal ethnography with its incredible attention to social actors on the ground and their complex motivations may well mystify our understanding of how the law works,[83] offering solutions that are incommensurate with feminist desires for change. Finally, empirical work may be especially insightful when we seek to resignify certain activities as 'economic' or in contexts such as the postcolonial, which demand new theoretical vocabularies or even the transnational setting of much feminist law-making. Here, Sally Merry's call for a deterritorialized ethnography identifying the 'flows' rather than 'sites' of 'processes of legal knowledge production, circulation and appropriation' is particularly resonant.[84]

Increasingly, transnational economic phenomena such as sex work, care work, trafficking, and surrogacy involve complicated global service chains.

78 id., at pp. 561–2.
79 K. Bedford and S. Rai, 'Feminists Theorize International Political Economy' (2010) 36 *Signs: J. of Women in Culture and Society* 1–18.
80 A. Stewart, *Gender, Law and Justice in a Global Market* (2011) 30.
81 Bedford and Rai, op. cit., n. 79, p. 7.
82 M. Safri and J. Graham, 'The Global Household: Toward a Feminist Postcapitalist International Political Economy' (2010) 36 *Signs: J. of Women in Culture and Society* 99–125.
83 Y. Blank, 'Critical Re-enchantment and the Seduction of Political Theology' (2013) 3 *UC Irvine Law Rev.* 6–7. Blank here is referring to the critical legal tradition rather than empirical legal work as such.
84 S. Merry, 'New Legal Realism and the Ethnography of Transnational Law' (2006) 31 *Law and Social Inquiry* 977.

Dominant strains of feminist legal theory and their anti-market stance have produced a political disconnect between feminists and reproductive labourers in these markets who are increasingly mobilizing outside women's movements. This is particularly true for sex workers, whose social marginality means they have little policy 'voice', but also applies to surrogates who have a significant 'collective action' problem. Empirical work undertaken with an ethnographic sensibility is one way to address this crisis of political representation for feminism. Further, where the 'hostile worlds' view of intimacy and the market have for long denied women remuneration,[85] feminist legal ethnography can restore economic agency by delineating how women are rational economic actors at least some of the time. Indeed, stay-at-home moms can be 'rational profit maximizers in an exchange in which they have their own moves to play'.[86] Rather than a straightforward capitulation to neo-classical economic logic, this offers possibilities for a renewed feminist research agenda.

In more concrete terms, ethnographic work can problematize the centrality of gender to feminist legal analysis. Indeed, feminist thought is no stranger to such provocations, which have emerged from a vast literature around difference and from queer theory. Davina Cooper, for instance, uses her case study of the Toronto Women's Bathhouse to argue against 'normative care', and its tendency to valorize rather than critique care.[87] Empirical work can further this impulse through renewed understandings of the varied material stakes of legal subjects in labour markets, their differential interests in the legal system, and how their interests intersect or conflict with those of female reproductive labourers and how these women's interests themselves far from align with each other. Thus the care-work debates can be recast as centrally being about intra-gender allocations between the nanny, au pair, housekeeper, all with a range of varied legal endowments, on the one hand, and the working mother, on the other. The sex work debates would particularly benefit from the knowledge that there is no one category of 'sex worker' and that sex workers' legal interests are often at odds with each other.

More broadly, empirical work can help de-exceptionalize the exclusive location of reproductive labourers in particular institutional settings and clarify the precise interrelations between these domains. Thus, sex workers do not work in a brothel all their lives; they marry and exit the sex industry but may return to sex work supplemented with income from the informal economy. Housewives meanwhile may perform regular or ad-hoc sex work to supplement their household income. Similarly, surrogates, often married mothers, straddle the institutional domains of the family and market. These

---

85 F. Block, 'Relational Work in Market Economies: An Introduction' (2012) 40 *Politics and Society* 135, at 137.
86 Tsoukala, op. cit., n. 32, p. 410.
87 Cooper, op. cit., n. 31, p. 254.

insights are not novel for feminists; materialist feminists were eloquent about the interrelations between the factory, marriage, and sex work, but these insights arose organically from their political lives in social movements. This lost dimension of feminist experience and theory is multiplied several times over in influential Western feminist interventions informed by what Valverde calls universalist and trans-historical ideas of gender and patriarchal power.[88]

Feminist legal scholars consistently draw on legal realism to delineate the complex web of background legal rules that affect women's lives. While ethnographic work is not essential to identify these rules, which may be numerous, it is invaluable in assessing their importance in a given context. Thus, during my field work in Sonagachi, a large Indian red-light area, it became apparent fairly quickly that the state's rent-control law and the social norms and economic stakes that had developed around it were equally if not more important than the anti-sex work criminal law. Perplexingly, no sociological or legal account of sex work in India or elsewhere had mentioned tenancy laws let alone rent-control laws, highlighting once again the crucial need for feminist legal ethnography. Feminist legal realists may have identified tenancy laws as well as contract law, family law, urban development law, and labour law as germane, yet only ethnographic work would point to the salience of investigating rent-control laws rather than, say, contract law. This becomes all the more significant when we approach law in legal pluralist terms, thus going beyond formal state law to capture a range of small-bore rules governing the household or pathways,[89] social norms, and market practices.

A significant drawback of the feminist legal scholarship on the market has been its inability to predict the unintended consequences of well-meaning legal reforms. Thus, in the sex-work debates, the internationally popular Swedish model of criminalizing the customer but not the sex worker is predicated on a radical feminist analysis of sex work. Yet, even a pre-liminary economic analysis will reveal that this model is highly likely to harm the very sex workers that it is meant to help. This is confirmed by sociological studies.[90] My analysis of its implications for Sonagachi enabled by a study of its complex political economy further suggested that the Swedish model, if enforced, would in fact produce windfall gains for the red-light area's landlords. It would eliminate brothels and free debt-bonded sex workers. Although the remaining independent sex workers in a stabilized post-enforcement scenario would probably earn more than before, they would lose the security of numbers in the red-light area and be subject to less risk-averse customers. Most likely, however, given the high levels of police corruption in this sector worldwide, the costs of increased criminalization in

---

88 Valverde, op. cit., n. 46.
89 Ellickson, op. cit., n. 42.
90 E. Bernstein, *Temporarily Yours, Intimacy, Authenticity and the Commerce of Sex* (2007).

the form of bribes would end up being borne by sex workers themselves. Such critique is not directed solely against radical feminist proposals for prostitution law reform. Against the sheer heterogeneity of sex workers in Sonagachi, I show how even labour rights legislation will in fact only benefit certain sex workers and hurt others.[91] Similarly, in the care-work debates, studies show that the more secure a homemaker in the post-divorce scenario, the more likely she is to stay at home. Thus, legal regimes that protect homemakers well upon divorce also produce the highest incidence of a traditional sexual division of labour.[92] It is precisely such counter-intuitive consequences of proposed regulation that feminist ethnographies can alert us to. In the following sections, I will take up the promise of legal ethnographic work in the context of trafficking and surrogacy.

TRAFFICKING

Some of the most significant feminist legal successes in the past decade have been at the international level. One such success was the adoption by the United Nations of the 2000 Protocol to Prevent, Suppress and Punish Trafficking Against Persons, Especially Women and Children ('UN Protocol')[93] supplementing the 2000 United Nations Convention Against Transnational Organized Crime.[94] Countries have signed and ratified it at a spectacular rate. Article 3(a) of the UN Protocol defines 'trafficking in persons' as broadly covering the recruitment, transportation or harbouring of persons, by means of the threat or use of force or other forms of coercion, of abduction, of fraud, of deception, of the abuse of power or of a position of vulnerability or of the giving or receiving of payments or benefits to achieve the consent of a person having control over another person, for the purpose of exploitation. Exploitation is listed as including the exploitation of the prostitution of others or other forms of sexual exploitation, forced labour or services, slavery or practices similar to slavery, servitude or the removal of organs. A victim's consent to the listed exploitation is irrelevant where any of the listed means of trafficking have been used.

The drafting and the implementation to date of the UN Protocol have been mired in deep ideological differences over the status of commercial sex work. Not unsurprisingly, trafficking has been regularly conflated with trafficking for sex work and trafficking for sex work with sex work, while trafficking for purposes other than sex work receives limited attention. The

---

91 Kotiswaran, op. cit., n. 9.
92 Tsoukala, op. cit., n. 32, p. 425.
93 G.A. Res. 25, Annex II, UN GAOR, 55th Sess., Supp. No. 49, at 60, UN Doc. A/45/49 (Vol. I) (2001).
94 Transnational Organized Crime, G.A. Res. 53/111, UN GAOR, 53rd Sess., 85th plen. Mtg., UN Doc. A/RES/53/111 (1998).

130

international anti-trafficking regime is also thought to promote Western states' agendas of migration and border control.[95] This critique of anti-trafficking law has been put forth by scholars and activists, feminists and non-feminists alike, who all resist the normative capture of the trafficking issue in terms of organized crime and want to reframe it fundamentally as an issue of labour migration.

Despite this ringing critique of anti-trafficking law, the jurisprudence around it is somewhat scarce. As the Open-ended Interim Working Group on the UN Protocol recently observed, 'important concepts contained in the Protocol are not clearly understood and, therefore, are not being consistently implemented and applied.'[96] Moreover, the central legal concepts in the definition of trafficking, namely, the means and purpose of trafficking both span a continuum of possibilities. The means of trafficking can involve anything from legally recognizable and fairly narrowly construed notions of coercion, deception, fraud, and abduction to the capacious outlier concept of the abuse of a position of vulnerability. Similarly, although Article 3 points to specific labour conditions that constitute exploitation and are understood as such under international law, this list is not exhaustive and could extend to working conditions best described as precarious, exploitative, and norma-tively reprehensible. Given this malleability of the offence of trafficking, states can tailor the trafficking offence to suit domestic conditions. Even as domestic legal regimes continue to negotiate these definitional parameters of the means and purpose of trafficking, there remains a tremendous disconnect between legal scholarship, on the one hand, and labour and migration studies, on the other. Labour and migration scholars continually delineate patterns of exploitation in labour markets without ever using the term trafficking. Legal scholars are meanwhile keen to identify discrete instances of trafficking but are frustrated by the unwillingness of labour scholars to draw relatively clear boundaries between trafficking and just 'bad work'. Legal ethnographers, I suggest, are well equipped to bridge this gap, given their familiarity with legal doctrine and the empirical lives of legal concepts so as to enable translations back into renewed conceptual understandings.

Rhacel Parreñas's recent book, *Illicit Flirtations*, on Filipina migrant hostesses working in Japan, exemplifies how ethnographic work can illumi-nate legal concepts.[97] In popular discourse, the sexualized nature of hostess work renders hostesses as trafficked sex workers although they are fully

---

95 J. Chuang, 'Rescuing Trafficking from Ideological Capture: Prostitution Reform and Anti-Trafficking Law and Policy' (2010) 158 *University of Pennsylvania Law Rev.* 1655; J. Hathaway, 'The Human Rights Quagmire of "Human Trafficking"' (2008) 49 *Virginia J. of International Law* 1–59.

96 UN Office on Drugs and Crime, *Issue Paper on Abuse of a Position of Vulnerability and Other 'Means' Within the Definition of Trafficking in Persons* (2012).

97 R. Parreñas, *Illicit Flirtations: Labor, Migration and Sex Trafficking in Tokyo* (2011).

aware of the nature of the work entailed when they apply for entertainer visas. Yet, the Japanese government recently tightened requirements for granting these visas, producing a sharp drop in the number of applications. This easy-fix solution, however, fails to address the indentured working conditions of migrant hostesses. Parreñas's ethnography exposes the labyrinth of contracts that hostesses enter into with the Japanese club, the Japanese promotion manager, and the Filipino recruitment agent and talent manager. Under these contracts and related social practices, hostesses bear all the costs of migration while receiving a fraction of what is legally due to them, resulting in what Parreñas calls 'indentured mobility'. Thus, the buffer of Filipino managers and agencies meant to safeguard migrants under Philippine emigration law creates the very conditions for trafficking.[98] Parreñas's work illustrates how an empirically informed understanding of labour markets can generate understandings of both the structural coercion that leads to trafficking (rather than one-off instances of deceit and fraud) as well as of the exploitation generated by a matrix of contracts legally entered into between parties.

Most significantly, ethnographies of labour markets challenge the simplistic remedies of rescue and rehabilitation proposed to target trafficking. Bonded labourers are known to mock the rescue efforts of NGOs who erroneously assume they were tricked into bondage;[99] some prefer not to be released, as they have no alternative.[100] In the United States, trafficked victims who availed themselves of a T-visa to continue living there find themselves prone not just to 'unsafe and dangerous working conditions but also to reexploitation'.[101] In a globalized economy rife with precarious labour, a robust redistributive agenda focused on workers' rights seems more compelling than rescuing trafficked victims and rehabilitating them by offering training for low-paying jobs.

TRANSNATIONAL SURROGACY

My second example for illustrating the empirical method pertains to the transnational surrogacy market of which India is emerging as a major hub. The normative landscape is familiar with scholars and activists who call for

---

98 id., pp. 51, 56.
99 J. Breman and I. Guérin, 'On Bondage: Old and New' in *India's Unfree Workforce: Of Bondage Old and New*, eds. J. Breman, I. Guérin, and A. Prakash (2009) 1, at 12.
100 I. Guérin and G. Venkatasubramanian, 'Corridors of Migration and Chains of Dependence: Brick Kiln Moulders in Tamil Nadu' in Breman et al. (eds.), id., p. 188.
101 D. Brennan, 'Key Issues in the Resettlement of Formerly Trafficked Persons in the United States' (2010) 158 *University of Pennsylvania Law Rev.* 1581, at 1600, 1602.

the ban of commercial surrogacy, terming it 'reproductive trafficking',[102] in contrast to medical professionals actively pursuing a surrogacy practice who call for its legalization. Most feminists, however, realize that banning commercial surrogacy is impossible at this stage of the industry's development and demand stricter regulation by the state. A permissive legal regime wherein non-binding guidelines of the Indian Council of Medical Research regulate surrogacy, coupled with competitive prices for medical services, have spurred a vibrant market for surrogacy in India. Far from engaging with the complexities of surrogacy as an issue, I will simply show how an economic sociology of law could alter a conventional feminist legal analysis that might get mired in a vortex of debates over objectification, commodification, subordination, and exploitation.[103]

Drawing on my recent interviews with seven prominent infertility clinics in four Indian cities, I offer some description of the market before returning to one of the key provisions of the proposed Assisted Reproductive Technologies (Regulation) Bill 2010 ('ART Bill'). Everywhere I went, there were already reams of newspaper reports covering surrogacy, not to mention blogs from commissioning parents and clinics, even as in-depth academic accounts of the industry's political economy are yet to appear. The media had come and gone. Even the Oprah show had visited, which some practitioners claim was a significant marker for the surge in international demand for surrogacy. Press coverage is currently preoccupied not with the novelty of surrogacy but with scandal – reporting on greedy surrogates, minors who had died donating their eggs too often and too soon, and of clinics sprouting in the hinterland where 'quacks' promised surrogacy but delivered babies born of mothers inseminated by local donors. The domino effects of a market gone wild are for all to see. As I spent time in waiting rooms for chronically over-booked fertility doctors, the pace of business was brisk. There were brochures to be handed out, 'packages' to be pitched, bills to be settled, medicines to be dispensed to expectant surrogates, babies to be delivered, and grateful parents to be sent back home to their countries with baby and exit visas in hand. Interestingly, the most successful fertility clinics that perform surrogacy in India today recruit surrogates and gamete donors, perform the in-vitro fertilization (IVF) procedures, operate a surrogacy hostel for surrogates and, finally, deliver the babies, apart from informally facilitating travel, accommodation, and birth registration and visa formalities for foreign couples.

102 M. Rao, 'Why All Non-Altruistic Surrogacy Should Be Banned' *Economic & Political Weekly*, 26 May 2012; U. Smerdon, 'Crossing Bodies, Crossing Borders: International surrogacy between the United States and India' (2008–2009) 39 *Cumberland Law Rev.* 15–85.

103 Kim Kraweic's work on ART is an exception: K. Kraweic, 'Altruism and Intermediation in the Market for Babies' (2009) 66 *Washington & Lee Law Rev.* 203–57.

The proposed ART Bill when passed by the Indian Parliament will be one of the most permissive laws in the world, permitting commissioning parents to remunerate surrogates for surrogacy services. The Bill, whose drafting committee included several pro-surrogacy medical practitioners, seeks to break the monopoly of the ART clinic over the surrogacy process. The goal is to achieve a functional separation between the ART clinic and ART bank such that the all-important job of recruiting gamete donors and surrogates is performed by the ART bank while the ART clinic is limited to performing only the IVF procedures. Yet even preliminary field-work suggests that this is unlikely to work, not only because it is relatively easy to legally register two separate entities controlled by the same enterprise. In a market where surrogates and commissioning parents are divided by huge disparities in power and social status, as well as cultural distance in the case of foreign commissioning parents, the role of the doctor is crucial to cementing a multi-faceted transaction that lasts over a fairly significant period of time, namely, ten months. The doctor has to mould the highly stigmatized act of reproducing for another into an act of altruism without upsetting the hetero-patriarchal deal at either end and while mobilizing racial difference so that the baby is ultimately handed over to the commissioning parents. Indeed, it is this mediating role of the doctor, which is a combination of maintaining and consolidating class interests but also exercising benevolent oversight over illiterate, yet equally devious surrogates (not unlike their domestic 'servants') that calls for performing an enormous amount of immaterial labour[104] and the building of emotional and cultural capital.

The surrogacy transactions I describe are best understood through Zelizer's concept of 'relational work', namely, a process of defining the nature of connections between the connected worlds of intimacy and the market by contrasting it with other known types of relationships, defining their transactions, and identifying the appropriate media of exchange.[105] The relational work performed by doctors at the reputable clinics explains at least in part their high rate of positive surrogacy outcomes and their steady supply of surrogates who recruit friends and relatives by word of mouth. Consequently, these clinics also had a strong aversion to any risk of reputational damage. The immaterial labours of doctors also explain why many of them felt that the proposed legislative aim to functionally separate the ART bank and ART clinic made little sense. On the flip side, the high level of relational work that a successful surrogacy practice demands meant that not all fertility doctors wanted to perform surrogacy. Both male and female doctors that I interviewed spoke of the 'headache' of managing surrogates and commissioning parents who were both demanding. Thus, any attempt to regulate transnational surrogacy would be misguided in not accounting for the pivotal

---

104 Parreñas, op. cit., n. 97, p. 90.
105 Block, this volume, p. 41.

role of doctors' relational work in facilitating the surrogacy transaction from beginning to end. Feminist legal scholarship informed by ESL's focus on the transaction at hand would then not only offer more tailored policy proposals (for example, regulate the surrogacy hostel, unionize surrogates, stipulate a minimum remuneration) but also temper overstated fears of the domino effect of the market.

CONCLUSION

In this article I have tried to delineate some of the ways in which American feminist legal scholars have theorized the market. Feminists made pioneering critical legal moves drawing on the legal realism of the 1930s, by deconstructing the family-market dichotomy and building a tradition of non-formalist legal scholarship. Thus, where an economic sociology of law has focused on the legal dimensions of the relationship between the economy and society refracted through the dichotomies of private/public, market/state, feminist legal scholars have powerfully introduced a third point of reference, namely, that of the household. Just as materialist feminists warned us that the exploitation of wage labour could not be comprehended without understanding women's domestic slavery, it seems clear that no plausible project for a contemporary economic sociology of law can afford to ignore the household.

Having made this crucial contribution, however, the family-market dichotomy has not only persisted within American legal feminism but has become consolidated under the watch of both cultural feminism and radical feminism. Feminists have either adopted a moralistic view of women's care work performed within the family or a structuralist opposition to the market as in the case of sex work. Here, the departures of American feminist legal theory from a mainstream social theory dominated by Marxism via cultural feminism and radical feminism were perhaps essential. Yet, there is a sense that feminists have outdone themselves. Thus Valverde reads MacKinnonite radical feminism as essentially Althusserian but without the benefit of the 'motor forces of history' and therefore universal and transhistorical, in effect, 'even more structured ... less "agentic", than that of the hardest of hard-line structuralist Marxists.'[106] The resultant theorization of the sexual subordination of women has led feminists down the path of carceral feminism,[107] with feminist calls on the state for increased criminalization. Similarly, care-work feminists need to be careful about valorizing care with emerging forms of 'inclusive neo-liberalism' which are reliant on 'female

---

106 Valverde, op. cit., n. 46, p. 8.
107 E. Bernstein, 'The Sexual Politics of the "New Abolitionism"' (2007) 18 *Differences: J. of Feminist Cultural Studies* 128–51.

135

altruism at the service of the state'.[108] Against this backdrop, I have argued that an economic sociology of law pursued in ethnographic terms can render more complex feminist stories about the law and the varied institutional and transactional settings of the economy, while enhancing the feminist legal realist project of drawing out background rules and practices to assess the law's distributive effects on differentially situated groups of men and women. As feminist legal theory comes to power, it owes itself this.

108 Bedford and Rai, op. cit., n. 79, p. 8, citing Molyneux.

JOURNAL OF LAW AND SOCIETY
VOLUME 40, NUMBER 1, MARCH 2013
ISSN: 0263-323X, pp. 137–54

Law, Social Policy, and the Constitution of Markets and Profit Making

KENNETH VEITCH*

This article explores the relationship between law, society, and economy in the context of the contemporary British welfare state. Drawing on themes in Polanyi's The Great Transformation, *it identifies the constitutive role of contemporary social policy and law in the creation and maintenance of markets and opportunities for the private sector in the field of welfare, focusing on the institutional mechanisms being put in place to encourage this. What emerges is a reformulation of the function of the welfare state and related law, as these are no longer predominantly driven by a logic of social protection via redistribution to those in need, but increasingly reflect the state's desire to create openings for the private sector within welfare. The institutions that once contributed to ensuring the embeddedness of the market economy in society now play an important role in processes of disembedding – with potentially detrimental consequences for those seeking assistance from the welfare state.*

INTRODUCTION

Social policy and related legislation present an opportunity to consider fundamental issues of law, economy, and society and, importantly, the interplay between them. As such, they form fertile subjects for engaging with an economic sociology of law. In recent years, however, there has been a tendency in some academic literature to treat them as if they were distinct entities. The standard analysis and critique of neoliberalism, for instance, conceptualizes the development of the so-called self-regulating market as

* Sussex Law School, School of Law, Politics and Sociology, Friston Building, University of Sussex, Falmer, Brighton BN1 9SP, England
K.J.Veitch@sussex.ac.uk

I thank the organizers of the workshop on 'Towards and Economic Sociology of Law' – Amanda Perry-Kessaris, Diamond Ashiagbor, and Prabha Kotiswaran – and Scott Veitch for their helpful comments on a previous written draft of this article.

137

demanding a corresponding diminution of the social or welfare state. The result is that the social and the economic appear in conflict with each other, with the economic sphere being viewed as unable to function properly where the social persists.[1] This article challenges this portrayal of neoliberalism by exploring the connections between law, economy, and society. Specifically, it identifies the constitutive role of contemporary law and social policy in creating and maintaining markets and opportunities for profit making within the welfare sector.[2]

In one sense, social policy has always been bound up with questions and problems of economy. The welfare state illustrates this vividly. Thus, through discharging its core function of protecting citizens against the economic and social risks of capitalism, welfare institutions indirectly assisted the capitalist mode of production. For instance, publicly funded health care and education benefited employers by ensuring a flow of healthy, knowledgeable, and skilled workers. What can be witnessed today, however, is a more direct role for social policy and related legislation in supporting capital – something that has implications for assumptions surrounding the traditional functions of the welfare state. Via a focus on recent developments and reforms within health care and unemployment policy and law, the article develops an analysis of the types of institutional mechanisms that are being deployed to facilitate the implementation of this more direct role of social policy and law.

In order to frame the discussion and analysis, the article draws on some themes and concepts from a work that has to a degree inspired the development of economic sociology and the nascent economic sociology of law – namely, Karl Polanyi's *The Great Transformation*.[3] Two specific features of Polanyi's work render it useful in the present context. The first is his idea of the embeddedness of the market economy in society and social relations; the second is the stress he places on state intervention as an indispensable element in the construction of markets. Those features of his work provide a conceptual framework through which to reflect on the important changes in the roles of current social policy and law. On the one hand, it allows for a focus on their constitutive functions in respect of markets and opportunities for profit making for the private sector within the field of welfare. Specifically, it directs us to consider the types of institutional mechanisms – including the forms of law and social relations – that have, and are being,

1 See, for example, D. Harvey, *A Brief History of Neoliberalism* (2007).
2 The article is therefore in keeping with literature that stresses the centrality of the state and social relations to the development, maintenance, and success of markets and neoliberalism. See, for example, N. Fligstein, *The Architecture of Markets: An Economic Sociology of Twenty-First-Century Capitalist Societies* (2002); L. Wacquant, 'Three Steps to a Historical Anthropology of Actually Existing Neoliberalism' (2012) 20 *Social Anthropology* 66; and P. Bourdieu, *The Social Structures of the Economy* (2005).
3 K. Polanyi, *The Great Transformation: The Political and Economic Origins of Our Time* (2001/1944).

created for the purpose of facilitating such objectives. On the other hand, it confronts us with key questions regarding the degree to which the welfare state continues to operate as a source of social protection for citizens against the consequences and risks flowing from capitalism. As we will see, in some circumstances today's social policy and law are being deployed in ways that create conditions for precisely the production of such consequences and risks.

THE RECIPROCAL RELATIONSHIP BETWEEN SOCIAL AND ECONOMIC POLICY

One of the many virtues of Polanyi's *The Great Transformation* is its insight that a self-adjusting market (what he also calls the market economy) cannot exist for any length of time before it results in the destruction of natural and human life.[4] This state of affairs would mean:

> no less than the running of society as an adjunct to the market. Instead of economy being embedded in social relations, social relations are embedded in the economic system ... For once the economic system is organized in separate institutions, based on specific motives and conferring a special status, society must be shaped in such a manner as to allow that system to function according to its own laws.[5]

Famously, Polanyi goes on to illustrate this scenario by reference to the dangers arising from the fictitious commodification of land, labour, and money that emerged at the end of the eighteenth century and tightened its grip during the nineteenth. Rather than land and labour 'form[ing] part of the social organization itself',[6] as was the case in the mercantile system, these natural and human elements of society became subject to the price mechanism, the operation of which was to have devastating social consequences. Disembedded from social organization and thrust under a system operating on the principles of gain and 'unconscious growth',[7] the functions of land and labour shifted from the non-economic to the economic, and society had to take measures to protect itself. Moreover, Polanyi stresses that the self-regulating market was not some sort of free-floating entity that emerged out of thin air and operated without support of any kind. Rather, state intervention was crucial in establishing and enforcing the doctrine of laissez-faire and the operation of the self-regulating market. As Polanyi notes of the 1830s and 1840s, there emerges 'an enormous increase in the administrative functions of the state, which was now being endowed with a central bureaucracy able to fulfil the tasks set by the adherents of liberalism.'[8]

4 id.
5 id., p. 60.
6 id., p. 72.
7 id., p. 35.
8 id., p. 145.

Against this backdrop, Polanyi's thesis is that the economic system must always be embedded in social relations if it is to function for the benefit of society. He notes the types of measures society was adopting to protect itself against the self-regulating market. Thus, for example, he charts the development from the 1870s of strong trades unions that negotiate wages and conditions of labour outside of the self-regulating market. Moreover, such measures had as their objective non-monetary interests such as 'professional status, safety and security, the form of a man's life, the breadth of his existence, the stability of his environment'.[9] It was the need for social protection to address the 'social interests of different cross sections of the population [...] threatened by the market' that mattered.[10] According to Polanyi, such measures had restored the social embeddedness of market economy and thereby ensured the indivisibility of the economic, the political, and the social. This, he said, reflected Robert Owen's insistence 'on the *social* approach'[11] within New Lanark in Scotland:

> New Lanark had taught [Owen] that in a worker's life wages was only one among many factors such as natural and home surroundings, quality and prices of commodities, stability of employment, and security of tenure ... The education of children and adults, provision for entertainment, dance, and music, and the general assumption of high moral and personal standards of old and young created the atmosphere in which a new status was attained by the industrial population as a whole.[12]

For present purposes, two aspects should be noted from Polanyi's book: the first is the importance placed on the social embeddedness of markets as the sine qua non of the maintenance of society; the second, related to this and especially relevant here, is that for the social embeddedness thesis to be meaningful, the self-protective measures adopted by society from the 1870s onwards had to serve non-economic interests ('the form of a man's life, the breadth of his existence', and so on.). That is, they had to ensure that markets and the economy were rooted in the organization of society and reflected the non-economic interests and values associated with man's life.

Published in 1944, Polanyi's book appeared just before the establishment in the United Kingdom of the institutions of societal self-protection that have come to be known collectively as the welfare state. Before assessing whether and how some recent examples of social policy and law sit within Polanyi's embeddedness framework, it is necessary to get a sense of how the relationship between economic and social policy has played out over the course of the welfare state's history. We can usefully do so by referring to some of Bob Jessop's work on the capitalist state.

9 id., p. 161.
10 id., p. 162.
11 id., p. 178 (emphasis in original).
12 id.

In *The Future of the Capitalist State*,[13] Jessop develops an ideal typical analysis of what he identifies as the two dominant forms of capitalist state in the post-war era – the Keynesian Welfare National State (KWNS) and the Schumpeterian Competition State or Schumpeterian Workfare Postnational Regime (SWPR). Two points from his analysis are relevant for present purposes. First, Jessop stresses what he calls 'the regulation approach' to capitalism, which posits that stable capital accumulation is unlikely to result from the operation of market forces alone. Rather, it requires the intervention of the state and other 'non-market mechanisms'. These 'shap[e] the dynamic of accumulation as well as being shaped by that dynamic.'[14] In other words, accumulation (economic) regimes and political regimes coevolve. Moreover, 'choices among economic and social policies are typically linked to prevailing accumulation strategies, state projects, hegemonic projects and more general philosophical and normative views of the good society.'[15] Secondly, in this context, Jessop explores the changing productive role of social policy in capital accumulation regimes since the war – something he argues is often overlooked in analyses that concentrate on the decommodifiying and redistributive features of the welfare state. Let us now look briefly at this second aspect of his work in the context of the two features of social policy that will form the focus of the reflections in the remainder of the article.

Jessop first discusses what he calls 'the social reproduction of labour-power as a fictitious commodity'. In the era of the KWNS, the state, rather than families and/or liberal market forces, becomes the key player in this reproduction. Here, the socialization of life risks occurs via a system of comprehensive and (near-)universal measures designed to redistribute wealth to those in need. Access to these measures was based mainly on 'past, present or future participation in the labour market and/or on national citizenship.'[16] In contrast, within the SWPR or Workfare State we have witnessed what Jessop describes as 'the increasing subordination of social policy to economic policy'.[17] This occurs primarily as a result of internationalization and the need for national states to remain economically competitive, lest they risk capital flight. In those circumstances, the welfare state comes to be viewed as both an onerous cost of production and an obstacle to a flexible labour market – the latter deemed to be necessary in order to remain economically competitive. The welfare state was therefore redesigned in order to reduce costs and to help facilitate and enhance the establishment of flexible labour markets. One of the mechanisms through

---

13 B. Jessop, *The Future of the Capitalist State* (2002).
14 id., p. 1.
15 id., p. 44.
16 id., p. 150.
17 On this theme, see J. Clarke, 'Subordinating the Social? Neo-liberalism and the Remaking of Welfare Capitalism' (2007) 21 *Cultural Studies* 974.

which this occurred was (and is) workfare – a social policy that makes the receipt of state unemployment benefit conditional upon signing, and complying with, a contract stipulating a variety of work-related activities to be undertaken with a view to returning the unemployed to the labour market. Those 'active' labour policies differ from the KWNS's 'passive' system of unemployment support, where the unemployed were effectively unconditionally entitled to receive state support. Today, the discourse is firmly one of obligation and Jessop notes that it reflects 'a general movement away from the social democratic tradition'.[18] We will return to workfare later.

Jessop also highlights the shift away from 'collective consumption' in today's SWPR. Collective consumption – the publicly organized and financed provision of goods and services, such as education, health, and housing by a particular form of national state – has given way 'to more market- and/or third sector solutions to the socialization of consumption'.[19] Features indicative of this trend include the following: (i) an increased role for the private and third sector[20] in the provision of social services, which may involve, for instance, outright privatization or such provision by those sectors combined with public payment, or the application of market discourse and practices within a publicly funded and provided service (such as the implementation of the internal market within the United Kingdom's National Health Service (NHS) in the 1990s); and (ii) greater reliance on public-private partnerships as a mode of governance within the welfare sector. In other words, the function of social policy is no longer simply to ensure the public financing of publicly delivered social services. The prising open of this monopoly to include the involvement of the private sector means that social policy is, at least in part, now specifically designed to facilitate opportunities for profit making.

Jessop's work on the reciprocal relationship between economic and social policy since the 1940s presents two key issues that might fruitfully be refracted through the prism of Polanyi's work, outlined earlier. First, there is a suggestion that social policy and the institution created for the purpose of society's self-protection against the detrimental social consequences produced by capitalism – the welfare state – have been redesigned in order, predominantly, to support the very source of those consequences – that is, capitalism. This is at odds with the impact of the forms of social protection that Polanyi charted from the 1870s onwards as these, he argued, ensured

---

18 Jessop, op. cit., n. 13, p. 155 (reference omitted).
19 id., p. 162.
20 According to the House of Commons Public Accounts Committee, the third sector includes 'voluntary and community organisations, charities and social enterprises, ranging from small local community groups to large, established, national and international organisations.' HC Public Accounts Committee, Thirty-seventh Report, *Building the Capacity of the Third Sector* HC (2009) 436, 1.

142

that the economic system became re-embedded in the social – that is, that those measures protected non-monetary interests, such as 'the form of a man's life' and 'the breadth of his existence'. In Polanyi's terminology, this contemporary shift in the predominant function of social policy and the welfare state from a source of social protection for citizens to a facilitator of markets and opportunities for profit making represents a disembedding of the economy from social relations, resulting in 'the running of society as an adjunct to the market'. Moreover, we encounter here a reversal of Polanyi's double movement thesis, in which forms of social protection are created in order to ameliorate the deleterious effects of markets; rather, the institutional forms of social protection today shed at least part of this protective function and are deployed, instead, towards ends the social consequences of which the welfare state traditionally offered protection against. The result is a disembedding of the economy by means of, among others, institutions formerly associated with ensuring its embeddedness.

If establishing markets and facilitating opportunities to obtain profit are core functions of social policy today, then a second issue arises. This involves identifying what kinds of mechanisms, including legal ones, are used for this purpose, and what forms of social relations are expressed through those mechanisms. Here, we are less concerned with Polanyi's concept of embeddedness and more with his observation, reiterated by Jessop, that state intervention is crucial in establishing and maintaining markets and possibilities for capital accumulation. In particular, it is the *political* formulation and deployment of a variety of institutions and institutional mechanisms, and through these, the construction and use of specific forms of social relation, that must be the focus of attention here. As Loïc Wacquant argues, what is required when trying to grasp the slippery phenomenon of neoliberalism is a shift from 'a "thin" economic conception centred on the market to a "thick" sociological conception centred on the state that specifies the institutional machinery involved in the establishment of market dominance ...'.[21]

By reference to two examples from recent social policy and law, the following section illustrates the relevance of those two themes in Polanyi's work for understanding the constitutive role of social policy and law in establishing and maintaining markets and opportunities for profit making within the welfare sector.

21 Wacquant, op. cit., n. 2, p. 71.

143

CONSTITUTING MARKETS AND PROFIT MAKING OPPORTUNITIES – HEALTH CARE AND WORKFARE

1. *Solidarity and reforming the National Health Service (NHS)*

The first mechanism that is increasingly deployed for the purpose of establishing and maintaining markets and opportunities for profit accumulation is the monetary fund through which social services within the welfare state are traditionally paid for. The operating principle of this type of fund is solidarity. This denotes that citizens' resources are pooled for the purpose of spreading risk and that there is an element of redistribution within society. The management of social risks is therefore not merely the preserve of those who can afford to purchase private insurance; rather, it is undertaken by the state on behalf of non-owners of insurance. While this redistributive aspect of the fund has traditionally implemented an underlying concern for social justice and the protection against social risk of those lacking means, as Alain Supiot notes, there is also an impersonal element to this 'welfare state' form of solidarity. For while founded on the redistributive ethos described, the system posits a formal set of social relations amongst citizens, rather than one based on close local or customary social bonds. Citizens therefore make payments to bureaucratic institutions and then bring claims for access to social goods and services such as health care and pensions. This lends a technical quality to the system.[22]

The argument advanced here is twofold. First, there is evidence in contemporary social policy that points to the use of this monetary fund and certain types of law to create and sustain markets and opportunities for profit making within the field of welfare. The result is a novel form of redistribution – that is, from the public to the private sector – which, as we shall see, has implications for our understanding of solidarity and the use to which the social relations characteristic of this principle are put. Secondly, the impact of these changes has the potential to result in a disembedding of the economy from society as the resources of the welfare state no longer necessarily operate to protect those in need from the consequences of capitalism.

Some recent developments in the NHS serve to illustrate those arguments. One is the prominent role of public-private partnerships (PPPs, formerly the Private Finance Initiative) as ways of funding new NHS hospital buildings. Here, private contractors raise the money to finance the construction of hospitals for the NHS and, via the PPP contract, own and manage the hospital. The NHS Primary Care Trust leases the hospital and staff, such as cleaners, from the contractors, paying what is known as a 'unitary charge' for these from their annual health care budget. Contracts last for periods

---

22 See A. Supiot, *Homo Juridicus: On the Anthropological Function of the Law* (2007) 207–12.

ranging from 25–30 years, although once they are paid off, the NHS does not necessarily end up owning the premises. The PPP scheme has been the object of cogent critique.[23] As well as being a social cost in monetary terms – that is, a mechanism by which to facilitate the accumulation of capital and profit via the redistribution of money from public funds[24] – it also has potential social costs in human terms, as the often onerous contractual obligations to pay for PPP financed buildings can jeopardize the existence of NHS hospitals, thereby endangering the treatment of patients.[25]

Aspects of the recent reforms to the NHS in England confirm this trend. The Health and Social Care Act 2012 replaces primary care trusts with clinical commissioning groups (CCGs) as the bodies responsible for commissioning (purchasing) most health care services within the NHS (a task that will involve responsibility for spending £80 billion of NHS resources). By 2016, it will become possible for CCGs to outsource their commissioning work to non-public bodies – including private firms. A market will therefore effectively be created for such services and be funded from the NHS budget. The legislation also promotes the 'any qualified provider' approach to the provision of NHS health care services – meaning there will be increased scope for, among other things, private health care providers to become involved in the provision of NHS health care. The scope for private sector involvement is also heightened by the promotion of 'fair and effective' competition and the application of competition law to the commissioning of NHS treatment for the first time. The sector specific regulator for health care – Monitor – is under a duty to promote provision of health care services which is 'economic, efficient and effective', and to exercise its functions in a manner that will prevent anti-competitive behaviour in health care provision that is against patient's interests.[26] It will also be able to tackle specific abuses and unjustifiable restrictions that demonstrably act against patients' interests by deploying its licensing powers and, where relevant, the Competition Act 1998. The effect will be to alter the current situation, in

23 See, for instance, A.M. Pollock, *NHS plc: The Privatisation of Our Health Care* (2004).
24 An analysis by the *Guardian* newspaper in 2012 found that the current 717 PFI contracts, while having a total capital value of £54.7bn, would have an ultimate cost of £301bn once paid off: *Guardian*, 6 July 2012, 1, 18. As Hellowell and Pollock note, one of the reasons for this inflated cost is that 'the cost of finance on PFI schemes is higher than is the case for publicly financed schemes ...': M. Hellowell and A.M. Pollock, 'The Private Financing of NHS Hospitals: Politics, Policy and Practice' (2009) 29 *Economic Affairs* 13. There is also evidence of a so-called secondary market in PFI shareholdings in hospitals, schools, roads, and prisons. See BBC Radio 4's *File on 4* programme 'PFI Profits', broadcast 19 June 2011.
25 The recent placing of South London Healthcare Trust into administration owing to an unsustainable deficit created by the contractual obligation to pay PFI costs is a case in point. Also, see Hellowell and Pollock, id.
26 Health and Social Care Act 2012, s. 62. What the phrase 'against patients' interests' means is unclear.

145

which the bulk of NHS services are commissioned from public bodies, by creating a level playing field in which private providers of health care can compete to deliver NHS healthcare services. CCGs will need, in effect, to ensure that a tendering process for the provision of NHS services is in place, if they are not to fall foul of competition law.

Those developments and reforms do not mean that redistribution in the original sense of that term, described above, no longer occurs within the NHS or that patients must now pay to access NHS services; access to treatment based on clinical need rather than the ability to pay continues to be advanced as a core principle of the NHS across the political spectrum.[27] Nor is it claimed that those recent policies disclose the first instance of any type of relationship between the NHS and capital. For instance, it could be argued that since its inception the NHS has maintained in good condition what Marx referred to as 'a disposable industrial reserve army'.[28] But the NHS was not originally designed to be a source of capital accumulation and profit making in itself – that is, as an institution the private sector became directly involved in running or helping to manage. The policies and legislation described above indicate that this has changed.

The shift entails a political reformulation of the ends to which public resources are directed. This manifests itself in the public fund being made to adopt another redistributive dimension – namely, to act as a direct source for the extraction of private wealth. It also has implications for the idea of the socialization of risk that lies at the heart of the principle of solidarity, as its meaning is no longer confined to describing the community's pooling of resources to the end of protecting its members against the risk of *social* misfortune (such as illness); rather, as, for example, PPPs demonstrate, it also incorporates the deployment of this common fund to protect those in the private sector from a variety of *economic* risks. As Pollock et al. note of PFI (now PPP) contracts, they rarely transfer economic risks to the funding consortium, with the result that these usually fall on the public and its purse. For instance: 'Where a Trust wishes to terminate a contract, either because of poor performance or insolvency of the private consortium, it still has to pay the consortium's financing costs, even though the latter is in default.'[29] This social protection from economic risk might be thought to have a more general meaning too in that making available the welfare state's public funds for the private sector opens up an invaluable source of income and potential

---

27 'It is our privilege to be custodians of the NHS, its values and principles. We believe that the NHS is an integral part of a Big Society, reflecting the social solidarity of shared access to collective healthcare, and a shared responsibility to use resources effectively to deliver better health.' Department of Health, *Equity and Excellence: Liberating the NHS* (2010; Cm. 7881) 7, para. 1.1.

28 K. Marx, *Capital: A Critique of Political Economy, Volume 1* (1976) 784, and, generally, 781–802.

29 A.M. Pollock et al., 'Private Finance and "Value for Money" in NHS Hospitals: A Policy in Search of a Rationale?' (2002) 324 *British Medical J.* 1205, at 1208–09.

146

market and profit-making opportunities at times, such as the present, of sluggish economic growth at the macro level. Importantly, though, this shift in the function of the socialization of risk has the concomitant effect of exposing the community and its members to a diminution in the level of social protection as money is diverted away from core services to the interests of capital – something that dilutes the original redistributive objective of the fund.

Legally, this novel function of the socialization of risk might be conceptualized as a case of joint and several liability, not merely in the familiar sense of debtors being held jointly and severally liable only for their own debts, but in the sense of a group being ascribed such a liability for the debts or costs or harms of others outside of the group too. In the context of the foregoing examples, this means that, by the medium of contract, taxpayers become jointly and severally liable for repaying the significant costs of PPP building projects, including costs flowing from any default on the part of the private funding consortium. In turn, and perversely, citizens also become liable for the *social costs* they themselves suffer (lack of access to adequate health care, say) as these flow from the liability to pay the financial costs of PPPs from public resources. Andreas Wildt's description of the Roman Law concept from which the idea of solidarity originates – *obligatio in solidum* – assists in highlighting some of the themes involved in this contemporary set of arrangements:

> To be the cosignatory of a loan means that one is liable for the reversals of fortunes of another; that one's own economic well-being is no longer completely in one's own hands ... The bonds of fraternal recognition ... are not blood bonds in this Roman conception, nor are they affective. Neither genes nor love, but liability is the bonding force. We are bound together with those with whom, like it or not, our own fates and our own well-being are interwoven. That, and not a sum of money to be repaid, is the sense of the acknowledgement of debt.[30]

The developments described above demonstrate the state's extension of the type of solidarity associated with the operation of a welfare institution such as the NHS. For no longer is the community of taxpayers solely 'liable for the reversals of [social] fortunes' of others within the group – that is, those who become ill. Additionally, through the legal institution of contract, this community's liability is extended to embrace the costs and risks and harms of those operating in the private sector. And while sums of money do indeed need to be repaid (and paid) by the community to this sector, the underlying source of this obligation is the political creation of a bond between the public and the private, the social and the economic. Through its contracts with the private sector, the state increasingly binds the social and economic 'fates' and 'well-being' of its citizens to the private sector, its agents, and market

---

30 A. Wildt, 'Solidarity: Its History and Contemporary Definition' in *Solidarity*, ed. K. Bayertz (1999) 6 (reference omitted).

147

mechanisms such that they become interwoven, or inextricably linked, with these.

What this scenario reveals then is the indispensability of a key welfare institution and its large fund of public resources for the prospects of capital and profit accumulation within the NHS. It also demonstrates how the state moulds this welfare institution and its underlying mode of social relations (solidarity) to work towards those ends. Together with competition and contract law, these become crucial institutional mechanisms for realizing the political desire to develop markets and increase the role of the private sector.

2. Workfare, contract, and social relations

We saw earlier that workfare serves capital by supporting the flexible labour markets that are deemed necessary to ensure countries' economies are, and remain, competitive.[31] But what does this social policy reveal about the type of institutional mechanism deployed by the state to produce this market-friendly outcome? And what form of social relations is expressed through this mechanism?

The workfare contract – or 'claimant commitment', as it is now known after the implementation of the Welfare Reform Act 2012 (WRA 2012) – is the social policy mechanism used by the state to support flexible labour markets. The choice of contract is important as it presents a powerful image of the person and social relations that is intuitively attractive and worthy of support, especially in today's consumer-driven society. This image is founded upon a liberal political rationality that conceives of the self as a rational, self-determining agent, who makes autonomous choices about whether to enter agreements based upon self-assessments of individual utility. As such, the workfare contract does not, in theory at least, compel welfare beneficiaries to sign up to it; rather, it emphasizes the importance of consent, negotiation, and reciprocity in the construction of the agreement. In other words, it envisages formal equality between the contracting parties. This is important as it means that, by being deemed to have voluntarily chosen to enter into the contract, welfare recipients can be taken to have freely negotiated and accepted the responsibilities under the agreement. In other words, they can be assumed to have bound themselves to the obligations in the contract – which are that they work, seek work, or undertake training with a view to working in a flexible labour market. As a number of scholars have pointed out, the empirical reality of workfare and other 'social control contracts' does not reflect any practical implementation

---

31 This justification can be seen in the current British government's White Paper on welfare reform, where the existing welfare system is said not to 'reflect the needs of a flexible labour market'. Department for Work and Pensions (DWP), *Universal Credit: Welfare that Works* (2010; Cm. 7957) 10. The new system of Universal Credit will, in contrast, 'drive dynamic labour market effects' (id., p. 58).

148

of the theoretical contract norms such as reciprocity and consent.[32] The truth is that, if the unemployed wish to obtain benefits, they have little option but to accept the conditions in the workfare contract. There is a vast inequality of bargaining power between welfare beneficiaries and welfare state administrators. In one sense, however, this does not really matter, for the crucial point is that, whether or not those contractual norms are replicated in practice, they are treated as if they are. It is the ideological dimension of the workfare contract – that is, its ability to represent unemployment and the solutions to it as revolving around a formally equal set of social relations characterized by matters of individual choice and responsibility – that is important here. Possible structural causes of unemployment, such as flexible labour markets themselves, are obscured, allowing politicians to claim these markets as solutions to the problem, rather than as the problem itself.

Consistent with the ideological dimension of the workfare contract is the threat of the application of financial sanctions for either breaches of the contract or a failure to enter into it at all. This has been a core feature of workfare and has been continued and deepened in the WRA 2012.[33] Essentially, unemployment benefit is reduced in stages depending on the severity and number of contractual breaches, the classification of claimant, and the type of workfare programme. While the presence of those sanctions may confirm the critique that workfare contracts are not based on the norm of consent (for the inevitable reduction in or removal of one's unemployment benefit in the event of non-compliance effectively leaves the claimant with no practical alternative but to agree to the conditions), again it is the ideological aspect of contract – that you must suffer the consequences of breaches of your voluntarily assumed obligations – that is crucial in lending legitimacy to a policy designed to entrench flexible labour markets. Moreover, this punitive element of the workfare contract feeds into more populist notions surrounding those groups assumed to be heavily reliant on welfare benefits – that they are up to no good, lazy, cheating the system, and so on. The call for them to find a job and relieve the taxpayer of unnecessary costs also serves to further contemporary social policy's aim of securing the presence of flexible labour markets and, hence, a more competitive economy.

It could be argued that other mechanisms, such as the Mandatory Work Activity scheme, have been developed with the same objective of maintaining flexible labour markets in mind. Purportedly designed for jobseekers

---

32 See, for example, P. Vincent-Jones, *The New Public Contracting: Regulation, Responsiveness, Relationality* (2006) ch. 9; M. Freedland and D. King, 'Contractual Governance and Illiberal Contracts: Some Problems of Contractualism as an Instrument of Behaviour Management by Agencies of Government' (2003) 27 *Cambridge J. of Economics* 465.

33 For more detail on this, see ss. 26 and 27 of the WRA 2012 and the Act's preceding White Paper, DWP, op. cit., n. 31, ch. 3.

who would 'benefit from experiencing the habits and routines of working life',[34] viewed from another angle it is simply a mechanism for ensuring the flow of free labour for employers operating within flexible labour markets.[35] What all of these mechanisms demonstrate however, is the crucial constitutive role the state plays through its social policy in developing and maintaining flexible labour markets. In that sense they bear out Polanyi's observation that the state's intervention is crucial in establishing and maintaining a market economy.

Workfare also contains elements pointing to a Polanyian disembedding of the economy from society; in other words, the policy is not necessarily designed to protect society and its members from the deleterious human consequences of the operation of markets. On the one hand, this can be seen in the provision for the removal of benefits from those failing to discharge their contractual workfare obligations. On the other hand, by binding beneficiaries to flexible labour markets, jobseekers become subject to the economic and social insecurity associated with this type of market. I have described elsewhere empirical evidence suggesting that those entering the labour market through workfare programmes often find themselves in precarious forms of employment and, eventually, back on benefits – the so-called revolving-door syndrome.[36] Consequently, workfare is very different from the types of protective measures Polanyi described as emerging from the 1870s. Importantly, it would not appear to serve the types of non-economic interest – 'safety and security, the form of a man's life, the breadth of his existence, the stability of his environment' – Polanyi viewed as a condition of embeddedness. Indeed, quite the opposite would appear to be the case, as workfare jeopardizes those interests and threatens to produce what Robert Castel has described as the individual's 'disaffiliation':

> that is, *rupture of the bond within society*. The final outcome, the end of this process, is that economic insecurity becomes destitution and fragility of relationships becomes isolation ... Poverty is revealed as the outcome of a series of breakdowns in belonging and failures to establish bonds, which finally throws the person concerned into a floating state, a sort of *social no-man's land.*[37]

Revealingly, the possibility of disaffiliation in the present context arises through the intervention of the welfare state and its objective of supporting flexible labour markets. It is a social cost *written into the state's social*

---

34 DWP, id., p. 29.
35 The Mandatory Work Activity scheme involves an unpaid full-time work placement lasting a maximum of four weeks.
36 K. Veitch, 'Social Solidarity and the Power of Contract' (2011) 38 *J. of Law and Society* 189.
37 R. Castel, 'The Roads to Disaffiliation: Insecure Work and Vulnerable Relationships' (2000) 24 *International J. of Urban and Regional Research* 519, at 520 (emphases added).

policy – a form of policy originally designed to ameliorate the worst social and economic consequences of capitalism. In Polanyi's terms, not only is this an example of 'the running of society as an adjunct to the market'; it also reveals that the institutions most traditionally associated with embeddedness have today themselves become important vehicles of disembeddedness.

The next, and final, section draws together the article's themes by reflecting upon what implications they might have for our understanding of the relationship between law and the welfare state today.

LAW AND THE CONTEMPORARY WELFARE STATE

Historically, what were the effects of the emergence of the welfare state upon law? Having identified formal rational law as the form of law characteristic of Western modernity and the rise of the capitalist economy, Weber notes the challenges being made to the formal qualities of modern law. With the emergence of the 'modern class problem', there arose '[n]ew demands for a "social law" to be based upon such emotionally colored ethical postulates as "justice" or "human dignity", and directed against the very dominance of a mere business morality'.[38] This results in what Weber calls the materialization of formal law, as law's formal and abstract system of general rules becomes, among other things, more particularistic (designed to further specific economic or social purposes within commercial or labour law, for instance) and involved in the management of class conflict. This dilutes its formal, impartial, and technical character as its function shifts from ensuring the equality of legal subjects before the law to the implementation of particular governmental social policies designed to redress the inequalities arising from capitalism. In other words, with the arrival of the welfare state, the form and function of law alter from those characteristic of the liberal state.[39]

How might the legislation considered in this article fit within this historical trajectory from formal rational law to social law? The first point to note is that it displays elements of social law. Thus the Health and Social Care Act 2012, for example, depicts a welfare system that, despite cuts in expenditure, continues to operate on the principle of solidarity – in the sense

---

38 M. Weber, *Economy and Society* (1978) 886.

39 Weber's identification of the materialization of law has given rise to a sizeable literature on this topic, largely taken up via a focus on the phenomenon of juridification. See, for instance, J. Habermas, *The Theory of Communicative Action – Volume 2: Lifeworld and System* (1987) 356–73; G. Teubner, 'Juridification: Concepts, Aspects, Limits, Solutions' in *Juridification of Social Spheres: A Comparative Analysis in the Areas of Labor, Corporate, Antitrust and Social Welfare Law*, ed. G. Teubner (1987) 3–48; F. Ewald, 'A Concept of Social Law' in *Dilemmas of Law in the Welfare State*, ed. G. Teubner (1986) 40–75. Limitations of space do not allow for a discussion of this literature here.

151

of a social fund in which the community pools risks and there is an element of redistribution. For instance, in principle at least, access to NHS services continues to be based on clinical need, rather than the ability to pay.

But this Act and the WRA 2012 also contain evidence of elements of formal rational law and an image of social relations influenced by the liberal political rationality associated with this form of law. Thus, the possibility of applying competition law to ensure the absence of anti-competitive behaviour introduces a degree of formal equality into the NHS commissioning process, and the use of contract law as the legal mechanism upon which PPPs rest stresses the importance of the formal notion that agreements freely entered into between parties must be upheld. The fact that the outcomes of the implementation of these formal legal processes may not lead, in Weber's words, to "justice" or "human dignity", does not affect their legal validity. This differs from social law, which, François Ewald argues, operates on the basis of "solidarity contracts" – a notion of contract 'founded on ideas of fair distribution or equitable allocation of social burdens and profits'.[40] Similarly, the workfare contract and claimant commitment, while not strictly legal entities, are founded on the same idea of social relations – characterizing jobseekers as self-determining, self-interested actors who freely enter into contracts and accept obligations with a view to maximizing their individual utility. Once again, while entering into the contract or commitment may result in injustice or human indignity (one might think, for instance, of the lack of pay for work undertaken through the Mandatory Work Activity scheme), founding these contracts and commitments upon both this idea of social relations and the formal properties of contract law means that those types of social consequences have no bearing on the legal validity of workfare mechanisms.

Those Acts therefore display elements of both social law and formal rational law. Importantly, the latter functions as a central institutional mechanism through which the welfare state establishes, supports, and maintains markets today (flexible labour markets in the case of workfare and a market for the provision of services and infrastructure in the field of health care). Within the sphere of social policy, formal rational law and its associated liberal form of social relations are therefore constitutive of the development of markets and opportunities for capital accumulation and profit making. Those functions demonstrate one of Polanyi's key arguments, namely, that state intervention is crucial to the establishment and continuation of free markets. Laissez-faire did not require the withdrawal of the state in order to flourish; instead, it demanded constant state policing and assistance. Law, of course, had, and has, an integral role to play in this. Contract and property law, for example, are essential not only in providing, through principles such as freedom of contract, for the protection of private

40 Ewald, id., p. 43.

property rights within an already existing market; they are foundational in *establishing* markets. As Paddy Ireland notes:

> [P]roperty and markets are legal, political and social constructs – the products as well as the objects of regulation; and thus, as a result, not only is the goal of 'deregulation' absurd, the dynamics and rationalities of particular markets are themselves inevitably political and legal products which vary according to the legal rights-obligations-regulatory structures that constitute them.[41]

This brings us to one of the central points to emerge from the analysis undertaken in this article. For the creation of markets and the carving out of opportunities for capital accumulation and profit making in the welfare arena are not the products of formal rational law alone. Rather, they are also 'political and social constructs'. In order to function effectively, formal rational law requires a propitious political and social environment. In the present case, this takes the form of a combination of a large communal resource, based on the principle of solidarity, from which funds can periodically be extracted by the private sector, and the institution of a liberal political rationality within social policy that views social relations as being based on an image of people as self-determining, self-interested actors who voluntarily create their responsibilities through consensual agreements. Given that, politically, it would be unfeasible simply to dismantle welfare institutions and move to a system of private insurance, the desire to use these institutions as sources of economic growth for the private sector requires the careful construction of a legal, political, and social system geared towards this end (a 'state-crafting', to deploy Loïc Wacquant's phrase[42]). While this includes implementing what for the post-war welfare state are new legal mechanisms and political rationalities (albeit they have a much older provenance), it also involves putting what might be called the existing system of public or social wealth at the service of markets, capital accumulation, and profit making. The result is that the solidarity fund takes on an additional redistributive function – redistributing wealth *away* from those for whom it was originally intended and *towards* those who operate the system, namely, the capitalist economy, responsible for producing the need for a welfare state initially. While redistribution to the non-owners of capital still occurs through the welfare system today, there is greater potential for recent social policy, and the type of law it institutes within the welfare system (formal rational law), to produce injustice and human indignity as a result of its concern to further Weber's 'business morality'.

This raises a final point, which is that the form of law increasingly to be found within social policy and legislation becomes complicit in the tendency of the welfare state to produce conditions of social suffering rather than the

41 P. Ireland, 'Law and the Neoliberal Vision: Pension Privatisation, Investor Protection and the Ownership Society' (2011) 62 *Northern Ireland Legal Q.* 1, at 5.
42 Wacquant, op. cit., n. 2.

social protection one had come to expect of it. As social policy becomes concerned with issues of reducing costs by, among other things, furthering the role of the private sector, and with sustaining flexible labour markets, so the form of law deployed to support those objectives begins to become constitutive of an erosion of social protection and the consequences, such as social dislocation and economic insecurity, identified earlier. Here, the law of the welfare state begins to exhibit what Alain Supiot has described in the context of labour law as 'the separation of things and persons'. There, he argues that today 'work figures as a thing divested of the person and available for purchase and sale, and the person features only in the case of "needs" which are so compelling that they cannot be ignored by the collectivity.'[43] But as welfare policy itself is increasingly tailored towards private ends, it too becomes 'divested of the person', as the approach to unemployment benefit via workfare demonstrates. Unlike the protective legislation at the end of the nineteenth century that Polanyi discusses, the legislation described in this article is not exclusively concerned with the protection of non-economic interests, despite the fact that one might consider welfare as indispensable to what Polanyi describes as 'the substance of society'. For welfare – 'the state of faring or doing well: freedom from calamity, etc.'[44] – is inextricably linked to providing the conditions for human beings not simply to exist, but to flourish (of 'doing well'). Health care, education, decent work, and shelter are all preconditions for the realization of this flourishing. The rise of formal rational law within the welfare sector operates as part of an institutional framework responsible for the steady erosion of such an understanding of, and aspiration to, welfare, and its replacement with one in which Weber's 'business morality' begins to dominate.

43 A. Supiot, 'The Dogmatic Foundations of the Market' (2000) 29 *Industrial Law J.* 321, at 339.
44 *Chambers English Dictionary.*

JOURNAL OF LAW AND SOCIETY
VOLUME 40, NUMBER 1, MARCH 2013
ISSN: 0263-323X, pp. 155–71

The Legal Construction of Economic Rationalities?

Andrew T.F. Lang*

This article makes the claim that certain strands of thinking within the sociology of knowledge, including the sociology of science, may provide some of the most powerful intellectual resources for rethinking the role of law within economic life. Starting with an understanding of the 'rationality' of economic actors as a situated social construction, this literature encourages us to explore law's role in the construction, dissemination, and evolution of the structures of knowledge which form the foundation of particular market rationalities. It offers one potential avenue for answering recent calls for further research into the constitutive role of law in economic life.

I. LAW'S CONSTITUTIVE ROLE IN THE ECONOMY

The question of law's constitutive role in economic life was first posed by the institutional economists and legal realists of the early twentieth century. Reacting against mainstream economic thought of the time, which tended to naturalize the market as an essentially spontaneous order, the institutional economists foregrounded questions around the origins, nature, and evolution of the institutional foundations of modern market economies. Veblen, Commons, Mitchell, Ely, Ayres, and others all sought to show how the apparently independent and autonomous sphere of market relations was neither natural nor spontaneously generated, but required a great deal of collective effort to create and sustain. This core thesis was later memorably elaborated in Karl Polanyi's *The Great Transformation*, and is now entrenched as a core tenet of much sociological thinking about economic life.

Within the tradition defined by classical economic thought and its subsequent developments, law is understood as primarily regulative in its effects on economic life. That is to say, it is a mechanism of public

* Department of Law, London School of Economics and Political Science, Houghton Street, London WC2A 2AE, England
a.lang@lse.ac.uk

intervention into a pre-constituted economic sphere, acting to modify pre-existing market logics and pre-existing behavioural dispositions of economic actors. However, once we adopt the anti-naturalizing approach of the institutionalists, and accept the socially and institutionally constructed nature of markets, then our understanding of the relationship between law and markets also changes: markets, it becomes clear, should not be imagined as existing prior to law, but are in part constituted by law. Law's relationship to economic life is both regulative *and* constitutive.[1]

It was the legal realists – especially Robert Hale – who first explored in detail what it meant for law to help 'constitute' economic life. Hale showed, for example, how the relative bargaining power of parties to a market transaction is legally constituted. By defining the rights, duties, privileges, powers, and so on of each party with respect to all economic resources, law bestows different capabilities on each party, fundamentally shapes the alternatives available to each party, and defines the various ways in which (and extent to which) each party can pressure each other in the course of negotiation. Against mainstream economic and political thought of the time, which drew a clear distinction between the 'freedom' of markets and the 'coercion' of government interference through law, Hale argued that 'free markets' were themselves shot through with coercion – and that the state was implicated in such coercion through, among other things, the legal institutions of contract, property, tort, and their associated mechanisms of state enforcement. Similarly, he also showed that market prices are also legally constituted, in part because they represent the expected value stream of specific legal rights associated with the good or service which is the subject of the transaction, and thus depend fundamentally on the content of those rights.[2]

It was a formidable intellectual achievement of this 'first great law and economics movement'[3] simply to draw attention to the constitutive role of law in economic life, and the insights it has yielded are powerful and enduringly relevant. If market prices are themselves recognized to be the product of legal 'intervention', and if free markets are understood to be premised on politically sanctioned coercion, then the distinction fundamental to many contemporary economic debates, between 'free' markets on the one

---

1 For an account which usefully distinguishes between not only the regulative and constitutive but also the facilitative role of law, see L.B. Edelman and R. Stryker, 'A Sociological Approach to Law and the Economy' in *The Handbook of Economic Sociology* (2005, 2nd edn.) 527–51.

2 See, for example, R.L. Hale, 'Coercion and Distribution in a Supposedly Non-Coercive State' (1923) 38 *Political Sci. Q.* 470–94; R.L. Hale, 'Bargaining, Duress, and Economic Liberty' (1943) 43 *Columbia Law Rev.* 603–28; R.L. Hale, 'Force and the State: A Comparison of "Political" and "Economic" Compulsion' (1935) 35 *Columbia Law Rev.* 149–201. See, also, B. Fried, *The Progressive Assault on Laissez Faire: Robert Hale and the First Law and Economics Movement* (2001).

3 H. Hovenkamp, 'The First Great Law & Economics Movement' (1990) 42 *Stanford Law Rev.* 993–1058.

hand and 'coercive' regulatory intervention on the other, makes little sense. Given how far an awareness of law's constitutive role in the economy has drifted from the mainstream of modern economic and legal thought, it is an important insight to recover and develop in contemporary law and economics scholarship. The purpose of this article – in the specific context of a conference on a 'New Economic Sociology of Law' – is to draw attention to one possible path for such development.

II. THE QUESTION OF THE CONSTRUCTION OF THE RATIONAL ECONOMIC SUBJECT

The anti-naturalism of the institutional economists extended not just to their thinking about the nature and evolution of markets, but also to the nature and evolution of individual market *participants* – that is to say, of the rational 'economic man' of mainstream economic thought. Against the mainstream assumption of (a particular form of) rational action, in other words, the institutionalists preferred to 'regard rationality as a phenomenon that varies across actors and social arenas and, therefore, as a phenomenon to be studied and explained'.[4] In common with a number of classical economic socio-logists working around the same time, many of the institutionalists therefore emphasized the constructed nature of *homo economicus*, seeking to show how the particular forms of economic rationality we associate with market behaviour are not natural and unchanging but, rather, emerged historically as the product of particular socio-cultural formations characteristic of early industrializing nations.[5] Veblen, for example, famously explored the cultural foundations of consumption behaviour.[6] Simmel too, working within the closely cognate discipline of sociology, sought to explain the social foundations of the emergence of pecuniary rationality, in part by linking it to the emergence of the institution of money itself.[7] A foundational insight of this period was that the constitutive infrastructure of modern markets – that is, the infrastructure needed to bring markets into being and enable them to function effectively – includes what we might call the motivational founda-tions of modern economic rationality. Markets, in other words, rest not only

---

4 L.B. Edelman, 'Rivers of Law and Contested Terrain: A Law and Society Approach to Economic Rationality' (2004) 38 *Law & Society Rev.* 181–98.

5 G. Hodgson, *The Evolution of Institutional Economics* (2004); W.C. Mitchell, 'The Rationality of Economic Activity' (1910) 18 *J. of Political Economy*1 97–216; W. Sombart, *Der moderne Kapitalismus: Bd. Die Theorie der kapitalistischen Entwicklung* (1902).

6 T. Veblen, *The Theory of the Leisure Class: An Economic Study of Institutions* (1912); T. Veblen, *The Instinct of Workmanship: And the State of Industrial Arts* (1914); T. Veblen, 'The Limitations of Marginal Utility' (1909) 17 *J. of Political Economy* 620.

7 G. Simmel, *The Philosophy of Money* (2004, 3rd edn.).

157

on a bedrock of legal rules which help to define the relations between market participants, but also on the ongoing production of market participants with the recognizable dispositions, motivations, and cognitive characteristics of the calculative *homo economicus*.

Although these and other writers did not say much about it directly, their work on the socio-cultural construction of economic rationalities raised the question of the nature of the relationship between the legal and motivational foundations of markets. More specifically, it raised the prospect that markets are legally constituted 'all the way down': law may be involved, that is to say, not only in constituting the relations between market participants, but also in helping to constitute the habits of thought and forms of rationality characteristic of individual economic agents themselves.

This was not an issue which preoccupied the early twentieth-century legal realists. Even as they showed the ways in which relations between market participants are structured and constituted by law, their analysis tended to take the (rational) individual economic actor herself as given and pre-constituted. That is to say, the individual economic agent appeared in their accounts already encumbered with pre-existing motivations, preferences, and ways of interpreting the world, with law appearing for the most part as a resource to be deployed by such agents in their interactions with one another. Perhaps this is not so surprising, as their task of discrediting the naturalizing impulse of classical economic thought could be performed perfectly well without trespassing on such tricky terrain. Moreover, none of the institutionalist and sociological accounts of the social origins of *homo economicus* had placed law at the centre of their story, so few intellectual resources existed for properly theorizing the relationship between the legal and motivational foundations of markets.

For at least half a century, if not longer, broader intellectual currents conspired to keep the issue of the social-institutional construction of market rationalities out of the mainstream of the disciplines of economics, law, and sociology. In mainstream economics, institutionalism was famously marginalized in favour of highly formalized mathematical approaches which took both the existence of markets and of the stylized rational economic actor as given for the purpose of analysis.[8] For neoclassical economics, rationality was to be assumed, not explained, and research into the motivational foundations of markets came to be seen as falling largely outside the domain of economic analysis. In the discipline of law, the next generation of law and economics scholarship, dating from around the late 1960s, took a similar turn: inspired by neoclassical economics, it also took both markets and rational market participants as given for the purpose of analysis.[9] As a

---

8 G. Hodgson, *How Economics Forgot History: The Problem of Historical Specificity in Social Science* (2001).
9 See, generally, R.A. Posner, *Economic Analysis of Law* (2010, 8th edn.).

158

result, it focused exclusively on the regulatory role of law in the economy, and had little if anything to say about its constitutive aspects. Even subsequent generations of law and economics scholarship, inspired by developments in economics which depart from neoclassical assumptions, have generally not been able adequately to pose the question of law's relationship to the habits of thought of market participants. For example, subject to the qualifications made below, even if the new institutional law and economics has successfully renewed inquiry into the institutional foundations of markets, it has done so in a way which has kept the methodological assumption of the rational actor largely intact.[10] In addition, behavioural law and economics, while centrally concerned with the cognitive processes of economic actors, is focused almost exclusively on cataloguing and explaining real-world departures from theoretical models of economic rationality, and therefore has hardly addressed the construction of rationality itself.[11] Furthermore, because behavioural approaches tend to see cognition and perception as occurring exclusively in the individual's mind, and focus on the *biological* structures of the brain as determinants of cognition, they have also had comparatively little to say about the specifically *social* construction of economic rationality. Finally, even where the rationality assumption was challenged, this was done in a way which put the question of the social construction of rationality to one side. For example, within sociology, particularly after Parsons, work on the socio-cultural foundations of economic rationality was subordinated to an alternative line of attack on rational choice theory: namely, that its image of the self-interested, calculating individual paid inadequate attention to social norms, values, and roles as structural determinants of social behaviour.[12] To say that the assumption of rationality is unrealistic is quite different from saying rationality is socially constructed, and takes one down very different paths of enquiry.

It was in this context that a debate emerged over the course of the 1980s and 1990s between the new institutional economics and the new economic sociology.[13] The new institutional economics crystallized around the late 1970s as an explicit reaction to the acknowledged blind spots of neoclassical economics, and sought to reintroduce the institutional foundations as a legitimate topic of economic analysis. But it did so in a way which self-

---

10 See text accompanying nn. 23–27 below.
11 See, generally, C. Jolls, C.R. Sunstein, and R. Thaler, 'A Behavioral Approach to Law and Economics' (1998) 50 *Stanford Law Rev.* 1471–550; R.B. Korobkin and T.S. Ulen, 'Law and Behavioral Science: Removing the Rationality Assumption from Law and Economics' (2000) 88 *California Law Rev.* 1051–144.
12 See Hodgson, op. cit., n. 8.
13 See, for example, V. Nee and R. Swedberg, 'Economic Sociology and New Institutional Economics' in *Handbook of New Institutional Economics*, eds. C. Ménard and M.M. Shirley (2005) 789–818; J.N. Baron and M.T. Hannan, 'The Impact of Economics on Contemporary Sociology' (1994) 32 *J. of Economic Literature* 1111–46.

159

consciously distanced this new work from the earlier sociological and institutionalist traditions mentioned above. This distance was achieved primarily through the adoption of certain core tenets of neoclassical thought – most importantly, a clear commitment to methodological individualism, as well as a commitment to rational choice and utility maximization as its theory of social action. New institutional economics understood itself, then, to be applying the rigorous methods of neoclassical economics to many of the questions raised by the 'old' institutionalists.[14]

This caught the eye of some contemporary sociologists, and was one of the most important factors which provoked the emergence of the new economic sociology in the 1980s. Granovetter's seminal article introducing his notion of the 'embeddedness' of economic action is one of the classic texts of this period.[15] Taking Williamson as his prime representative of, and interlocutor within, the field of new institutional economics, Granovetter argued that the new institutionalists wrongly adopted an 'undersocialized conception of human action' in which economic actors were imagined as 'affected minimally by social relations'.[16] By contrast, he noted, economic action is and always has been deeply embedded in social relations – by which he meant primarily that the choices and behaviour of economic actors is deeply shaped by their concrete personal relationships and social ties. The networks of social relationships in which economic actors are embedded, he has since argued, affect their access to economic information, help to determine whom they do (and don't) trust in their commercial relationships, and provide meaningful sources of reward for conformity with socially-approved behavioural norms.[17]

Almost three decades later, it goes without saying that Granovetter's intervention was a tremendously productive one, which has led to a rich and diverse literature. For the purposes of this article, however, I simply wish to note that Granovetter's notion of 'embeddedness' did not, in fact, have the effect of returning the question of the social construction of economic rationality to the centre of work in economic sociology. This was because in important ways it represented a development of, rather than a full break from, earlier sociological critiques of rational choice models.[18] Granovetter, it is true, offered the concept of embeddedness as an alternative not just to

---

14 E. Furubotn and R. Richter, *Institutions and Economic Theory: The Contribution of the New Institutional Economics* (2005), especially ch. 1.
15 M. Granovetter, 'Economic Action and Social Structure: The Problem of Embeddedness,' (1985) 91 *Am. J. of Sociology* 481–510.
16 id., at pp. 483, 481.
17 M. Granovetter, 'The Impact of Social Structure on Economic Outcomes' (2005) 19 *J. of Economic Perspectives* 33–50.
18 For a different reading of Granovetter, which sees his work as precisely the forerunner of the work that I shall be drawing on in the next section, see M. Callon, 'Introduction: The Embeddedness of Economic Markets in Economics' in *The Laws of Markets*, ed. M. Callon (1998) 1–57.

160

the 'undersocialized' vision of economic man adopted in rational choice theory, but also to the 'oversocialized' vision of man offered by many sociologists, in which individual choices and actions are largely determined by the norms and values we have internalized from the society in which we live.[19] Nevertheless, there is an important family resemblance between Granovetter's criticism of rational economic man on the one hand and, of the other, those sociological approaches which emphasized the importance of norms, values, and roles in the determination of social action. Put simply, both make the claim that rational choice theory fails to take into account important constitutive forces shaping individual economic action – social norms and values on the one hand, and social relationships on the other – and that certain kinds of rational choice theory as a result provide an *inaccurate* portrait of actual real-world economic behaviour. Just like the earlier emphasis on values and norms, in other words, the notion of embeddedness was used to show that economic actors are not *purely* instrumental, not *purely* rational – at least not in the narrow economic sense – but instead are also subject to 'broader social influences', and pursue 'non-economic' alongside 'economic' goals.[20] This is very different, however, from showing that the meaning of 'rational' action and the content of 'economic' interests are themselves social constructions. For all its advances over the parsimony of rational choice, the theory of embeddedness still takes an apparently unproblematic and uninterrogated vision of pure economic rationality as its point of departure.

Another way of putting this point is to distinguish two different criticisms of undersocialized conceptions of the individual. The first notes that the atomistic vision of materially self-interested calculative rational individuals is a theoretical fiction, that individuals are always subject to influences from their social context, and that it is only once these social influences are taken into account that a fuller, richer, and more realistic account of social action can be developed. The second acknowledges the reality of calculative rationality as a governing principle of economic behaviour, but seeks to enquire into the underlying social processes and formations which enable calculative behaviour, produce atomized individuals, and give the notion of 'rationality' meaning in particular contexts. Although I acknowledge that there are parts of Granovetter's work which support both approaches,[21] my argument here is that it is the first claim which Granovetter articulates most explicitly – and certainly it is the first claim which Granovetter's work has most often been taken to represent by those who have subsequently drawn on his work.

Surprisingly, it was the new institutional economics which took us further down the second line of enquiry than the notion of embeddedness. While I

19 Granovetter, op. cit., n. 15, pp. 483–87.
20 M. Granovetter, 'Economic Institutions as Social Constructions: A Framework for Analysis' (1992) 35 *Acta Sociologica* 3–11, 4.
21 See Callon, op. cit., n. 18.

161

noted earlier that new institutionalist writers in economics explicitly adopted many of the assumptions and methodological commitments of the neoclassical economic tradition, it is also true that there were a number of key respects in which they departed from that tradition. One was the renewed attention that some of them gave to the cognitive and interpretive foundations of rational economic action. Neoclassical economic thought had been able to ignore the problem of cognition and interpretation in economic life largely by two means: first, by assuming that economic actors had complete information; and second, by assuming that processes of feedback and selection would over time serve to correct (at the aggregate level) any significant misperceptions of individual economic actors.[22] Put another way, it was thought that what constitutes 'rational action' in any particular market context would either be self-evident or would reveal itself over time as market actors learnt from experience. On these assumptions, problems of cognition and interpretation thus could be safely ignored, provided only that analysis remained at the aggregate level and focused on medium term outcomes. The possibility of multiple rationalities never arises, and the problem of how 'rationality' is given meaning in a specific market never needs to be addressed.

Crucially, the new institutional economists relaxed these neoclassical assumptions of complete information and perfect rationality in favour of assumptions of *in*complete information and *bounded* rationality.[23] (A consequence of these two moves is the third, and most well-known, departure from neoclassical theory, namely, the assumption of positive transaction costs.) This made it impossible any longer to bracket the question of perception. If economic actors only ever have access to significantly incomplete information, if there are significant limitations on their ability to compute the likely outcomes of their actions, if the economic environment they seek to interpret is increasingly complex, non-ergodic, and subject to continual change, if they are constantly being asked to make once-in-a-lifetime choices for which they have neither experience nor precedent, and if their ability to 'learn' from their mistakes is seriously impeded by confirmation bias and other cognitive blindnesses, then benign assumptions about convergence towards essentially 'correct' interpretations of the causal dynamics of economic life are impossible to sustain.[24] It follows that any theory of economic action must take into account the multiple ways in which economic agents perceive and interpret cause-effect relationships in the economic sphere in which they operate, and the ways in which certain

22 For example, Korobkin and Ulen, op. cit., n. 11, pp. 1070–74.
23 Ménard and Shirley, op. cit., n. 13; Furubotn and Richter, op. cit., n. 14; O.E. Williamson, 'The New Institutional Economics: Taking Stock, Looking Ahead' (2000) 38 *J. of Economic Literature* 595–613.
24 A.T. Denzau and D.C. North, 'Shared Mental Models: Ideologies and Institutions' (1994) 47 *Kyklos* 3–31.

162

perceptions become more dominant or persuasive than others. It becomes necessary, in other words, to build into one's theory of economic life an account of the cognitive frames available to economic agents: the means by which they imagine a particular range of alternative options available to them, and the mental techniques they use to compute the likely consequences of each in relation to their preferences.

Amongst the new institutional economists, it is North who has attempted to develop this line of thinking the furthest, in a series of publications over three decades.[25] His core claim (in this respect) is that any dynamic account of economic life must have at its centre the changing perceptual experience of economic actors: 'the key to understanding the process of [economic] change is the intentionality of the players enacting institutional change, and their comprehension of the issues.'[26] What matters, in other words, are the structures of knowledge available to actors, which make available a limited set of visions of how the economy works, on the basis of which preferences are formulated and strategies adopted. Fundamental economic changes, he argues, are impelled and given direction by underlying transformations in operational knowledge about how the economy works. According to North, therefore, what is needed is an 'explicit specification' of 'what we mean by rationality', which in turn means 'specification of the subjective models people possess' through which they seek to operationalize the content of norms of rationality in specific circumstances.[27] More than that, according to North, we need an account of the social foundations of these models: an account of how they develop, are propagated, given durability, shared amongst social groups, and embedded in the institutional infrastructure of economic life.

North, then, has succeeded in posing precisely the kinds of questions that in my view are usefully raised by the second line of criticism of the undersocialized economic actor set out above – and he has done so from a place not so far from the economic mainstream. However, as North himself has recognized, there is very little within the discipline of economics – certainly within the last 100 years or so of economic thought – which can provide us with adequate theoretical tools. North has turned predominantly to cognitive psychology for inspiration. In my view, however, developments in recent decades in the 'new sociology of knowledge',[28] including the sociology of science, are at least as valuable a resource in this respect as the

---

25 D.C. North, *Understanding the Process of Economic Change* (2005); Denzau and North, id.; D.C. North, *Institutions, Institutional Change and Economic Performance* (1990); D.C. North, 'Economic Performance Through Time' (1994) 84 *Am. Economic Rev.* 359–68; D.C. North, 'Institutions, Ideology and Economic Performance' (1992) 11 *Cato J.* 477–88.
26 North, id. (2005), p. 3.
27 id., p. 64.
28 I take the term from E.D. McCarthy, *Knowledge as Culture: The New Sociology of Knowledge* (1996).

163

insights of cognitive psychology. In the following section, I sketch the outlines of one possible approach to these questions, inspired in part by the work of such figures as Callon, Latour, Knorr-Cetina, Mackenzie, and others who have begun in the last fifteen years or so to deploy the conceptual tools they developed in the sociology and anthropology of scientific knowledge to the analysis of markets and market behaviour.[29]

III. THE COGNITIVE INFRASTRUCTURES OF MODERN MARKETS

In their 2005 article, 'Economic Markets as Calculative Collective Devices', Callon and Muniesa draw attention to what they regard as two different risks to be avoided in the analysis of calculative behaviour in markets.[30] The first, associated with the economism of traditional rational choice theory, is to treat calculative competence as an inherent component of the human brain, and a necessary part of human action. The second is to discard calculation altogether, in favour of models of human decision making based on notions of judgment, intuitive 'feel', rules of thumb, and other not-strictly-calculative processes. Callon and Muniesa attempt to avoid both mistakes by offering a very broad definition of calculative economic action:

> Calculating does not necessarily mean performing mathematical or even numerical operations. Calculation starts by establishing distinctions between things or states of the world, and by imagining or estimating courses of action associated with those things or with those states as well as their consequences.[31]

Calculative action, in this model, is understood in very general terms as goal-oriented action, or action oriented towards a project. Importantly, while their adoption of this starting point does rest on the (intuitively plausible) empirical claim that much social action in the marketplace is calculative in

---

29 See, for example, K. Knorr-Cetina and U. Bruegger, 'Inhabiting Technology: The Global Lifeform of Financial Markets' (2002) 50 *Current Sociology* 389–405; K. Knorr-Cetina and U. Bruegger, 'Traders' Engagement with Markets: A Postsocial Relationship' (2002) 19(5–6) *Theory, Culture & Society* 161–85; K. Knorr-Cetina and U. Bruegger, 'Global Microstructures: The Virtual Societies of Financial Markets' (2002) 107 *Am. J. of Sociology* 905–50; K. Knorr-Cetina and A. Preda, eds., *The Sociology of Financial Markets* (2005); D. MacKenzie, *Material Markets: How Economic Agents Are Constructed* (2008); D. Mackenzie, *An Engine, Not a Camera: How Financial Models Shape Markets* (2006); D. MacKenzie and Y. Millo, 'Constructing a Market, Performing Theory: The Historical Sociology of a Financial Derivatives Exchange' (2003) 109 *Am. J. of Sociology* 107–45; M. Abolafia, *Making Markets: Opportunism and Restraint on Wall Street* (2001); Callon (ed.), op. cit., n. 18; M. Callon and F. Muniesa, 'Peripheral Vision: Economic Markets as Calculative Collective Devices' (2005) 26 *Organization Studies* 1229–50; M. Callon, 'Actor-Network Theory, the Market Test' in *Actor Network Theory and After*, eds. J. Law and J. Hassard (1998) 181–95.
30 Callon and Muniesa, id.
31 id., p. 1231 (references omitted).

this general sense, they do not claim that calculativeness is an *inherent* property of human action, nor that it is the only form that human action can take. Rather, their purpose in proposing such a broad definition of calculation is precisely to set aside questions concerning the nature and various forms of human agency, so as to focus attention on the conditions – in particular, the ideational conditions – which make calculative action possible in the first place.

Calculative action, first of all, requires causal models: a calculative actor, seeking to maximize her utility in a given situation, must deploy causal models of some sort in order to assess the likely consequences of different courses of action available to her, and therefore to choose between them. Take, for example, the practice of trading in foreign exchange markets. A trader's decision to buy or sell a particular currency will depend, self-evidently, on her view of likely future price movements of that currency in light of contemporary economic conditions. Most professional traders will be able articulate their view of the likely effects of (say) a recession in the United States, or a spike in global commodity prices, or a housing crash in Spain, on the price of a range of different major global currencies. Importantly, the causal models that economic actors deploy do not just perform the function of connecting certain actions to certain expected outcomes, they also help to *limit* the set of outcomes which are treated by actors as relevant to their decision-making processes. Precisely because the consequences of any individual action ramify in an almost infinite and certainly incalculable number of directions, if meaningfully calculative action is to be possible, it is necessary to select only a few such consequences for direct consideration. For example, the decisions of traders of futures in certain minerals may well profoundly affect the direction of research and development in the mobile phone industry, with unknowable consequences for the direction of technological development in telecommunications, but if such consequences are invisible to these traders at the moment of decision, or if no clear heuristic is available to estimate meaningfully its nature and magnitude, then it cannot and will not be treated as significant or relevant, and it will not be taken into account in calculative decision making in the market.

Causal models themselves depend for their existence on at least two more basic elements. Operationalizing a causal model in the context of financial trading, to continue the example, requires access to an array of *facts*, as well as an accompanying set of rules for assessing the relevance and significance of each of these facts. Thus, for example, a bond trader needs not just a causal model which connects current economic trends with likely price movements in the bonds she trades, but also the facts about the current economic trends themselves: unemployment rates, rates of growth, interest rates, minutes of Federal Reserve meetings, share prices, inventory levels, and so on. This factual infrastructure, in turn, rests on underlying *practices of categorization and classification*. Calculation starts, as noted above, 'by

165

establishing distinctions between things or states of the world'.[32] Unemployment, for example, must be defined, and particular real-world working practices must be categorized as formal employment or not in the practical production of an official unemployment rate. The value of a company must be defined through particular accounting practices, which classify the various assets, expenditures, and revenues of a business in complicated and not self-evident, but highly consequential, ways.[33]

The first proposition I wish to draw attention to, then, is that behaviour of calculative economic agents in modern economies rests on a vast cognitive infrastructure – causal, factual, and classificatory – which is constantly being put into practice as they go about their various tasks of trading, producing, consuming, managing, and investing economic resources. This cognitive infrastructure helps to constitute particular kinds of economic rationality in the sense that it gives meaning to what counts as 'rational' action in different market contexts. Note that this claim does not proceed by questioning whether or not human beings actually behave in real life in accordance with assumptions of economic rationality, however conceived. Rather, the argument is that norms of rational economic action – defined in such abstract terms as utility maximization and the pursuit of self-interest – are *open-ended*, and that one therefore needs the frameworks of knowledge just described to operationalize and make meaningful an abstract notion of utility maximization in any particular real-world context. Such frameworks of knowledge are necessary, for example, to establish the categories which I use to define my utility, to determine the proximate outcomes which can usefully stand in as a proxy for the attainment of that utility, to determine what actions I can take which are likely to achieve those outcomes, and so on. In this sense, rational economic action is constituted (given meaningful and concrete form in specific contexts) through the structures of knowledge and cognitive infrastructures operating in a particular field of economic practice.

This cognitive infrastructure is informal as well as formal, tacit as well as explicit, local as well as standardized, and lay as well as expert. For example, the knowledge necessary to act competently as a bond trader includes not only official economic data but also such everyday knowledge as the best times of the day to buy or sell, or the etiquette of transactional conversations. It includes not only a knowledge of the core analytical concepts and categories used in professional vocabularies but also a feel for habitual ways of applying such concepts and categories to the facts of everyday life. It includes not just formalized explicit pricing algorithms but also the 'rules of thumb' and habits of mind by which pricing decisions are sometimes instinctively made. And it includes not only generic data sources (unemploy-

32 id.
33 See, for example, P. Miller, 'The Margins of Accounting' in Callon (ed.), op. cit., n. 18, pp. 174–93.

166

ment rates, interest rate spreads, news reports of recent political events) but also local knowledge, including knowledge of the specific way in which certain data tends to be given specific meanings in particular market contexts. For example, a Brazilian bond trader will know that certain types of Brazilian bonds are treated in the market as benchmark assets for emerging-market government bonds as a whole, with the consequence that a very particular array of economic data may be relevant for his valuation of that asset.[34]

A second proposition is that this cognitive infrastructure stands in more than just an instrumental relationship to individual economic actors. It is certainly possible to view calculative technologies as little more than tools in the hands of pre-constituted agents, serving only in marginal ways to shape the decision-making processes of such agents. But this ignores the extent to which the nature and shape of calculative processes themselves are in fact constituted in the organized relation and interaction between an individual and a calculative technology.[35] ('Calculativeness', Callon also reminds us, 'couldn't exist without calculating tools.'[36]) Indeed, the constitutive influence of the cognitive infrastructure described above extends in significant ways to the motivational and evaluative disposition of economic actors. In practice, goals and preferences are often an outcome of calculation and deliberation rather than their starting points.[37] In a similar way, facts tend in practice to be transmitted to an actor in and through a normative frame: 'facts' typically confront actors as part of a causal claim, causal claims are typically formulated in the context of an exhortation to forms of action, and such exhortations presuppose certain evaluative dispositions on the part of the actors they confront. Similarly, economic actors often come to know the world through such mental phenomena as problem definitions, which inseparably combine the production of facts about the world with the diagnosis of a problem, and therefore the implicit or explicit suggestion of possible solutions. The kind of factual knowledge which is deployed in the market, in other words, is always 'knowledge-in-motion', or 'knowledge-with-a-purpose', in the sense that it is never completely divorced from an implicit, accompanying logic of action, and an assumed motivational disposition.

A third and crucial proposition is that these frameworks of knowledge are *social,* in at least three senses. One sense is simply that they are broadly shared – that is to say, different individual economic actors in a particular marketplace tend to operate on the basis of a similar set of facts and conceptual categories, and tend to deploy similar kinds of calculative technologies in similar ways to similar effect. Indeed, this is not merely a

34 MacKenzie, op. cit. (2008), n. 29, p. 91.
35 See id., pp. 13–16; Callon, 'Introduction', op. cit., n. 18.
36 Callon, id., pp. 23 ff.
37 Searle makes this point in J.R. Searle, *The Construction of Social Reality* (1996) 30 ff.

167

happy coincidence but, rather, a crucial condition of possibility of market coordination, since it provides a degree of relative predictability of others' behaviour without which commercial decisions could not be made.[38] Another sense is that the cognitive infrastructure of markets is collectively produced – through statistical agencies, organized market analysis, in the back and forth of water-cooler conversations and email exchanges, and in myriad other contexts – as well as socially distributed. And a final sense in which the cognitive infrastructure of markets is social is that it has an existence 'outside' the heads of individuals.[39] Calculative tools need not always be consciously present in individuals' minds in order to exert a shaping influence on their behaviour. For example, an experienced trader may at times make decisions in the moment on the basis of a 'feel for the market' – an embodied sense of the dynamics of the market – without ever consciously calculating the likely outcomes of her actions. Similarly, a novice trader may initially feel her way through her initial transactions on the basis of what she understands to be a competent performance of being a professional trader. In both cases, the cognitive presuppositions on which such action was based may subsequently be articulated, but they are not directly operative at the moment of decision. Instead, such frameworks are best understood as embedded in the social and physical organization of the trading room, and working through the social and material interactions characteristic of the social practice of trading.[40]

38 See, for example, MacKenzie, op. cit. (2008), n. 29; B.G. Carruthers and A.L. Stinchcombe, 'The Social Structure of Liquidity: Flexibility, Markets, and States' (1999) 28 Theory and Society 353–82.

39 It is worth noting that the opposite view – the 'mentalist' view that locates structures of knowledge exclusively inside the minds of individuals – is perfectly possible, and has the advantage of a kind of common sense: where else can we locate thought other than in peoples' minds? On this view, structures of knowledge are not really structures at all but rather aggregations: they are, in other words, entirely decomposable into a multitude of individual states of mind. This perspective leads us away from enquiry into the social foundations of rationality towards enquiry into its biological foundations. If all thought is subjective, then to understand the process of knowledge construction, it is necessary to peer inside the minds of individual agents. And to understand the origin, nature, and dynamics of knowledge structures, it is necessary first and foremost to understand the structure of the mind, and the ways that the human brain is wired to process the sensory information it receives about the outside world. Mentalist presuppositions of this kind have informed a great deal of work on the structures of knowledge deployed by economic actors, particularly in the contemporary field of behavioural economics.

40 Mackenzie, op. cit. (2008), n. 29.

168

IV. THE LEGAL CONSTRUCTION OF ECONOMIC RATIONALITIES

I began this article by recalling the work of the legal realists of the early twentieth century, who succeeded in drawing attention to the crucial *constitutive* role of law in economic life. I argued that more needs to be done to recover and deepen our understanding of this constitutive function of law, especially in the contemporary context of economic transnationalization. I then tried to suggest, in broad terms, one way of doing so. While the legal realists provided keen insight into the role which law plays in shaping the relative bargaining power of economic actors in the marketplace, and in structuring market prices, they tended to take the rational economic actor herself as given for the purposes of their analysis, and therefore had relatively little to say about the processes by which rational economic agents are produced, or about the social-institutional formations in which specific forms of market rationality are constructed, contested, and sustained. I drew attention to a body of more recent work in the tradition of the sociology of knowledge which seeks to show the important role that cognitive technologies – institutional facts, frameworks of knowledge, and techniques of calculation – play in the constitution of the kinds of calculative rationality characteristic of modern markets. This body of work focuses attention squarely on the cognitive – as opposed to biological or cultural – construction of economic rationality.

The cognitive infrastructures of modern markets matter a great deal. By structuring the way we measure the perceived relative value of economic resources, they profoundly affect the way in which those resources are distributed between different individuals and social groups.[41] By selectively defining which of the many consequences of our actions we take into account as we make economic choices and define our strategies in the marketplace, calculative technologies simultaneously render *in*calculable, and therefore invisible and undervalued, particular kinds of impacts that our choices may have on others. More concretely, macroeconomic stability can be deeply affected by the algorithms used to calculate the risk associated with financial products and transactions. Major periods of industrial change are frequently associated with shifts in strategic thinking about the most effective forms of business organization and the most important sources of competitive advantage for firms.[42] Conversely, taken-for-granted ways of

41 Again, Callon: 'Imposing the rules of the game, that is to say, the rules used to calculate decisions, by imposing the tools in which these rules are incorporated, is the starting point of relationships of domination which allow certain calculating agencies to decide on the location and distribution of surpluses.' (Callon, 'Introduction', op. cit., n. 18, p. 46.)

42 For a vivid example, in the context of transformations of Japanese labour relations after the Second World War, see B. Gao, 'Efficiency, Culture and Politics: The Transformation of Japanese Management in 1946–1966' in Callon (ed.), id., pp. 86–115.

169

classifying the world, and of understanding its dynamics, can significantly impede processes of economic transformation.

I can now state more clearly the question to which I think a new 'economic sociology of law' might usefully turn its attention. It is this: in what ways, if any, are the cognitive infrastructures of modern markets – and therefore the particular forms of calculative rationality characteristic of such markets – created, entrenched, and mobilized through law and legal practices? What, in other words, is law's role in the construction, maintenance, and transformation of frameworks of knowledge and their associated practices of economic rationality in particular market contexts?

Importantly, a very similar set of questions has emerged in the context of a relatively recent line of law and economics research inspired by organizational sociology and the sociology of law, of which Edelman is probably the key proponent.[43] Edelman's starting points are, in broad terms, precisely those which characterize this article: she starts her analysis of economic life not with a pre-constituted rational actor but rather a 'social actor whose thinking incorporates institutionalized notions of rationality', and she sees markets as 'social arenas in which the dynamic interactions of law, norms, culture, power, and even science, technology and religion all help to construct our understandings of rational action.'[44] Her research is therefore focused on 'explaining how law interacts with social structure, social norms, and culture to produce the meaning of rationality'.[45] Her claim is that law in fact plays a powerful role in constituting the meaning of rationality in at least two related ways: first, by incorporating ideas about rational economic behaviour that originate in economic fields, and thereby reinforcing and legitimating such ideas;[46] and second, through the work of legal and managerial professionals who help to define what it means in organizational terms to comply with the law, and who in doing so help to shape circulating norms of business rationality.[47] While the centrality given in this article to calculative technologies marks something of a different emphasis from this body of work, it remains an important source of inspiration for the line of enquiry I am suggesting.

43 Edelman, op. cit., n. 4; Edelman and Stryker, op. cit., n. 1; L.B. Edelman, 'Legal Ambiguity and Symbolic Structures: Organizational Mediation of Civil Rights Law' (1992) 97 *Am. J. of Sociology* 1531–76; L.B. Edelman and M.C. Suchman, 'The Legal Environments of Organizations' (1997) 23 *Annual Rev. of Sociology* 479–515.
44 Edelman, id. (2004), p. 188.
45 id, p. 187
46 id. See, also, Edelman, op. cit. (1992), n. 43; L.B. Edelman, S.E. Abraham, and H.S. Erlanger, 'Professional Construction of Law: The Inflated Threat of Wrongful Discharge' (1992) 26 *Law & Society Rev.* 47–83.
47 Edelman et al., id; Edelman, id.; L.B. Edelman, 'Legal Environments and Organizational Governance: The Expansion of Due Process in the American Workplace' (1990) 95 *Am. J. of Sociology* 1401–40.
48 T. Veblen, 'Why Is Economics Not an Evolutionary Science?' (1898) 12 *Q. J. of Economics* 373–97, at 391.

170